Pergamon Titles of Related Interest

Raufer FIGHTING TERRORISM: THE EUROPEAN EXPERIENCE
Rapaport & Alexander THE MORALITY OF TERRORISM
Shultz & Sloan RESPONDING TO THE TERRORIST THREAT

Related Journals
(Free specimen copies available upon request.)

DEFENSE ANALYSIS

NUCLEAR Terrorism
Defining The Threat

Edited by
Paul Leventhal and Yonah Alexander

The Nuclear Control Institute and
The State University of New York
Institute on Studies in International Terrorism

Published with the cooperation of
The W. Alton Jones Foundation

PERGAMON-BRASSEY'S
International Defense Publishers Inc.

Washington • New York • London • Oxford
Beijing • Frankfurt • São Paulo • Sydney • Tokyo • Toronto

Pergamon Press Offices:

U.S.A. (Editorial)	Pergamon-Brassey's International Defense Publishers, 1340 Old Chain Bridge Road, McLean, Virginia 22101
(Orders & Inquiries)	Pergamon Press, Maxwell House, Fairview Park, Elmsford, New York 10523, U.S.A.
U.K. (Editorial)	Brassey's Defence Publishers, Maxwell House, 74 Worship Street, London EC2A 2EN
(Orders & Enquiries)	Brassey's Defence Publishers, Headington Hill Hall, Oxford OX3 0BW, England
PEOPLE'S REPUBLIC OF CHINA	Pergamon Press, Qianmen Hotel, Beijing, People's Republic of China
FEDERAL REPUBLIC OF GERMANY	Pergamon Press, Hammerweg 6, D-6242 Kronberg-Taunus, Federal Republic of Germany
BRAZIL	Pergamon Editora, Rua Eça de Queiros, 346, CEP 04011, São Paulo, Brazil
AUSTRALIA	Pergamon Press (Aust.) Pty., P.O. Box 544, Potts Point, NSW 2011, Australia
JAPAN	Pergamon Press, 8th Floor, Matsuoka Central Building, 1-7-1 Nishishinjuku, Shinjuku, Tokyo 160, Japan
CANADA	Pergamon Press Canada, Suite 104, 150 Consumers Road, Willowdale, Ontario M2J 1P9, Canada

Copyright © 1986 Pergamon-Brassey's International Defense Publishers, Inc.

All rights reserved. No part of this publication may be reproduced, stored in a retrieval system or transmitted in any form or by any means: electronic, electrostatic, magnetic tape, mechanical, photocopying, recording or otherwise, without permission in writing from the publishers.

First printing 1986

Library of Congress Cataloging in Publication Data

Nuclear terrorism.

"Published with the cooperation of the W. Alton Jones Foundation."
Proceedings of the Conference on International Terrorism: the Nuclear Dimension, held June 24-25, 1985, Washington, D.C.
Bibiography: p.
1. Nuclear terrorism--Congresses. 2. Nuclear terrorism--Prevention--Congresses. I. Leventhal, Paul. II. Alexander, Yonah. III. Nuclear Control Institute (Washington, D.C.) IV. State University of New York College at Oneonta. Institute for Studies in International Terrorism. V. Conference on International Terrorism: the Nuclear Dimension (1985 : Washington, D.C.)
HV6431.N83 1986   363.3'2   86-12332
ISBN 0-08-034323-6

Printed in the United States of America

CONTENTS

INTRODUCTION

Paul Leventhal and Yonah Alexander   1

RAPPORTEUR'S SUMMARY

Robert L. Beckman   5

Chapter One. Is Nuclear Terrorism Plausible?

Brian M. Jenkins   25
Responses by:
David Mabry   33
Yuval Ne'eman   35
Mason Willrich   37
John Peter Goss   39
Bertram Brown   43
Louis René Beres   45

Chapter Two. What Nuclear Means and Targets Might Terrorists Find Attractive?

Thomas D. Davies   54
Responses by:
Merrill Walters   67
Guenter Hildenbrand   70
Theodore B. Taylor   78
William J. Dircks   79
D. A. V. Fischer   84
Peter Stockton   89

Chapter Three. How Can Government and Industry Effectively Respond?

Louis O. Giuffrida	92
Responses by:	
James K. Asselstine	99
Donald Devito	102
Jacques Meurant	105
Steven Goldberg	118
André Kleinman	121

Chapter Four. How Can Nuclear Violence Be Prevented?

Bernard O'Keefe	124
Responses by:	
Harold Agnew	128
William O. Doub	131
Bernard T. Feld	138
Paul Warnke	139
Amiram Nir	141

Chapter Five. Two Congressional Perspectives

Richard A. Gephardt and Jeremiah Denton	144

Appendix A. World Inventories of Plutonium

David Albright	159

Appendix B. U.S. Exports of Highly Enriched Uranium

David Albright	193

Appendix C. World Spent Fuel Reprocessing Plants	199
Appendix D. The World Enrichment Picture	205
Selected Bibliography	209
About the Editors and Contributors	213

Introduction

Paul Leventhal
Yonah Alexander

Terrorism is not new in history. Through the centuries, it has been used as a political expedient in the struggle for power within and among nations. Established regimes and opposition groups, functioning under stress, have utilized extra-legal instruments of psychological and physical force against indigenous populations or targets elsewhere to gain tactical and strategic advantage. Intimidation, coercion, repression and, ultimately, destruction of lives and property have been the terrorists' means to attain ideological, political, social and economic ends.

Today's terrorists enjoy the advantage of combining high technology with mass communications to introduce an unprecedented intensity and ubiquity of violence into everyday life. In terms of popular perception, if not actual effect, we have entered a new "age of terrorism" with frightening ramifications. The most disturbing is the possibility that terrorists soon may have the means, and indeed the motivation, to engage in nuclear violence. By "nuclear violence" we mean the sabotage of nuclear facilities or shipments, the detonation of homemade or stolen nuclear weapons or the use of devices for dispersal of stolen radioactive nuclear materials.

Terrorism as practiced with conventional means by ideological revolutionaries or religious extremists already has the potential to disrupt societies worldwide. The staggering growth in terrorist activity over the last two decades is menacing. The Rand Corporation estimates that the number of terrorist incidents involving fatalities has been increasing about 20 percent a year since the early 1970s. Over the past 15 years, according to Risks International Inc., some 25,000 domestic and international terrorist incidents occurred. Nearly 46,000 individuals have been killed and another 28,000 wounded, with property damage estimated at over $1 billion. Although no single terrorist attack has yet resulted in catastrophic disruptions or casualties, the level of violence has been increasing, and future incidents could be much more costly. A single nuclear incident could match or dwarf the casualties and property damage caused worldwide by terrorists to date.

But is nuclear terrorism plausible? There is no consensus on this issue. Some observers see nuclear terrorism as implausible, others see it as possible but not imminent and others are convinced it is inevitable—perhaps just around the corner. It is generally acknowledged that terrorists thus far have been constrained either by a lack of capability, a lack of motivation, or a combination of the two. The key issue is whether these technological and self-imposed constraints are eroding as a result of technological and political developments.

Given the potentially cataclysmic consequences of an act of nuclear terrorism, and the chaos that would ensue from even a credible terrorist nuclear threat, a major effort to develop a multidisciplinary strategy for preventing nuclear terrorism would appear to be warranted. However, the popular perception of nuclear terrorism as a high-consequence but low-probability event serves to inhibit such preventive action. Yet inaction may prove perilous; there are no guarantees that the present constraints on terrorist groups will persist indefinitely.

The world is potentially vulnerable to nuclear terrorism as the consequence of two concurrent developments: the growing sophistication and boldness of terrorist organizations, attributable in some measure to state financial, technical and logistical support of their activities; and the increasing availability of nuclear know-how and materials and of deployed nuclear weapons throughout the world. The vulnerability of civilian and military nuclear assets to attack, sabotage or theft by terrorists is a matter of growing concern, as is the possibility that terrorist or other third-party nuclear weapons could be used in an attempt to trigger a U.S.-Soviet or other nuclear exchange.

In assessing the risk of nuclear terrorism, there is a technical and a political side of the equation. There are factors on each side of the equation that can influence whether terrorists actually will "go nuclear."

First, on the technical side, there are inherent links between civilian nuclear programs and the capabilities and materials needed to build nuclear weapons. To the extent such capabilities and materials come within reach of terrorists or their state sponsors, the risk of nuclear terrorism is increased.

Within the next decade, for example, there will be more explosive nuclear materials introduced into world civilian commerce than now exist in the arsenals of the superpowers. These civilian materials are nuclear fuels dedicated for peaceful purposes; if obtained by terrorists, however, they could be turned into crude but devastating nuclear weapons. Efforts to minimize production and use of explosive nuclear materials in the civilian sector have not been effective, largely because of the commitment of Europe and Japan to use plutonium as fuel in nuclear power reactors. Some progress is being made, albeit slowly, to eliminate use of the other nuclear explosive material, highly enriched uranium, as fuel in civilian research reactors.

Second, there is the risk of sabotage of nuclear reactors and related fuel facilities, of which there are several hundred in industrialized nations and a growing number in developing areas of the world. The level of protection attending these facilities, and attending the thousands of shipments of nuclear materials between and among them each year, varies by country and region. A key factor is that such protection is usually provided by companies that own the facilities and materials, not by police or military forces.

Third, there is growing concern that some nuclear weapons, particularly the relatively mobile tactical types, are insufficiently protected against theft or sabotage by terrorists. There is the related concern that a number of tactical weapons lack self-protecting devices that would render them inoperable if stolen by terrorists. Out of some 50,000 nuclear weapons possessed by the United States and the Soviet Union, about 13,000 are tactical.

Fourth, beyond the potential vulnerability of nuclear weapons in transit, in storage or deployed, there is continuing U.S. congressional concern about security against terrorist attack at American weapons laboratories and production facilities.

On the political side of the equation, there are a number of factors bearing on the question of whether terrorists will utilize the nuclear option.

First, it is likely that opportunities for conventional terrorism increasingly will be contained in the foreseeable future through tighter security and enforcement measures. Terrorists tend to attack "soft targets"—those with relatively little apparent security. Consequently, many business firms are following the lead of military, police and diplomatic establishments by upgrading their security. This could have the unintended effect of hastening the advent of nuclear or other forms of mass-destruction terrorism. As conventional targets are increasingly hardened, other targets created by technological advances are likely to become more attractive to terrorists.

Second, there is the propaganda and psychological-warfare value to terrorist groups that could result from shifting from conventional to mass-destruction violence. Since the strategy of terrorism does not prescribe instant victories over adversaries, an extension of the duration and impact of violence is indispensable. Should effective governmental and intergovernmental responses deny terrorists their sought after publicity, they may well change tactics, increase their audacity and escalate the symbolic orientation of their acts through nuclear or other high-technology weapons, if available.

Third, ideological and political violence often is a means to an end and progresses in proportion to the aims envisioned. If the goals escalate, the level of terrorism may also escalate. The principal constraint on such violence is the types of weaponry available. It is conceivable, therefore, that a highly motivated and desperate terrorist group with substantial technological and financial assets will attempt to improve its bargaining leverage by resorting to threatened or actual mass destruction. Such a determined group would be willing to take large risks in acquiring and using such weapons.

Many groups see themselves in an "all-or-nothing" struggle to bring a government to submission. It is prudent to anticipate that such groups might actually use nuclear or other weapons of mass destruction and, in the process, bring devastation to many lives, including their own. Surely, for such terrorists, the fear of deadly force used for deterrence or in retaliation does not exist as it does in the case of states. A principal danger is that if one sub-national group succeeds in achieving its goals by such means, the temptation for other terrorist groups to use, or threaten to use, similar weapons may become irresistible.

There are serious concerns about the adequacy of intelligence resources, protective and safeguards measures, and public awareness, and about the extent of progress toward international cooperation (particularly between the United States and the Soviet Union) to reduce the risk that international terrorism will acquire a nuclear dimension.

If modern society is to provide a reasonable degree of protection against this and other forms of "superterrorism," policymakers and the public must take note of the threat and respond appropriately. Effective preparedness and countermeasures must necessarily include contingency planning and crisis management policies at various governmental, inter-governmental and non-governmental levels.

It is out of these concerns that in June 1985, the Nuclear Control Institute and the State University of New York Institute for Studies in International Terrorism co-sponsored a multidisciplinary conference, "International Terrorism: The Nuclear Dimension," in Washington, D.C. The conference was held in association with the University of Chicago Institute for Social and Behavioral Pathology, the City University of New York's Ralph Bunche Institute on the United Nations, the Strategic Study Center of SRI International, and Atlanta University's Criminal Justice Institute.

The conference addressed the potential for state-sponsored and sub-state nuclear terrorism. Some 150 experts from 13 countries addressed four basic questions:

- Is nuclear violence plausible?
- What might the means and targets be?
- How can governments and industry effectively respond?
- How can nuclear violence be prevented?

This volume records the papers and deliberations of the conference and represents the first phase of a longer term project to recommend ways to prevent nuclear terrorism. An International Task Force on the Prevention of Nuclear Terrorism, comprised of 26 experts from 9 countries, has been formed to follow up on the work of this conference. Its findings and recommendations will be published in a separate volume.

Rapporteur's Summary

Robert L. Beckman

The 1980s may well be remembered as the decade of terrorism. Because of the extraordinary frequency and boldness of recent terrorist acts and of the growing intensity of government responses, many experts are concerned that terrorists will exploit their role on a world stage by escalating to threats or acts of mass destruction. One clear concern is the threat of nuclear terrorism, which would put at risk many lives and the future course of industrial civilization.

In response to this concern, the Nuclear Control Institute and the State University of New York's Institute for Studies in International Terrorism convened a conference, "International Terrorism: The Nuclear Dimension," at the Sheraton-Carlton Hotel in Washington, D.C. on June 24 and 25, 1985. Participants included members of the multinational business community and specialists in international terrorism, nuclear weapons design and deployment, civilian nuclear commerce and proliferation, international law, national and industrial security, crisis management and civil defense. The national security implications of terrorism were heightened by the coincidence of the conference with the airline hostage crisis in Beirut and the Air India disasters over Ireland and in Japan.

The conference was opened by the co-chairman, Paul Leventhal, president of the Nuclear Control Institute. He recalled the choice posed in 1946 by Bernard Baruch before the United Nations in presenting the U.S. plan for international control of the atom—the choice "between the quick and the dead." The basic choice, Leventhal said, remains "alacrity and wisdom on the one hand, death and destruction on the other."

The object of the conference, Leventhal said, was "not to unduly alarm, but to *duly* alarm" policymakers and the public in the interest of alerting them to the dangers of nuclear terrorism and the means available for preventing its occurrence. He cited the risks of explosive nuclear fuels being stolen from commerce and made into bombs; of actual weapons or weapons components being stolen and exploded; and of nuclear facilities being sabotaged or conventional industrial installations being subjected to nuclear sabotage.

How great are these risks in the context of current terrorist behavior and future trends? In particular, to what extent does state support of terrorist activities exacerbate these risks, and what can be done to counter the threat? Leventhal raised the problem of engaging in effective counter-terrorism in the nuclear arena without doing violence to basic democratic institutions. He warned against playing "catch-up ball" in the area of nuclear security and stressed the need to prevent, not manage, nuclear terrorism.

Professor Yonah Alexander, director of the State University of New York's Institute for Studies in International Terrorism and co-chair of the conference, explored state-sponsored terrorism and its goals of undermining psycho-social stability and exploiting the political vulnerability of pluralist democracies. Terrorism continues to increase, Dr. Alexander said, partially because the international community does not view it as criminal behavior or as warfare. The use by terrorists of mass destructive weapons—nuclear, biological and chemical—may be inevitable. Particularly troublesome are the claims by state sponsors of terrorism that they are entitled to nuclear assistance by virtue of their adherence to the Nuclear Non-Proliferation Treaty or membership in the International Atomic Energy Agency.

The conference was divided into four panels. Each panel addressed one of the four basic questions posed above by responding to a principal paper and then to questions from the audience. What follows is a summary of the four principal papers and of the major issues that emerged in discussions during the course of the conference.

PRINCIPAL PAPERS

Is Nuclear Terrorism Plausible?

Dr. Alexander, the chair of Panel I, introduced Brian Jenkins of the Rand Corporation, who presented the principal paper, "Will Terrorists Go Nuclear?"

According to Jenkins, a current poll by George Gallup of opinion leaders in the United States indicates that a nuclear incident in the U.S. involving terrorists is viewed as a more imminent danger than a nuclear war between the superpowers. Ten years earlier, Jenkins said, he had found no convincing evidence that a disastrous nuclear incident perpetrated by terrorists was likely. Over the last two years, the number of nuclear-related incidents has sharply decreased and hoaxes have virtually ceased. At the same time, however, terrorism has become bloodier.

State sponsorship reduces the constraints on terrorists and permits them to operate at a higher level of violence, emboldened by more resources, money, intelligence and technical expertise. There have been few credible instances of threatened nuclear terrorism. Yet a credible threat of nuclear terrorism would provide enormous coercive power. Consequently, the nuclear dimension might become attractive because terrorists, rather than wanting a lot of people killed, want a lot of people watching. On the other hand, the possibility of an actual act of nuclear violence should not be discounted. Even though terrorists generally operate on the principle of the minimum force necessary, this seems to be changing: the number of incidents of large-scale, indiscriminate violence with multiple fatalities has increased in the 1980s.

In Jenkins' opinion, nuclear terrorism could take a number of forms: attack or seizure of a nuclear facility; theft of nuclear materials or weapons; radioactive contamination of a target; an explosion or the threat to detonate a nuclear device. Consequences would vary, from no panic to catastrophic loss of human life. Acts of nuclear terrorism could be committed by criminals, lunatics, anti-nuclear extremists or authentic political terrorists. Because of the complexity of the problem, Jenkins chose to focus on the motives of political terrorists who might use a nuclear explosive to threaten violence.

Moral and political considerations have traditionally constrained terrorist violence. An internal self-checking tends to make terrorist decision-making somewhat conservative. This may change as the composition of a group changes or as frustration and zealotry make terrorists bolder. Certainly the likelihood of nuclear terrorism will increase as nuclear bomb materials become ubiquitous, as nuclear knowledge spreads, and as some groups turn to "pure terrorism": indiscriminate violence calculated to create panic and a popular clamor for political change.

Jenkins imagined that certain conditions or circumstances would erode constraints, making killing easier: numbness from battle; revenge; the need for increased violence to hold the public's attention; struggles within a group leading to the ascension of ruthless leaders; or last-ditch desperation. Terrorists might use increased violence against members of a different ethnic group. On the other hand, terrorists might target a large, remotely sited industrial installation if they wanted to keep the number of deaths down but still cause enormous economic disruption or property loss.

Terrorists imitate governments, Jenkins said. Thus, it is not inconceivable that use of a nuclear weapon by a superpower would lower constraints against nuclear terrorism. Since governments tend to view nuclear arsenals as "legitimate" but widely condemn chemical and biological weapons, there may be fewer constraints against nuclear violence than against violence using chemical or biological agents. Also, as bomb-usable material is introduced into civilian commerce, a black or grey market in nuclear materials may develop, thus increasing the likelihood of nuclear violence.

What would terrorists hope to gain by threatening an act of nuclear violence? The coercive potential of a credible nuclear threat is problematic: If the nuclear threat strikes at the heart of social order—the ability of a government to govern, for example—then an appropriate response becomes hard to imagine. The weapon need not be built; a nuclear threat that is taken seriously would provide plenty of leverage and publicity for terrorists with minimal personal or political risk.

In summary, Jenkins said that as opportunities for theft of fissionable material or nuclear weapons become more common, nuclear terror becomes more plausible. Still, it is by no means imminent or inevitable.

What Might the Means and Targets Be?

The chair of Panel II, Victor Gilinsky, former commissioner of the Nuclear Regulatory Commission, introduced Rear Admiral Thomas Davies (USN, Ret.), former assistant director for non-proliferation of the Arms Control and Disarmament Agency.

In his paper, "Terrorism's Nuclear Potential," Davies explored the vulnerability of nuclear facilities, materials, and weapons to terrorism. Since one third of all terrorist attacks worldwide are against U.S. citizens and interests, concern within the U.S. government over potential acts of nuclear terrorism is running high. Nuclear theft and sabotage are real concerns.

In 1978, the CIA identified nuclear storage depots in Western Europe as vulnerable to terrorist attack. Stealing a ready-made bomb is preferable, from a terrorist's perspective, to building one, according to the CIA. Terrorist groups in Europe have shown interest in the theft of nuclear weapons. In the United States, congressional investigators have found that plutonium and nuclear test devices could have been stolen from Department of Energy facilities. One "black-hat" team was able to penetrate a building where a nuclear test device was stored and could have made off with it several minutes before arrival of a response force. Physical security should be tightened at both weapons-production facilities and storage depots. There are some 50,000 weapons in the nuclear arsenals of the superpowers.

Other prime targets of theft and sabotage are found along the nuclear fuel cycle, at the more than 260 commercial nuclear power plants throughout the world, at the fuel enrichment, reprocessing and fabrication plants that service them, and along transportation routes. No one can say for certain what has become of the more than 9,000 pounds of nuclear material that are unaccounted for in U.S. civilian and weapons facilities through 1981.

Highly enriched uranium (HEU) and separated plutonium, both bomb materials, have been injected into world commerce as civilian fuels — HEU in research reactors and plutonium in power reactors. They are vulnerable to hijackings when transported to and from reactors. The HEU is particularly vulnerable on virtually undefended campuses. Industrial nations have been slow to face up to the risks of shipping bomb-grade plutonium, as indicated by the October 1984 shipment of about 30 bomb's worth of U.S.-origin plutonium from France to Japan. The original security plan was so lax that the shipment had to be delayed for two years until agreement could be reached on a plan costing millions of dollars and involving American, French and Japanese military forces.

The safeguards system of the International Atomic Energy Agency is incapable of coping with such shipments, mainly because it is not designed to pursue or retrieve missing material. Even the United States continues to have trouble tracking and assuring the physical security of the transportation of over one ton of exported HEU annually.

Terrorists who can obtain explosive nuclear material can build a nuclear bomb—not a highly effective bomb, perhaps, but one that will explode. The task of converting civilian fuel containing explosive uranium or plutonium into bomb material has been likened to converting morphine base to heroin.

The potential for sabotage of civilian nuclear facilities has received too little attention. Light water reactors are inherently susceptible to sabotage. The most serious reactor accident, a core melt, can be caused by sabotage of vital reactor systems by insiders or even by the placing of explosives outside the perimeter fence of a plant. Effective physical protection of nuclear plants should include a rethinking of the limitations on the use of deadly force by private guards. It should also include better design of plants against the kinds of attacks terrorists are capable of mounting.

Davies concluded that those responsible for nuclear security have been too prone to traditional concepts of physical security, especially to "mirror-image treatment of the adversary." He called for imputing the audacity, motivation and ingenuity of contemporary terrorists to the threat of nuclear terrorism. He also stressed the need to minimize and eventually eliminate explosive nuclear fuels from civilian nuclear programs and commerce.

How Can Governments and Industry Effectively Respond?

Paul Leventhal, chair of Panel III, introduced Louis Giuffrida, director of the Federal Emergency Management Agency, to present the principal paper, "How Terrorism Can Be Stopped: The Domestic Front."

General Giuffrida summarized his thoughts on the threat of terrorism to democratic societies: There are no guarantees that terrorism can be stopped from spreading once it starts, even with massive use of security forces; it is impossible to protect everyone and everything from a terrorist attack. Societies should define the maximum level of illegitimate violence they can tolerate and still remain free. Terrorism goes beyond that line: It is organized, illegitimate violence aimed at achieving specific change, with an intended audience larger than the direct victims of the violence.

Americans have acted under the illusion that the United States is immune from terrorism. While all dissenters are not terrorists, neither should society and the media mistake criminal misfits like the Symbionese Liberation Army for folk heroes. Uncoordinated acts of terror using conventional technology probably will be supplanted in the future by highly organized terrorist incidents of greater frequency and severity. This bodes ill for an open, vulnerable society like the U.S. High-technology societies have too many "choke points" for adequate protection. Nuclear, biological or chemical terrorist incidents are certainly possible.

State-sponsored terrorism inevitably will increase. Europe, long an easy target, is toughening up its defenses; terrorism can be expected to gravitate to the United States.

The United States must assume worst-case scenarios for planning purposes, including prevention of nuclear violence and attacks with chemical or biological (CB) agents. Experts are agreed that terrorists already have the technical capability to construct CB weapons. The difficulty of preventing nuclear terrorism or attacks with CB agents necessitates an early decision about the concessions society will be prepared to make. The kind of emergency services required flows from that decision, and from available resources.

To be both effective and acceptable, the essential components of a counterterrorism program should include:

- securing continuous intelligence on terrorist groups;
- identifying and isolating terrorist groups and preventing terrorist actions by denying them food, money, shelter, weapons, medical treatment, etc.;
- capturing and bringing to trial terrorist leaders.

Coordinated planning demands dialogue among involved agencies, all operating with the best intelligence. Nuclear terrorism presents unique planning problems. By law, the FBI is responsible for incident management. However, FEMA and the NRC may encroach on the FBI's area of responsibility because of overlapping jurisdictions and because they are better prepared for the multitude of responses associated with a nuclear incident. Planners need to ask some fundamental questions: who has ultimate decisionmaking authority during a nuclear incident with regard to release of information and decisions about public safety and relocation and, ultimately, regarding who covers the costs?

FEMA has been building an Integrated Emergency Management System over the past four years, along with Emergency Operating Centers, a National Emergency Management System, a National Emergency Training Center, and an Emergency Information and Coordination Center. FEMA coordinates all federal responses to consequences of terrorist incidents, including nuclear-related ones. The physical consequences of such an incident and the response are generic in nature, irrespective of the precipitating event.

Response to terrorist acts is not solely a federal problem. State and local governments must also participate. The public needs to be kept informed and supportive. Accordingly, FEMA negotiates and signs a Comprehensive Cooperative Agreement with the governor of each state. States make their own vulnerability assessments. FEMA and the states together implement and test contingency response plans, including a recent one at the St. Lucy nuclear power plant in Florida and another just prior to the Los Angeles Olympics. The Integrated Emergency Management System is a direct outgrowth of dialogues with states on real and hypothetical catastrophes.

How Can Nuclear Terrorism Be Prevented?

The chair of Panel IV, Ray Cline, former CIA deputy director for intelligence and now with the Georgetown University Center for Strategic and International Studies, introduced Bernard O'Keefe, a nuclear weapons expert who is chairman of the Executive Committee, EG&G, Inc. O'Keefe presented the principal paper, "What Can Be Done to Prevent Terrorist Nuclear Violence?"

O'Keefe stated that little can be done to prevent a skilled, determined, well-organized terrorist organization from setting off a nuclear explosion on U.S. territory. Given this vulnerability, the best strategy would be to ensure that such organizations do not exist or, if this is not practical, to deter them by demonstrating that any attempt at nuclear violence will be counterproductive to their goals and objectives.

Any modern industrial nation can build a nuclear weapon (given the fissile material). Hundreds of kilograms of fissionable material have been lost, stolen or misdirected from international commerce. It has been speculated that a kilogram of cocaine and a kilogram of fissionable material sell for the same amount on the black market. And it would not be difficult to smuggle nuclear explosives across international borders. United States borders would be as permeable to nuclear weapons as they currently are to bales of marijuana.

Threats of nuclear terrorism will probably always be with us; there have been over 100 hoaxes already. As in the past, they are being handled expertly by the U.S. Nuclear Emergency Search Team (NEST). The task is not simple because weapons emanations are fairly easy to shield. An example of international cooperation and of the skills involved in such detection work (albeit applied to other than a weapons threat) occurred in 1978, when a joint U.S.-Canadian NEST team located and cleaned up the debris from a Soviet nuclear-powered satellite that scattered over a 1,500-square mile area in the Canadian woods.

Nations must be deterred from assisting terrorist organizations in acquiring a nuclear capability by the certainty of devastating retaliation. Any nation that helps a terrorist group to mount a nuclear attack should be on notice that it does so at its own peril: It invites a nuclear attack on its own territory. To deter nuclear terrorism, nations must agree in advance on the actions they are prepared to take and publicize their retaliatory commitments in advance.

The key to international cooperation to prevent nuclear terrorism is the Soviet Union, O'Keefe observed. The Soviets recognize that their greatest danger is not from a first strike from the United States, but from accidental or terrorist-inspired nuclear conflagration. They are likely to abide by an agreement on countering nuclear terrorism because it is in their interest to do so. Because of their freedom to act independent of domestic political constraints, they can move immediately to retaliate. The threat of retaliation by the Soviet Union will be taken much more seriously by terrorists than such threats by the United States.

The United States is psychologically unprepared to deal with nuclear terrorism, mainly because the probability of a domestic terrorist nuclear attack appears so slight. The United States is more worried about the possibility of a Soviet nuclear attack on the United States or Europe. In fact, a more likely scenario is the "decapitation" of command and control systems in Washington or Moscow by terrorist nuclear detonations. The resultant confusion could easily escalate into full-scale thermonuclear war. Although this is our greatest danger, it receives minimal attention.

Intelligence-gathering must be enhanced. Upgrading the hotline and putting up geosynchronous satellites to detect explosions and establish their source can enhance intelligence.

But counter-terrorist measures are likely to conflict with our current constitutional concepts of civil liberties, O'Keefe warned. The debate on the trade-offs between intelligence gathering and civil liberties should begin immediately. The press should be alerted to the probability and the implications of nuclear terrorism. Popular support should be enlisted for effective action against nuclear terrorism.

PRINCIPAL AREAS OF DISCUSSION

The panels and audience raised a number of issues in responding to the formal presentations. There was a wide range of viewpoints on the likelihood of nuclear terrorism and on the motivations of those who might sponsor or engage in nuclear violence. There emerged from the discussions a concept of successive lines of defense against the nuclear terrorist threat: intelligence, physical security and crisis management. Of particular interest to the participants were security concerns relating to the protection of nuclear weapons, the use of explosive nuclear fuels in civilian programs and the degree of difficulty in using such civilian materials to build nuclear weapons. There also were discussions of particular needs: for cooperation among nations, between the United States and Soviet Union in particular, to counter the threat of nuclear terrorism; for adequate attention to civil-liberties concerns; and for increased public awareness of the threat.

The Likelihood and Character of Nuclear Terrorism

No one at the conference expressed the view that nuclear terrorism would not take place. Opinion ranged, however, from those who thought it not terribly likely to one panelist who concluded that a nuclear terrorist incident was likely to occur before the end of the decade. This panelist anticipated religious fanaticism coinciding with the availability of scientific and technical competence to bring about an act of nuclear terrorism.

Some panelists anticipated a chemical or biological threat, or continuing acts of product contamination, as more likely than a nuclear terrorist incident. There have been several fatal instances of chemical and biological terrorism. One member of the audience listed some aborted examples: an effort to raise typhoid bacillus to contaminate Chicago water supplies in 1972; the canning of nerve gas in aerosol containers in Austria in the 1970s; and the smuggling of botulism and tetanus viruses into Canada last year. But others asserted that such acts lacked the potential appeal of nuclear violence to terrorists in a number of respects: controllability, the legitimacy of nuclear weapons by virtue of their status in superpower arsenals, and the explosive impact of bombs. Terrorists, like war planners, believe they can control what they start, one expert observed, and CB seems too uncontrollable.

One panelist spoke of an apparent shift in "the psychology of treason." Citing the recent case of Navy personnel who betrayed military secrets not for ideological reasons but for money, he said that selling out a country or a mass of people becomes easier as a system of social checks breaks down. A psychotic on the inside might be as likely to engage in an act of nuclear terrorism as a high military official who would sell secrets. Thus, an act of nuclear terrorism is as likely from the "sane" as from the psychotic.

Another panelist asserted that terrorists generally seek to influence people rather than to exterminate them. Still, he warned, Iran and Libya seem ready at least to encourage acts of nuclear terrorism. Citing religious fundamentalism in the region, one panelist observed that the moral forces that might inhibit terrorists from engaging in mass destruction might push others to kill "everybody who belongs to the other religion." Another panelist observed that unprecedented panic resulting from media coverage of a threat of nuclear violence might alone be sufficient to serve the objectives of the terrorists without their carrying out the threat.

Intelligence to Detect and Deter Nuclear Terrorism

The conference identified a number of basic approaches to reducing the threat of terrorist violence generally and the nuclear threat in particular: changing the politics and pathology that give rise to terrorism; playing the role of "locksmith" by constructing better barriers against terrorists; and "managing a miracle" by instituting measures to limit the physical, institutional and psychological damage once terrorists strike.

One panelist asserted that societies blind themselves if they do not actively collect intelligence to preempt terrorists. States should send clear and unmistakable messages to international terrorists and their state sponsors. Counter-terrorism must emphasize strengthening field intelligence, that is, real-time intelligence gathering.

Another panelist observed that cooperation to deter nuclear terrorism should include not just states involved in nuclear activity, but any state concerned about terrorism. This will require a close working relationship among government intelligence agencies in coordination with private industry, particularly with nuclear companies and multinational corporations. The State Department's recent convening of major corporations into an Overseas Security Advisory Council and the FBI's seminars for industry on deterring terrorism were cited by one panelist as important steps in the right direction.

One participant observed that nations cannot do away with terrorism; at most, they can "score points." He said that classic methods of combatting terrorism involve defense against the terrorist; an offense to stop the terrorist before he strikes; and intelligence to anticipate and preempt. He stressed the need to collect basic information on terrorist organizations and their capabilities, the black market in nuclear materials, and links between terrorist organizations and states involving supply of nuclear material or weapons design.

A major problem for one panelist was the high degree of secrecy that surrounds intelligence information on terrorist activities and capabilities. Such information is needed by corporations to determine the level of threat to be protected against. Sometimes companies engaging in nuclear activities are directed to upgrade security systems without being told why. The intelligence information is withheld to protect sources and methods.

Although there were disagreements over how far intelligence-gathering agencies should be permitted to go to preempt terrorism—nuclear threats in particular—the conferees were generally agreed that better intelligence was needed to anticipate and preempt terrorist acts. One panelist asserted that on the domestic front there is no fundamental incompatibility between good intelligence and civil liberties. Another panelist emphasized the importance of cooperation among national intelligence services and the danger in lack of cooperation. He cited as examples the Soviets alerting the United States to the preparations for a South African nuclear test in 1979, but not warning the United States of the Yom Kippur surprise invasion of Israel by Egypt in 1973, an exercise that nearly resulted in a nuclear confrontation between the superpowers.

Physical Security of Nuclear Facilities and Materials

One panelist said an independent assessment commissioned by the Department of Energy (DOE) in 1980 to evaluate security at DOE's nuclear weapons facilities had found "a disaster waiting to happen." These facilities contain complete nuclear weapons, test devices, bomb-grade plutonium and uranium, and highly classified information. Although some improvements have been made since a 1982 congressional investigation, there remain attitudinal problems throughout the system that include lying to congressional committees and the use of secrecy to cover up misfeasance.

Several panelists complained of overclassification and a resulting lack of accountability by those charged with protection of nuclear materials, facilities and weapons. One questioner asserted that the performance of officials in charge of nuclear security is not subject to sufficient public accountability. Secret investigations of secret matters can often be secretly thwarted by those being investigated. He suggested that the security apparatus of an agency can be used to protect and promote the agency's political objectives.

A panelist responded by acknowledging past security deficiencies at the weapons facilities but asserted that citizens must trust in the integrity of the system and that intelligence and security had to be placed in the hands of experts. Some officials are bound to use the classification system to cover up incompetence or malfeasance. Yet laws intended to overcome this problem, such as the Freedom of Information Act, make the jobs of intelligence and security much more difficult. As long as national security is at stake, this panelist felt, certain rights must be surrendered in order to guarantee that security.

Countering nuclear terrorism was described by some as more a technical than a political problem. One panelist said terrorists already have taken action against the nuclear fuel cycle, in West Germany, for example, but not against operating reactors. West Germany asserts that it has in place much higher standards for protection of the nuclear fuel cycle than are found elsewhere. Standards for physical security generally involve minimum times for which barriers must prevent forcible entry. Multiple barriers and redundancy of alarm and detection systems are used as basic physical protection measures.

There was wide agreement that improvements in physical security measures and changes in organizational structures must keep pace with available nuclear targets. Unfortunately, according to one panelist, the accident at Three Mile Island showed that even the rules and procedures designed to prevent a meltdown were not sufficient in the face of operator carelessness and complacency. One panelist noted that the Nuclear Regulatory Commission (NRC) is upgrading physical security and safeguards regulations to meet "design basis threats" that reflect the changing threat environment. The required changes will not be inexpensive and may require a sharing of costs by the government. One panelist remarked that plutonium should be guarded at least as well as the gold in Fort Knox.

One member of the audience asserted that physical security measures must be improved to prevent destruction of a reactor with conventional explosives. Such an event could result in a release of radioactivity comparable to the fallout of several nuclear detonations. Destruction of a spent-fuel pool also would release radioactivity, but not of the same magnitude. Another panelist noted that although such worst-case scenarios involve substantial radioactive releases, reactors and spent fuel cannot explode like nuclear weapons. Another panelist noted that the particulars are too sensitive to be dealt with in open session, but that the possible catastrophic scenarios for sabotage of nuclear power plants are endless.

It was generally acknowledged that it would be difficult to prevent terrorist actions against nuclear plants in countries where extremists operate freely or where there is civil war or insurrection. U.S. physical-protection regulations assume a state of "civil order"; they would have to be tightened drastically in the event of civil disorder. One participant described how Basque terrorists in Spain caused the shutdown of an uncompleted nuclear power plant by murdering key plant personnel, actions that were premised, he said, both on the plant being a convenient political target and on anti-nuclear activism.

There was disagreement as to the desirability of the U.S. government establishing a special federal security force charged with all aspects of protecting nuclear materials at facilities and in transit. There was disagreement as well on the question of who should be financially responsible if nuclear materials are stolen and used for violent ends. Panelists observed that a federal security force had been proposed some years earlier, but that it had been rejected largely because of constitutional and jurisdictional considerations.

One panelist recommended that what was needed, if not a national security force, was an international nuclear "priesthood" dedicated to securing nuclear materials for centuries in the global interest.

Protection of Nuclear Weapons

Although conferees were of several minds about the civilian nuclear power industry as either a logical or attractive target for nuclear terrorism, there was wide concern that terrorists at some time would attempt to steal a nuclear weapon. As noted above, the conference heard descriptions of weak security at Department of Energy weapons facilities and questions as to whether all of the weaknesses have been corrected. Concerns were also expressed about the adequacy of security at NATO weapons installations and along transportation routes in Europe and throughout the world.

One expert said it would be foolish to discount the possibility of a terrorist attack against nuclear weapons in Europe. Such an attack would have a very high public and political impact. Any act that undermines the ability of the United States to deploy nuclear weapons has strategic and national security consequences for the United States. An attack on storage sites or deployed forces could raise to a politically unacceptable level the public's anxiety about nuclear weapons. An actual nuclear detonation would not be required to obtain this objective. It could be achieved by other means, such as an attack on a nuclear site, blackmail or radiation poisoning.

Fixed storage sites are highly visible and potentially vulnerable, even though a large-scale effort since the 1970s has succeeded in radically upgrading security. A senior-level weapons-protection group is working to anticipate and prepare for future threats by raising the risk to any terrorist threatening an attack against fixed facilities. The high visibility of deployed forces on the move on the roads makes them an easier target still; an attack against them is particularly troublesome. Even an unsuccessful attack could cause hysteria among citizens and governments of alliance partners on whose territory nuclear weapons are deployed.

Terrorists' capabilities have been significantly strengthened in recent years. But, on balance, "the risk is high" to terrorists who would attack nuclear forces in NATO. Were the Soviets to support such organizations, the balance of costs/benefits might change. However, there is no sign of such support from the Soviets, nor would it appear in their interest to undertake such an operation.

The conference was advised that anti-theft devices known as permissive action links (PALs) are being upgraded continually to prevent nuclear weapons from being detonated if stolen. Some participants expressed concern that progress was slow and that some weapons lacked such protection. One panelist suggested that this technology should be shared with any country with nuclear weapons. The equivalent safety feature for nuclear power plants would be to put them underground and to make their operation independent of any human or mechanical failure.

Regarding design safety of nuclear weapons, the conference was advised by one specialist that U.S. nuclear weapons are "inherently one point safe": that is, they will not go off if accidentally dropped. New weapons are made of an insensitive high explosive that cannot detonate even if hit by a bullet or if caught in a fire. Another expert suggested that one-point detonations were possible and that this was significant not only with regard to weapons safety but to the likelihood that terrorists could build a crude bomb that would produce a significant yield.

Although the discussion was necessarily limited because of the sensitivity of the subject, participants were agreed that the highest priority should be placed on rendering nuclear weapons as safe and secure as possible.

Use of Explosive Nuclear Fuels in Civilian Commerce

Strong concerns were raised about the weapons potential of the nuclear fuel cycle—in particular, the civilian use of weapons-usable materials and the blurring of lines between civilian and military programs.

A number of participants saw the advent of plutonium in the civilian nuclear fuel cycle as contributing substantially to the danger of nuclear terrorism. Terrorists, in their view, will have more opportunities to steal plutonium once it comes into worldwide circulation. A few panelists asserted that nations with scarce energy resources deem the use of plutonium to be an immediate necessity for energy-security reasons and that the associated security risks were manageable. Others disagreed, citing the abundance of uranium as making the use of plutonium unnecessary, either for recycling in light water reactors or in breeders. Because plutonium use is unjustifiable economically and too risky in the face of contemporary terrorism, reprocessing of spent fuel to obtain plutonium is, in their view, unwarranted.

A number of participants suggested that the best intervention would be to remove all bomb-usable material from commercial circulation. One panelist, however, considered that to be a broad question of non-proliferation policy relating to the risk of diversions by nations, and not a matter of directly deterring or preventing terrorism.

One panelist recalled the lack of U.S. success in seeking to persuade other countries to refrain from reprocessing spent fuel, recycling plutonium and developing the breeder reactor. In his view, institutional mechanisms, physical security measures and the strengthening of treaties and international organizations constitute a better approach than efforts at technology denial. In addition, potential fossil-fuel shortages, coupled with the health hazards of burning these fuels, legitimate the use of nuclear power and of plutonium fuel as a base for energy independence. This panelist acknowledged that the IAEA and the NPT presently were insufficient to the task of preventing theft of fissionable material. However, the recent rash of terrorist acts would probably stimulate international cooperative efforts to deal with the danger.

Others questioned the industry view that it was futile for the United States to try to discourage commerce in plutonium and highly enriched uranium. One participant asserted that this argument will seem hollow following an actual nuclear terrorist event involving such material, by which time it may be too late to establish effective controls. Consequently, the Department of State and Department of Energy should not acquiesce in the plans of allies to use U.S.-origin explosive nuclear materials, and the Department of Defense should serve as a check on such acquiescence by pressing national security concerns.

Some saw a general erosion of the psychological firebreak that has evolved over the years to establish a fundamental civilian/military distinction in nuclear programs. France's insistence on reserving the option to use its breeder reactor program as a means to produce plutonium for weapons was cited by one panelist as particularly troublesome. Since the French will not renounce the military use of civilian plutonium, and since there is a degree of cross-over between civilian and military programs in all the nuclear weapon states, some thought it unreasonable to expect a number of emerging nuclear states to act differently.

Some panelists asserted that the light water reactor fuel cycle is simply not an attractive target for terrorist activity; licensing standards reflect this. Also, the nuclear power industry in the United States does not use separated plutonium for fuel. The principal countries that do—France, Britain, Japan and the Soviet Union—have impressive non-proliferation credentials. One participant expressed the contrary view that plutonium produced and transferred by these countries was still a potential target of terrorists.

The conference was briefed on a number of steps taken by U.S. government agencies to minimize the risk of theft of nuclear materials. The Nuclear Regulatory Commission is about to issue a rule requiring the conversion of test and research reactors from HEU to low-enriched uranium (LEU) fuel. Transportation of nuclear materials was described as being much more terrorist-resistant than presumed. For example, multiple shipments of less-than-strategic amounts of material (one or two kilograms) are not allowed by the United States on the grounds that a strategic quantity could be obtained through a series of coordinated, well-timed thefts.

The Atomic Energy Act (Sec. 127) requires that the executive branch make a finding that adequate physical protection is provided for shipping and use, as well as retransfers and reprocessing, of U.S.-origin nuclear materials. American technical experts visit other countries to make these determinations and to help in upgrading physical protection. Exchanges of experts and information are common. The State Department was responsible for initiating the Convention on the Physical Protection of Nuclear Materials, which defines specific criminal acts involving shipments of nuclear materials. The convention has not yet come into force for lack of signatories.

Reducing potential sources of nuclear materials and know-how available to terrorists was a principal concern of a number of participants. In their view, exporters of sensitive nuclear technology, facilities and materials should refrain from making shipments to the Middle East and other troubled areas. In addition, there should be general restraint on exports of plants capable of processing explosive materials, as well as on transfers of the materials themselves.

One expert asserted that more work needs to be done to ascertain the extent of a black market in fissionable material. To deter such activities, he advocated the enactment of extremely severe penalties (at a minimum, life imprisonment) for illegal possession of plutonium or highly enriched uranium. An effective complementary measure would be a complete prohibition against exports of plutonium and highly enriched uranium for any purpose.

Building a Nuclear Weapon

There was a diversity of opinion about how easy or difficult it is safely to make a crude nuclear explosive device. Specifically at issue was the quality of material and level of expertise needed to do so. A number of participants asserted that many of the facts necessary for thorough and realistic assessment of this terrorist threat needed to be made public. There was wide agreement that dedicated terrorists would not be impeded by the secrecy and that terrorists with state support would be able to build a nuclear weapon. In European countries, according to one participant, terrorists have much greater access to high technology and to cooperation from friendly governments than they had only a few years ago.

On the specific issue of the usefulness of reactor-grade plutonium for building a weapon, a former weapons designer stated categorically that reactor-grade plutonium (the quality of plutonium typically produced by nuclear power plants), once separated from spent fuel, can be used for making militarily reliable, high-efficiency fission bombs. Another former weapons designer agreed on the suitability of the material, but suggested the task would be too difficult for even sophisticated terrorists in the absence of governmental or organizational backing. Both agreed that the first line of defense is to prevent unauthorized acquisition of nuclear material. Both also agreed that there was no economic justification for the use of separated plutonium in civilian power programs.

One participant suggested that the IAEA should be urged to engage the nuclear weapons states in discussions that would lead to a definitive statement about the utility of reactor-grade plutonium in explosives.

One panelist urged that plutonium should be recognized as the world's most dangerous substance, both for its weapons potential and for its toxicity if ingested. He accepted a clarification that plutonium was not the most poisonous of substances. Nevertheless, as an expert in the audience pointed out, in experiments on beagle dogs, one microgram level of aerosol exposure in the lungs led to 100 percent assurance of getting cancer.

Crisis Management

Panelists agreed that governments had to do worst-case planning because one could not predict all contingencies, nor expect foreign policy to avoid all conflicts, nor assume that all prospective demands by terrorists are negotiable. At some point, concessions might be impossible.

Still, panelists and audience alike were skeptical that federal agency planning for incident preemption, response or recovery was sufficient. The rise of state-sponsored terrorism and the limitations of intelligence gathering make early warning exceedingly difficult. Consequently, preventive measures must be instituted now, even before the threat is apparent. Contingency planning for effective incident response and recovery must also be enhanced.

Decisions about prevention or response are fundamentally political, not technical or scientific, according to one panelist. Emergency management becomes politically charged as it seeks to satisfy the three essential components of the problem: readiness, response and recovery. Planning is paramount, even more important in many cases than the actual response. There is no substitute for realistic training exercises and trial coordination between state and local jurisdictions to divulge potential glitches.

This political dimension is especially evident when decisions must be made among competing response alternatives, for example, whether or not to evacuate or what information to release. The same infrastructure that responds to hurricanes or floods also will have to cope with nuclear catastrophe. The same problems of coordination and allocation of resources arise. The basic maxim of emergency management will become all the more evident in the event of nuclear terrorism: "Murphy was an optimist."

An emergency management planner remarked that states have neither the resources nor the expertise to plan effective responses to nuclear terrorism. States have radiological protection programs to deal with accident situations, but the planned reduction of federal funding for these programs makes even these jobs virtually undoable. Another participant remarked that such budget cuts are shortsighted and lead to false economies, causing emergency planning to be sacrificed on the altar of deficit reduction. One panelist responded that the states would have to learn to do more with less.

Switzerland was cited as the best example of a national program to cope with nuclear catastrophe. In 1959, Swiss citizens voted to establish a civil defense program as part of national defense. The object was to reduce the possibility of an attack or an attempt at blackmail. The preparations, primarily the construction of civil defense shelters for all citizens, include protection against nuclear war and terrorism. One participant observed that Switzerland, a neutral nation with a small population, presented a unique situation not readily replicated by other nations.

The conference also considered the role of the media in nuclear emergencies. A number of participants observed that objectivity is always a concern, and emergency planners both need and fear the media's ability to present events and disseminate information. That they tend to sensationalize events is an inevitable adjunct of a free society. Yet the press serves a positive and indispensable role in such circumstances, even serving to draw attention to possible problems in advance of an emergency. One participant noted that the Federal Emergency Management Agency has put together and tested the concept of joint information centers to cope with some media problems.

In sum, the panel agreed that better coordination of emergency planning efforts would enhance the third line of defense against nuclear terrorism.

Bilateral and Multilateral Cooperation

A number of conference participants stressed the importance of the superpowers and nuclear suppliers becoming more credible in the arms control and non-proliferation fields. In their view, as long as industrialized nations continue to rely on nuclear weapons for their own security and to press ahead with development of explosive fuels for their nuclear programs, less advanced nations, including those of immediate proliferation concern, can be expected to emulate these "legitimate" steps toward nuclear capability.

One panelist saw superpower nuclear competition as a dangerous example to the rest of the world. Continued reliance on "nuclear terror" as the basis of mutual deterrence provides an incentive for terrorists and states to use nuclear weapons as a legitimate means to accomplish political ends.

One participant observed that arms control means taking non-proliferation seriously, and vice-versa. The growing legitimacy of nuclear weapons and the growing availability of materials needed to build them were seen by a number of participants as a dangerous example and as presenting tempting targets for terrorists.

A number of participants emphasized the importance of cooperation between the superpowers as the key to controlling both vertical and horizontal proliferation of nuclear weapons and to preventing their acquisition by terrorists. But others, perceiving the Soviet Union as the principal organizer, financier and sponsor of international terrorism, questioned the feasibility of U.S.-Soviet cooperation. This perception of Soviet sponsorship of terrorism moved another panelist to lament the "all-consuming anti-Sovietism" behind U.S. foreign policy. He asserted that anti-Sovietism impedes the United States from gaining understanding about the political roots of terrorism in certain countries, particularly Central America, and urged that U.S. foreign policy be evaluated for content that elicits terrorist actions against the United States.

Another panelist responded that a fair analysis of terrorists' motivations in the Middle East would recognize that the U.S. is beleaguered in the region more for its support of Israel than for its anti-Sovietism. Further, despite evidence cited by one panelist that a Palestinian group had made a decision to "go nuclear" in 1978, no Middle Eastern state, except for Israel, would have the wherewithal to produce nuclear weapons before the turn of the century. And Israel probably could be counted on to practice its own preemptive approach to non-proliferation (as it did in 1981 by bombing an Iraqi research reactor) if a regional adversary was on the verge of going nuclear.

One panelist maintained that the Soviet Union, whether or not it supported some terrorist activities, was unlikely to sponsor the construction or theft of a nuclear weapon. Iran, Iraq and Libya were mentioned as potential sponsors of nuclear terrorism or as states that might want to steal or acquire a nuclear weapon.

There was a suggestion that Western nations should consider emulating the USSR by leasing, rather than selling, fissionable material to clients. One panelist stressed the need for establishing multinational nuclear fuel cycle centers—in particular, the international management of spent fuel either for long-term storage or for ultimate separation and recycling of plutonium.

A member of the audience observed generally that because technological advances have overtaken political controls, national solutions will not work. The best hope, in his view, is international order. Terrorists act out of desperation and will resort to escalating violence until they feel their grievances are satisfied. Violent retaliation, and other more extreme anti-terrorist responses raised at the conference, should be contemplated only in combination with measures to rectify injustice.

There was support for bringing the International Convention on the Physical Protection of Nuclear Material into force and for updating the International Atomic Energy Agency's guidelines on physical protection. Several participants applauded the cooperation among nuclear suppliers to strengthen IAEA safeguards and to improve nuclear plant security and safety features. Mention was made as well of the voluntary offers of the Soviets and Chinese as nuclear-weapon states to place some of their civilian nuclear facilities under IAEA inspections. These and other efforts in support of the NPT/IAEA non-proliferation regime were seen by some participants as helping to deter state sponsorship of nuclear terrorism by raising the risk of being caught in violation of the treaty and being expelled from the agency.

Civil Liberties Concerns

The conference identified a range of views as to whether increased physical protection and surveillance activities to prevent nuclear terrorism would lead to conflicts with basic constitutional guarantees of civil liberties.

Some panelists preferred erring on the side of preserving the right of lawful, peaceful dissent and enhancing the social mechanisms for peaceful change. Others saw the issue as one of survival and suggested that there already was a need to restrict certain individual rights in order to provide better security at commercial nuclear plants. In this regard, security firms were petitioning to get access to FBI fingerprint data for use in hiring decisions, and a bill was pending in Congress to make this possible.

One panelist focused on both the use of computer files for intelligence gathering and the use of deadly force to protect nuclear installations as presenting important challenges to individual liberties. With regard to deadly force, the recent Supreme Court ruling in *Tennessee v. Garner* challenges the right of guards or police to use deadly force to prevent the escape of felony suspects, particularly in a case where the suspect does not appear to offer any threat to lives. Government liability for damage or loss of life in searching for stolen nuclear material would present important new legal problems as well.

Some members of the audience expressed concern that the security apparatus, rooted as it is in confidentiality, cannot be fairly judged, either for its adequacy or its fairness. One questioner commented that peaceful demonstrations against nuclear power, both in Europe and at Savannah River in South Carolina, had been curtailed because of claims that security would be jeopardized.

Civil liberties concerns were also raised regarding the infiltration of dissident groups by intelligence operatives and the placing of foreigners under greater domestic scrutiny. One panelist asserted, however, that there was no fundamental incompatibility between good intelligence and civil liberties, and that in the event of "clear and present danger," health, safety and security must take precedence over constitutional liberties.

Public Awareness of the Threat

There was considerable discussion of what the appropriate role of the media should be in alerting and informing, without unduly alarming, the public about the likelihood and consequences of nuclear terrorism. Many participants agreed that press coverage tends to dramatize terrorist incidents, thus adding to the sense of crisis. One panelist noted that in four past nuclear incidents, press attention, or the lack thereof, determined how the public perceived the incident. Another panelist said the press was instrumental, nonetheless, in providing vital information to the public during crises and was a valued ally of emergency managers. Press coverage can enhance or erode public confidence in government's ability to counter or respond to nuclear terrorism. More should be done, therefore, to alert the public to the means available to prevent nuclear terrorism and to respond to an actual crisis.

FOLLOWING UP THE CONFERENCE

Although governments can seek to deter terrorism by addressing underlying grievances and by better protection of vulnerable targets, there can be no guarantees that terrorists will not eventually resort to nuclear violence. Much still needs to be done to increase capabilities in the areas of intelligence, physical protection and safeguards, and crisis management. More can be done to minimize nuclear targets of opportunity.

As a follow-up to the conference, therefore, the Nuclear Control Institute and SUNY's Institute for Studies in International Terrorism have continued their collaboration by organizing an International Task Force on the Prevention of Nuclear Terrorism. The Task Force's report of findings and recommendations, along with a companion volume of support studies, will be released in mid-1986.

Chapter One

Is Nuclear Terrorism Plausible?

Brian M. Jenkins

Several cities, including the one where I live, have been destroyed by terrorists with nuclear weapons. Others have been held hostage to the whims of political and religious fanatics. Vigilant government agents, sometimes armed only with luck, have foiled schemes of mass destruction on dozens of occasions; there have been numerous close calls. We live on borrowed time. All on the pages of fiction. For novelists and screenwriters, the possibility of nuclear terrorism has provided a potent source of inspiration. It combines the two darkest fears of our era: fear of nuclear destruction and fear of increasing terrorism.

The speculation is not confined to fiction. Others besides novelists have warned of the dangers of nuclear terrorism. Some of these warnings are based upon sober analysis; much of the popular speculation falls within the realm of sensationalism.

The motives of the authors also vary. Some are concerned about the adequacy of security measures surrounding nuclear facilities; some worry that an adequate level of security cannot be attained without authoritarian methods of social control that are incompatible with a free society, if not for the public at large, at least for the employees of the nuclear industry, whose lives are increasingly subjected to close scrutiny and irritating security measures as attention focuses on the potential threat posed by "insiders." Others who oppose nuclear programs to begin with see the threat of nuclear terrorism as one way to increase public anxiety and resistance to nuclear programs.

As is often the case in our media-rich society, the line between fact and fiction blurs. In one case, the co-author of a best-selling novel about nuclear terrorism narrated a segment about the subject on a popular television news show. At the end, the viewer wasn't sure which part of the broadcast was fiction and which part was fact.

Whether their opinions are molded by paperback potboilers or the dried fruit of research, many people believe that nuclear terrorism of some sort is likely and may be inevitable. Reflecting the results of a poll conducted among 1,346 opinion leaders in the United States, George Gallup, Jr., in his recent book, *Forecast*

2000, wrote that "while a war between the superpowers, the United States and the Soviet Union, is a real cause for concern, [a disastrous nuclear incident involving terrorists in this country] seems to me to be the most imminent danger."

But will terrorists go nuclear? Ten years ago I was asked to tackle this question. The essay I wrote was unabashedly speculative.[1] Fortunately for society (although a problem for the researcher), there was little to go on. The historical record provided no evidence that any terrorist group had ever made any attempt to acquire nuclear material for use in an explosive or dispersal device. Apart from a few incidents of sabotage in France and the brief seizure of a nuclear reactor under construction in Argentina, political extremists had not attacked nuclear facilities. No criminal or terrorist group had demonstrated or claimed that it possessed nuclear material. If members of any such groups had ever seriously discussed the option of going nuclear, I knew of no such discussions.

There had been bomb threats against nuclear facilities, vandalism, token acts of violence, low-level sabotage, minor thefts of nonfissionable material. There had been nuclear threats, most of which could easily be dismissed as puerile hoaxes. In sum, the history of nuclear incidents up to 1975 provided no convincing evidence that more serious incidents were likely. As the nuclear industry expanded, we could anticipate that the number of low-level incidents would increase proportionately, but there was no basis for predicting escalation. From this tiny platform of actual history, one could only take a breathtaking inferential leap into a future based on the little we knew about the behavior of those we call terrorists.

In the intervening years, we have witnessed additional incidents of crime and violence in the nuclear domain, and a slight escalating trend in the late 1970s. However, the number of nuclear-related incidents has declined sharply in the last two years. Nuclear hoaxes, which occurred with increasing frequency during the last decade, also have virtually ceased. We have no explanation for this.

At the same time, however, terrorism has increased in volume and has become bloodier. And we have learned more about how terrorists decide to do what they do. Keeping these developments in mind, I have been asked to reexamine the question of whether terrorists will go nuclear.

We must keep in mind that nuclear terrorism can take many forms. Terrorists may attack or try to seize nuclear facilities. They may attempt to steal a nuclear weapon or nuclear material and offer to return it for ransom. They may contaminate some target with radioactive material. They may fabricate a hoax nuclear threat. If they have somehow obtained an actual nuclear explosive device, they may detonate it or threaten to detonate it.

The consequences of the potential actions also vary. A nuclear hoax poses no direct danger to human life, but if the threat is publicized and believed, panic could cause casualties. Sabotage of a nuclear reactor may result in a mere shutdown, or it could spread radioactive fallout the equivalent of many atomic weapons. The detonation of even a crude nuclear device could cause thousands of deaths.

While we are likely to label anybody who does any of these things a "terrorist," in fact, potential nuclear adversaries encompass a broad range: common criminals, individual lunatics, anti-nuclear extremists, as well as authentic political terrorists. We can speak of political terrorists only as we know them today, that is, as the groups that have carried out the campaigns of terrorist violence since the late 1960s, although we realize that nuclear terrorists of the future may not arise from those sources currently identified. New kinds of groups may appear that might be more likely to use nuclear means to achieve their objectives.

My remarks today will focus on the motives of political terrorists who might detonate or threaten to detonate a nuclear explosion.[2] In order to do so, they must first acquire a nuclear weapon. Can they do it?

There are several ways a terrorist group might acquire a nuclear weapon for its own use. They could steal a nuclear weapon from some military arsenal, attempt to bypass the elaborate devices that are designed to prevent tampering, and rearm it or use its components to construct a new weapon. Another way would be to steal weapons-grade nuclear material and use it to fabricate an improvised nuclear device. Either way would require attacking defended targets, something terrorists generally have not done. To avoid encountering defenses, terrorists could attempt to obtain the material surreptitiously by other means. These might include enlisting confederates within nuclear facilities who can supply the material or purchasing it on the black market, if such a market develops for nuclear material.

Assuming they had the necessary nuclear material, could terrorists make a nuclear bomb? This question remains a topic of debate within the nuclear community. I am not qualified to offer a judgment, so let me instead try to offer a consensus view. Although the ease with which a bomb could be made has probably been greatly exaggerated in the popular press, the notion that some group outside of government programs can design and build a crude nuclear bomb is certainly more plausible now than it was 30 or 40 years ago. At that time, the secrets of nuclear fission were closely guarded. However, much of the requisite technical knowledge has since gradually come into the public domain. There are a growing number of technically trained people who understand these basic principles and who, without detailed knowledge of nuclear weapons design, theoretically could design such a weapon.

Actually building even a crude nuclear bomb, however, poses a greater obstacle. Experts argue about the number of persons needed, the mix of specialized skills, and the probability of success. They agree that it would involve considerable risks for its builders. Its detonation and performance would be uncertain. Its yield would be low, probably in tenths of a kiloton.

Few terrorists as we know them today possess the requisite technical skills identified by experts. There are a few engineers and a handful of scientists within the ranks of contemporary terrorist groups, but most terrorists come from the departments of social sciences or the humanities, which may help to explain why terrorists thus far have not carried out more technically demanding operations. One recent development, however, is changing this picture, and that is the increasing direct involvement of governments in the business of terrorism, not merely as political or financial supporters, but as participants in the direction, planning, and execution of terrorist attacks. State sponsorship puts at the disposal of the terrorists more resources: intelligence, money, sophisticated munitions, technical expertise. It also reduces the constraints on the terrorists, permitting them to operate at a higher level of violence.

It seems to me that the real arguments arise not so much in the area of theoretical capabilities as in the area of intentions. The public utterances of terrorists include very few references to nuclear activity. Terrorist groups in Western Europe have demonstrated their opposition to the deployment of new nuclear missiles, but they have done so with the traditional terrorist tactics of bombings and assassinations. Basque separatists have carried on a very effective terrorist campaign against the construction of a nuclear power facility in northern Spain, again with traditional tactics.

In the late 1970s, the Red Brigades, in one of their strategic directives, reportedly urged action against nuclear power facilities in Italy, but the press account of this particular document could not be verified by Italian authorities. Puerto Rican separatists have also reportedly threatened action against nuclear facilities in the United States. Recognition that nuclear facilities may be attention-getting targets, however, does not readily translate into nuclear bomb threats.

Our insights into terrorists' contemplation of the use of nuclear weapons are limited to a few casual remarks, such as that of a former German terrorist who said that with a nuclear weapon, terrorists could make the chancellor of Germany dance on top of his desk in front of television cameras. This statement provides evidence that terrorists recognize the enormous coercive power a nuclear capability would give them. More recently, an "Armenian Scientific Group" warned that Turkey's largest cities would be destroyed by three small nuclear devices the group claimed to have at its disposal.[3] This raises an important point regarding motivation: Convinced that more than a million Armenians were the victims of Turkish genocide 70 years ago, some Armenians might now feel justified in using weapons of mass destruction in revenge, which is always a potent motive.

The obvious attraction to terrorists in going nuclear, however, is not that possession of a nuclear weapons capability would enable them to kill a lot of people. Simply killing a lot of people has seldom been a terrorist objective. As I have said on numerous occasions, terrorists want a lot of people *watching*, not a lot of people *dead*. Terrorists operate on the principle of the minimum force necessary. They find it unnecessary to kill many, as long as killing a few suffices for their purposes.

Statistics bear this out. Only 15 to 20 percent of all terrorist incidents involve fatalities, and of those, two-thirds involve only one death. Less than 1 percent of the thousands of terrorist incidents that have occurred in the last two decades involve 10 or more fatalities, and incidents of mass murder are truly rare.

We have to pause for a moment to define terms. By mass murder, I mean attempts to kill large numbers of persons in a single action outside of war. Let me set aside cases where governments have deliberately pursued genocidal policies, the cumulative body counts of terrorist campaigns, or the scores of serial murderers, not because I consider any of these things less reprehensible, but because they are not what we are talking about here.

Arbitrarily taking 100 deaths as the criterion, it appears that only a handful of incidents of this scale have occurred since the beginning of the century: a 1921 bombing in Bessarabia; a 1925 bombing of a cathedral in Sofia; a little-known attempt to poison German SS prisoners of war just after World War II; the crash of a hijacked Malaysian jet airliner in 1977; the 1978 bombing of an apartment building in Beirut; a deliberately set fire that killed more than 400 in Teheran; the 1983 bombing of the U.S. Marine barracks in Beirut that killed 241. Lowering the criterion to 50 deaths produces a dozen or more additional incidents. To get even a meaningful sample, the criterion has to be lowered to 25. This in itself suggests that it is either very hard to kill large numbers of persons or very rarely tried.

Unfortunately, things are changing. Terrorist activity over the last 20 years has escalated, both in volume and in bloodshed. At the beginning of the 1970s, terrorists concentrated their attacks on property. In the 1980s, according to U.S. government statistics, half of all terrorist attacks have been directed against people. The number of incidents with fatalities and multiple fatalities has increased. A more alarming trend in the 1980s has been the growing number of incidents of large-scale indiscriminate violence: huge car bombs detonated on city streets, bombs planted in airline terminals, railroad stations, and hotel lobbies.

These incidents make it clear that terrorists have the means to kill greater numbers of people than they do now, if they wanted to. Since the constraints are not technological, we must search for other reasons. For years, I have been convinced that the actions of even those we call terrorists are limited by self-imposed constraints that derive from moral considerations or political calculations. The growing volume of testimony from terrorists interviewed while still at large, interrogated in prison, or testifying at trials has, I believe, borne out that notion.

Many terrorists consider indiscriminate violence to be immoral. They regard a government as their opponent, not the people. They may also wish to behave like a government themselves. They use the language of government to justify their actions: robberies are "expropriations," kidnap victims are subjected to a "people's trial," enemies of the people are "condemned" and "executed." Wanton violence, in their view, would imperil this image.

There are also political considerations. The capability to kill on a grand scale must be balanced against the fear of alienating perceived constituents (a population that terrorists invariably overestimate), provoking widespread revulsion, and unleashing government crackdowns that have public approval. The practical consideration of maintaining group cohesion also tends to impose limits on terrorist violence.

Attitudes toward the use of violence not only vary from group to group but also may vary within the same group. We know now that within any terrorist group there are latent defectors who have lost faith in the cause or in the efficacy of terrorist tactics, or who find themselves repelled by escalating violence and would drop out or defect if the group goes too far. A proposal to kill indiscriminately on a grand scale might provoke sharp divisions among the terrorists, exposing the operation and the group itself to betrayal.

Obviously, not all groups share the same operational code. Subscribing, or at least paying lip service to the philosophy that power comes from the people, left-wing terrorists generally target their violence against the symbols and representatives of the state, taking care to avoid civilian casualties. However, not all left-wing terrorists share this caution—Marxist ideology, for example, did not prevent the Japanese Red Army from carrying out the Lod Airport massacre in 1972.

Right-wing terrorists generally regard the people as a disorganized, despicable mass that requires strong authoritarian leadership. These terrorist groups have shown themselves capable of "pure terrorism"—indiscriminate violence calculated to create panic and a popular clamor for a political strongman who will be able to impose order.

Certain conditions or circumstances also may erode the constraints. Like soldiers in war, terrorists who have been in the field for many years may be brutalized by the long struggle; killing becomes easier. A group may seek to avenge members who have been killed or a population that has been wiped out. Terrorists may feel compelled to escalate their violence in order to keep the attention of a public that has become desensitized by the growing volume of terrorism or to recover coercive power lost as governments have become more resistant to their demands. The composition of a terrorist group may change as the faint-hearted drop out or are shoved aside by more ruthless elements. The lack of success or the imminence of defeat may call for desperate measures.

The threshold against mass murder may be lowered if the terrorists' perceived enemies and victims are members of a different ethnic group. As we have seen throughout history, the presumed approval of God for the killing of pagans, heathens, or infidels can permit acts of great destruction and self-destruction. In addition, state sponsors might covertly use terrorists to carry out a nuclear threat (although it is hard to imagine the scenario in which a state would relinquish a nuclear capability to terrorists without retaining direct control over its use). Some suggest that terrorists might overcome taboos against weapons of mass destruction by targeting a large industrial site, for example, an oil refinery where the loss of life would be minimal but the destruction of property and consequent disruption could be enormous. The annals of modern terrorism provide ample precedents for such targeting.

Several changes in the environment might increase the possibility of terrorists going nuclear. As nuclear programs expand, nuclear material suitable for use in weapons could become more widely available than it is now. Expanding commercial traffic in explosive nuclear fuel will increase the opportunities for diversion, which in turn could lead to a nuclear gray or black market where terrorists could acquire nuclear material as they now acquire conventional weapons. As knowledge of nuclear weapons design increases, so do the chances of terrorists gaining access to it.

Some developments could also alter incentives. A sudden rush by governments to acquire or to announce that they already possess nuclear weapons might persuade terrorists to attempt to do likewise. In one generation, China advanced from a guerrilla army to a nuclear power. Terrorists could try to take a short cut. The use of a nuclear weapon in war would somehow seem to lower constraints against terrorists moving toward nuclear weapons, although I am not quite sure why. Certainly, it would depend very much on the circumstances and the results. Finally, an incident of nuclear terrorism, perhaps even an alarming hoax, would almost certainly increase the probability of other terrorists going nuclear.

The question often arises, "Why would terrorists choose nuclear weapons over chemical or biological weapons, which evoke great fear and are technically less demanding?" In several ways, these weapons also are less attractive. Terrorists imitate governments, and nuclear weapons are in the arsenals of the world's major powers. That makes them "legitimate." Chemical and biological weapons also may be found in the arsenals of many nations, but their use has been widely condemned by public opinion and proscribed by treaty, although in recent years the constraints against their use seem to be eroding.

But neither chemical nor biological warfare seems to fit the pattern of terrorist behavior. Terrorist attacks are generally intended to produce immediate, dramatic effects. Terrorist incidents have a finite quality—an assassination, a bombing, a handful of deaths, and that is the end of the episode. And the terrorists retain control. This is quite different from initiating an event that offers no bang but instead produces indiscriminate deaths and lingering illness, over which the terrorists would have little control.

If terrorists had a nuclear capability, they would be more likely to brandish it as a threat than detonate it, although one can conceive of a more emotional use of a nuclear weapon by a desperate group as the ultimate instrument of revenge or as a "doomsday machine." Translating the enormous coercive power that a nuclear weapon would give a terrorist group into concrete political gains, however, poses some difficulties. First, the terrorists would have to establish the credibility of the threat. The scenarists solve this problem by having them get away with a military weapon, thus removing the uncertainty of their possession, or by providing the terrorists with two weapons, one to be used as a demonstration.

Second, the terrorists would have to persuade the government that it has an incentive to negotiate. That may sound odd, given that they could threaten to cause thousands of casualties, but the "rules" of bargaining that have evolved from dealing with ordinary hostage incidents may not apply to nuclear blackmail. For one thing, we may assume that the terrorists' demands would be commensurate with the magnitude of the threat. Governments facing the threat of nuclear terrorism would paradoxically find it more difficult to refuse, yet more difficult to yield. Impossible demands, for example, that a government liquidate itself, could not be met even under a nuclear threat. Nor could terrorists enforce permanent policy changes unless they maintained the threat indefinitely. And if a government could not be assured that the threat would not be dismantled once the demands were met, it would have little incentive to negotiate. It thus becomes a matter not of concessions, but rather of governance. I am not suggesting that armchair extortionists cannot come up with solutions to these dilemmas—finite, irrevocable demands that governments could meet with adequate assurances that the threat would end once the demands were met. I am suggesting that it is not easy for terrorists, even if they are armed with nuclear weapons, to achieve lasting political results. They might find nuclear weapons to be as useless as they are powerful.

In my 1975 essay, I concluded that

> Terrorists may not be interested in or capable of building a nuclear bomb. The point is, they do not have to. Within their range of resources and technical proficiency, they may carry out nuclear actions that will give them almost as much publicity and leverage, with less risk to themselves and less risk of alienation or retaliation. As the industry expands during the next few years, we will probably witness a growing number of low-level nuclear incidents . . . There will be moments of alarm, but the inconvenience and political repercussions that these incidents produce will probably exceed the actual danger to public safety.

We did, in fact, witness more low-level incidents.

With regard to the possibility of serious nuclear incidents, I concluded that it would increase "at a far more gradual rate" if only because the opportunities for diversion and technical know-how would increase. "At some point in the future, the opportunity and capacity for serious nuclear terrorism could reach those willing to take advantage of it." But I did not see this as an inevitable development. Before then, the development of more effective safeguards could push that "point indefinitely into the future."

What do I conclude now? Despite the theoretical increase in opportunities as nuclear programs have grown, and the demonstrable escalation in terrorism, going nuclear still represents a quantum jump for terrorists, one that is not impossible but by no means imminent or inevitable.

NOTES

1. Brian Jenkins, *Will Terrorists Go Nuclear?* California Seminar on Arms Control and Foreign Policy, paper No. 64, Los Angeles: Crescent Publications, 1975. I returned to this topic in several subsequent essays and have drawn on these freely in the preparation of these remarks. Anyone interested in the evolution of my own thinking on various aspects of the issue may examine *The Potential for Nuclear Terrorism*, P-5876, Santa Monica: The Rand Corporation, May 1977, and *The Consequences of Nuclear Terrorism*, P-6373, Santa Monica: The Rand Corporation, August 1979 (also in John Kerry King [ed.], *International Political Effects of the Spread of Nuclear Weapons*, Washington, D.C.: U.S. Government Printing Office, 1979.
2. A number of my colleagues and friends provided comments and advice on the topic in the preparation of my previous essays as well as in this one. I would like especially to thank Konrad Kellen, Victor Gilinsky, Ariel Merari, and Paul Leventhal.
3. *Marmara,* Istanbul, January 14, 1985.

* * * * *

RESPONSES

David Mabry

I would be a fool if I did not say that this is very serious business in the Department of State and that we take the nuclear threat very seriously. I agree with Brian Jenkins that, basically, terrorists still have as their focus influencing people and not exterminating them. But I think that mass destruction is getting far more commonplace, and terrorists are becoming bolder and bolder. As Brian said in an earlier article that he wrote, staying in the headlines requires acts of greater and greater violence, and we are seeing that in what has happened in the past week.

I was up in the counter-terrorism office the night before last, and at 4:05 a.m. we got the first feed-in information via a Federal Aviation Agency channel that a plane had gone down. My first thought was it flew out of Montreal and it had a bomb on it. I mean, you can predict these things; at least, when they happen, you can almost tell what might have prompted the disaster.

We know that we have a serious incidence of state-sponsored terrorism, and there is no doubt in my mind that Libya or Iran wouldn't hesitate at least to encourage acts of nuclear terrorism. We at the State Department just cannot discount that possibility.

Our focus now is on contingency planning. I am very much involved in emergency action planning and crisis management—that's my role as a deputy director there—and we have to plan for the contingency that we are talking about here today.

The most popular act of a terrorist is bombing, and an extension of that act, it seems to me, is combining radioactive material with an explosive device. It would enable them to capture far bigger headlines. The media interest that we have seen the past week, and the numbers of callers who want to assist or who want to provide a solution or who are panicked, would be increased a hundredfold if we had such a threat. The cost of decontamination to the United States would be incredible. The lethal physical damage—it all poses a grave dilemma.

A major nuclear accident abroad, particularly involving terrorism, could seriously undermine the ability of our strategic and tactical nuclear capable forces to function effectively abroad in the furtherance of our national strategies. Also, I don't think that there is any question but that an incident of that type could adversely affect our current arms-control interests. So, I repeat again, we take this threat very seriously.

We have enacted memoranda of understanding between the FBI, the Defense Nuclear Agency, the Department of Energy and our department. The U.S. political response, as you know, focuses on, or falls upon, the local U.S. diplomatic mission. Its emergency action committee is the focus for all managership of a crisis. In an effort to train these emergency action committees in crisis response, we are reviewing their emergency preparedness throughout the world. We are conducting crisis management exercises at 36 posts in 1986, 22 in 1985.

The preparation of an emergency action committee to handle a nuclear incident is a logical extension of the exercises we are already conducting. Our military commands already plan extensively. They exercise regularly. Their unified and specified command structure has major on-scene responsibilities for handling a nuclear incident.

When we are talking crisis management at a foreign post, we are talking about dovetailing an embassy plan with the military plan. We have developed a model nuclear plan for the 19 key posts in the world that most probably could have a nuclear disaster. By the end of this month, those 19 key embassies will have provided to the State Department a copy of their nuclear crisis management annex. Later this summer, we will have an implementation visit by a team of the State Department and Defense Nuclear Agency visiting those commands, or at least some of them, to discuss the dovetailing of their plan with the military plan.

In 1986, we will be conducting crisis management exercises of a nuclear type at 10 foreign posts, and at another 9 in fiscal year 1987. We had a joint U.S.-U.K. exercise this past May; we are going to have another one with the Federal Republic of Germany in October.

Bilaterally, we have a relatively high level of cooperation with other countries. Technical consultations have taken place on a regular basis. In the last 10 years, there has been a very useful exchange of information, and we have discussed informal exercise and training responses with them.

In summary, I would like to say that we have an awful lot to do in the State Department. I would be kidding you if I said we were not very concerned at how much we have to do in the future, and I'm talking about the immediate future. We are very sensitive to that fact. We know we cannot eradicate this threat, and that the only thing we can do is prepare for it in as much detail as we can.

* * *

Yuval Ne'eman

Two topics have been discussed in Dr. Jenkins' paper, and I am in general agreement with him. However, I'll state those cases in which I find that my own reading of the situation leads me to somewhat different conclusions. One is the issue of the protection of nuclear plants, and the other is terrorism based on nuclear weapons. These are two very different issues. The prospective perpetrators of the terrorism acts are very different; the whole picture is a different one.

About the nuclear plants, one has to start considering terrorism as one more risk in designing a plant, notwithstanding the difficulty of adapting to such thinking in the beginning. Airlines were very reluctant to think of having to search luggage or fly with protection until they were forced to do it. And so there are considerations that will have to be taken in the future in the design of nuclear facilities. I would say that the American industry, having come to a standstill anyhow (no new orders for nuclear plants), may now have the opportunity to concentrate on trying to design reactors that would be much safer in several ways, including against terrorism, for instance, going underground with the nuclear parts or different fuel concepts, etc.

Now as to terrorism and the prospective use of nuclear weapons, I tend to agree with what Dr. Yonah Alexander has said, that, generally, as in the cited example of the attack on the Marines in Lebanon, most terrorism is state-sponsored. There may be here and there some lone groups working on their own, but I think that even when this happens for a while, in the end they all become linked into the terrorist internationale nowadays. There is a terrorist internationale, and the Soviets are responsible for creating it. They must have some branch in their secret services that took care to put such different and distant organizations as the Japanese Red Army, the Tupamaros in South America, the PLO, the Bader-Meinhof and the Italian Red Brigades together, and to organize it so that those bases that existed in Lebanon until three years ago could serve as the training grounds for everybody. How else can you have this Japanese Red Army, which had never heard about Israel, come and perpetrate the main action (1969) in an Israeli airport, etc. There have been many indications of these connections. Whoever has had some experience in what it takes to search for such an organization will realize that they couldn't just come to Japan and look for the Japanese Red Army, and vice versa. You need somebody who has a good protected base in each country with continuous collection and collation of information. Only then can one put all such groups together in contact.

So there is such an internationale. Now I think that the Soviets, in this case we are discussing (nuclear terrorism), do not represent an important danger. I think they are more careful, and they would not like to be at the mercy of these groups. Having a nuclear weapon in the hands of one of the terrorist groups would represent for them a danger as well, indirectly. Not that it would be used against them, since there has never been any terrorist act of any of these groups directed against any Soviet plane, for instance. Nevertheless, the terrorists would represent a danger, indirectly, for instance, of starting a war. So the Soviets have an interest in restraining such activities and are not a danger.

The question is, who does represent a threat? As things stand at present, I have to give a precise answer much as I don't like, as a scientist, to be specific. In physics you generalize and you write formulae that go for any situation; then you introduce boundary conditions that represent a definite situation. But in this field, I think that if you want to really be ready for what's coming, you've got to consider what is happening on the ground. I think the one danger is from states that have strong motivation, that are militant. For such states, the use of a terrorist organization would also be a method, and perhaps the only one, of acquiring nuclear weapons by stealing them or attacking an American or NATO base and getting them by force. Also, such states have an interest in using unidentified terrorist groups in order to evade possible retaliation. So these are really the possible sponsors of such an operation. Libya, for one, is very prominent in my mind as a candidate. There has been a lot of documentation about at least three attempts of Khaddafi to lay his hands on nuclear weapons. Of course, it would be easier for him to do it indirectly, without having the finger point to Libya for retaliation. It's got to be a state that has some special (though irrational) motivation and that is not industrialized, so that force is the only way for it to acquire nuclear weapons. It has to have money, so that it may spend it on things of that nature. It couldn't be a poor Bangladesh or a country that cannot really afford that kind of action. In a normal situation, I would say that countries such as Iraq and Iran would be obvious candidates, too, but now they are at each other's throats, and if one of them does get hold of a nuclear weapon, it will just throw it at the other immediately, without going through terrorists. Remember how Iraq has been using chemical weapons, as has been confirmed by the SIPRI Institute in Sweden these last days. If the situation were to arise where they were not at each other's throats, they might be similar candidates for international nuclear terrorism. So one has to look at such concrete situations. I think these are the key dangers.

I would only like to make one more comment to Dr. Jenkins' belief that there are moral limitations on terrorists in using nuclear weapons and that they would refrain from killing blindly. I am afraid that, sometimes, similar "moral" forces are the ones that push you to kill. I think that if you live in Lebanon in 1985, you don't have to be a terrorist to believe that the best thing you can do for your religion is to kill everybody who belongs to the other religion. So the motivation in that case is not limited by such "moral" considerations. I would not think, if terrorists acquire a weapon, that they would simply just ask for a price to give it back. They might indeed threaten the extermination of a city, and for that price ask for whatever can be asked for. But they could also use the weapons. So I think the danger of nuclear weapons being used by terrorists is perhaps small in terms of the technical possibilities, but it is certainly there, and I have pointed to the main direction where you should concentrate your attention, in my mind.

* * *

Mason Willrich

Like Brian Jenkins, I am re-visiting ground I have plowed before. I can't help but note, in passing, that the timing of this conference is abysmal in terms of what is going on in the external environment that is affecting the situation we are discussing.

In commenting on Jenkins' paper, I'd like to focus on three issues: incentives for terrorists to go nuclear; possibilities for terrorists to go nuclear; and what might be done about the threat. As far as the incentives are concerned, Jenkins noted how a sudden increase in the number of governments with nuclear weapons could increase the likelihood of terrorists following suit. It's interesting to note that the rate of spread of nuclear weapons among governments of the world has proceeded at a much slower pace than the potential for doing so, and the question arises, whether there is a likelihood of an acceleration in that rate in the near future. Perhaps the rate itself is a commentary, an assessment of the practical political and military utility of nuclear weapons acquisition by governments. Nevertheless, there are a number of disturbing situations around the world. Pakistan is one of them, and there the United States has leverage that, in my view, can and should be used effectively.

In terms of other countries that have been or are particular concerns, my reading of the situation in Latin America, which is obviously from some distance, is that there has been continuation of some unfavorable trends in terms of fuel cycle development. However, the political backdrop for perhaps reduced incentives for acquisition of nuclear weapons capabilities in that region seems potentially more favorable.

In terms of the larger issue of non-proliferation incentives, I think that the United States and the Soviet Union continue to present a bad example to the rest of the world in their continuing reliance on nuclear terror to deter each other. That kind of a backdrop cannot be ignored in terms of dealing with the incentives for terrorists to go nuclear.

Turning to the possibilities, I am not going to discuss the possibilities for theft of nuclear weapons from weapons stockpiles. Let me say a few words about the civilian fuel cycle, however, beginning with the growth of nuclear power worldwide. First of all, I think that it is important for the overall world energy situation that nuclear power development proceed on a safe and economic basis, so I am not an advocate, but a cautious supporter, of the development of nuclear power in appropriate circumstances. The rate of development of nuclear power has been substantially slower than we would have thought in the last 10 years because of slower economic growth, slower growth in electricity demands, increased construction costs of nuclear power plants and increased public concern with operational safety issues, and because of problems, particularly in the United States, with operational safety.

I think we need to distinguish carefully between reactors as a possible target for sabotage by terrorist organizations, and fuel cycle facilities, which may be a possible source of fissionable materials for terrorist organizations. The consequences of the slower growth rate in nuclear power is that there is, today, plenty of uranium. I don't think there is much economic justification, if you are starting out today, for any use of plutonium, either in a recycle mode in light water reactors or, particularly, in any sort of breeder-reactor program. For the time being, the United States is relying upon the once-through fuel cycle. Indeed, we are struggling to maintain the nuclear power option in the United States. So the once-through fuel cycle is something we need to clearly establish before we think about moving further, as far as the fuel cycle itself is concerned.

Nevertheless, there are reprocessing, breeder-reactor development programs and some use of plutonium for recycling in light water reactors, particularly in Europe and perhaps in the future in Japan. But this is on a stretched out schedule, and separated plutonium is not being transported to the extent we thought it would be at one time. Troublesome facilities, however, do remain in a variety of sensitive countries, and those are obvious sources of substantial concern.

Now what should be done about all of this? Well, I would say that the United States and the Soviet Union need to achieve meaningful arms control, based upon minimum levels of deterrent forces, rather than upon accelerating the arms race by pressing forward with the Strategic Defense Initiative (SDI), as currently proposed. Second, we need to strengthen the non-proliferation treaty and the IAEA system of safeguards. Third, as part of that, we need to restructure the nuclear power industry internationally, with a whole set of ideas that have been around for many years that have not been implemented: international custody of plutonium stocks, construction of fuel cycle facilities on the basis of multinational ownership, and the co-location of fuel fabrication facilities with reprocessing facilities, where that occurs. As I say, there isn't much justification for doing that, but where it does occur, that should be the mode. That kind of a framework, I think, is going to be more conducive to being able to apply strong physical security safeguards that will effectively prevent. I think that's what we need to focus on—the prevention of any terrorist inroads into civilian nuclear fuel cycle activities.

Basically, one of the best ways to proceed with nuclear power is to proceed with it on the basis of strong and broad economic justifications. We need to use restraints in terms of international nuclear trade, where necessary, to prevent using fuel cycle facilities as sweeteners. Such sweeteners are about as dangerous and about as ineffective in promoting the use of nuclear power in the world as deploying new strategic nuclear systems by the United States and the Soviet Union for use as bargaining chips in promoting arms control negotiations.

* * *

John Peter Goss

Before making my own comments, may I fix as my reference point a definition of terrorism. I view terrorism as a tactic used for specific purposes within a spectrum of political violence that runs from violent demonstrations through to armed insurgency. Through violence or threats of violence, terrorism is intended to coerce or intimidate individuals, a community or government in furtherance of political aims. Since, then, the essence of terrorism is violence, there is a certain logic that the terrorist will push terrorism to its extreme limits. Indeed, we have seen over the past 20 years an ineluctable progression in sophistication, violence and the spectacular nature of terrorist attacks.

I am fond of tracking this progression in "10-year slices." For example:

- *Prior to 1965*: Terrorism was essentially, but not exclusively, an element of rural insurgency in the campaigns against colonial powers, e.g., Indochina, Malaya, Algeria.
- *By 1975*: Urban terrorism had appeared and taken root. The main European terrorist groups had emerged; aircraft hijacking; kidnapping of government officials and businessmen; spectacular assassinations and hostage incidents (such as the 1973 massacre of Olympic athletes) had been staged.
- *By 1985*: The full international character of terrorism and state sponsorship had emerged. The ante of violence had been raised to include massive bombing attacks (Bologna station, 1980, and Beirut, 1983); ultra-spectacular assassinations or attempts, exemplified by Schleyer (1977), Moro (1978), the Pope (1983); and embassy hostage-taking (the Iranian Embassy in London, 1979, and Dominican Embassy in Bogota, 1980).

It is reasonable to suppose that this progression might continue in the decade to 1995. In this context, and with the increasing publicity offered to each subject, it might seem natural for the public to link the seeming omniscience of terrorism and the specter of a nuclear apocalypse (a symbiotic link of expectancy). Certainly, a terrorist threat involving use of nuclear material would cause unprecedented panic. We have also heard this morning of the availability of technical information for construction of a nuclear device and the inevitable increase in the types and quantities of radiated material within the nuclear industry and scientific fields that would tend to facilitate progress toward nuclear terrorism.

Nevertheless, and leaving apart consideration of external (e.g., security) controls, I believe that there are very real constraints upon the construction and use of nuclear devices by terrorists.

While technical theory may be available to terrorists, the logistical resources required by them for construction and deployment and operation would be considerable. (To take a conventional example, while the Beirut bombings of 1983/84 required considerable sophistication and resources, they were mounted in an ideal environment and would be extremely difficult to set up logistically outside of that operational area.)

While many terrorist groups appear to be (and are popularly publicized as) mindless, irrational killers, the activities of mainstream terrorist groups are anything but purposeless (even if that purpose is misguided). The killing of innocent victims is more often than not coldly calculated. While in some cases there have been instances of violent attacks designed specifically to cause extreme public reaction and Draconian countermeasures by government, most terrorist activities take into account the need to preserve a degree of public sympathy and to develop their constituency. This constraint leads them to seek some legitimacy in the type of target selected and the limitation of the scale of violence used. The use of a nuclear device would totally forfeit public support, whether national or international.

Another significant restraint must be the potential ideological divisions and stresses that exist within the terrorist groups and that, under even "normal" circumstances, inhibit decision-making and action.

Another constraint must be that of the actual risks incurred by the terrorists carrying out a nuclear operation. Whatever the claims of Iranian Revolutionary Guards and Lebanese Shiite extremist groups to be seeking martyrdom, it has been very rare for terrorists to lend themselves to suicide missions. Invariably they go for the "safer" option in their portfolio of potential targets. (The Japanese Red Army and Armenians have been notable exceptions in their willingness to go down with the target.) Security controls protecting nuclear weapon sites and material must provide a strong deterrent.

I must add some caveats to what I have said. While the exploitation of nuclear means by mainstream terrorist groups is unlikely at present, it is entirely possible that extremist and fanatical splinter groups or individuals would be willing to resort to such means; however, here *capability* is unlikely to match *intent*.

One might see the emergence of new groups willing to push terrorist violence to its limits. The history of many terrorist groups is characterized by divisions between protagonists of the use of violence and those favoring a more political approach (the IRA, ETA and PLO are good examples). It is a fact that, no matter what tactical successes terrorist groups achieved, not one has yet attained its long-term aims. It is arguable that sections of existing extremist organizations, or new groups, may take the view that the failure has been the result of a reluctance on the part of traditional leadership to go sufficiently far in the promotion of violence and that operations of mass destruction would be more effective. Most dangerous, perhaps, are the emerging groups with religious motivations, people who are not reading the same maps as we are.

Insofar as extremist splinter groups are concerned, the Lebanese Shiite "Islamic Jihad," to give this ill-defined group its umbrella home, is one that might favor the use of weapons of mass destruction. For the immediate future, happily, intent again is very unlikely to be matched by capability.

Turning from the mainstream groups themselves, would the *sponsor states* of terrorism be prepared to pass nuclear technology or means to their proxies?

The Soviet Union, undeniably dedicated to the wide support of international and indigenous terrorism through finance, training, equipment, etc., certainly does not exercise, in my view, the degree of close control of terrorist groups that would permit the passing of weapons or materials of mass destruction. The degree of Soviet control over nuclear weapon systems within the Warsaw Pact demonstrates this concern. The Soviets may also well feel that they are doing quite well with present conventional support and its appropriate exploitation.

Iran may appear totally irresponsible in its conduct of international relations and its actions, but I would suggest that there is a great difference between the sponsorship of bombing, hostage-taking and kidnapping and the encouragement of nuclear terrorism on the part of its adherents. Whatever the pull of religious fanaticism, I do not see the Iranians (or Syrians) providing Lebanese Shiite extremist groups (such as Hispallah) with the means of nuclear mass destruction, even if these were available to them. I should add a caveat that if such groups were able to gain independent access to nuclear material, they would have considerably fewer inhibitions.

Libya, on its track record, must be considered a rogue element on the terrorist scene. While no responsible government (including the USSR) would wish to see Colonel Qadaffi provided with nuclear means, there is always the possibility that a regime as dedicated to clandestine activity as it is and with such formable financial resources as it has might succeed in acquiring radioactive material. One should note that, apart from account-settling with its own dissidents, Libya tends to operate through proxies.

To look at another dimension of the problem, what demand or ultimate aim would favor the use by terrorists of nuclear devices or material (as opposed to conventional means)? Among them may be:

- The bringing down of a government or its leadership by exposing the regime's incompetence or impotence. However, other means (e.g., systematic attacks on the government structure or the national economy, assassination or even large-scale hostage-taking) may also achieve this end.
- Palestinian aims in resolving the Israeli problem. They are unlikely to be achieved by an act of nuclear terrorism. Indeed, however, it is highly likely that it would be counter-productive. The same could be said of an attempt, for example, on the part of Sikh extremists to gain independence for Khalistan.
- The release of convicted terrorists, of political prisoners, provision of welfare, etc. All are other subjects of possible demand, but ones that could equally well be obtained by more conventional means.
- The raising of extremely large financial ransoms for terrorist funding purposes.

While the actual detonation of a nuclear device as an act of terrorism is, I believe, most unlikely at present, there are nuclear-associated means further down the scale of violence that could be exploited by extremist splinter groups or "crazies":

- The use of hoaxes (which could be extremely elaborate and sophisticated) utilizing contaminated material (with a sample to be provided to demonstrate capability). The particular problem of dealing with this type of threat (as in conventional bomb and product extortion) is the assessment of capability and intent. The stakes for guessing correctly would be extremely high, and the temptation to concede equally so.
- Actual contamination by radioactive materials, e.g., of buildings, symbolic targets, water supplies.
- More conventionally, occupation of a nuclear plant.
- Low-level bombing or sabotage of nuclear plants or sites.

I would again make the point that the threat to use nuclear means is likely to be as effective as the actual carrying out of the attack. The factor of media publicity (the "Hexagon" element in the mixture) would invest the threat with an added dimension of credibility; the pressures generated upon governments to concede would be enormous.

I have confined my remarks to the nuclear threat. I believe, however, that the use of chemical and biological warfare (CBW) agents may be in fact more attractive to terrorists. While some of the same practical political and moral restraints remain, CBW agents are certainly much cheaper and easier to produce, to steal and to put into effect.

There are other conventional means and targets open to terrorists, short of those weapons of mass destruction, that I can foresee being exploited over the next decade in preference, at least temporarily, to nuclear terrorism.

They include:

- Shipjacking—LNG and LPG ships and storage facilities
- Attacks on power grids
- Attack on pipelines
- Attacks on communication systems
- Attacks on computer centers
- Mass hostage-taking
- Mass assassination (e.g., by bombs detonated on aircraft in flight).

To look beyond the next decade is highly speculative. However, given the continuation of terrorism, one must say that the likelihood of resort to nuclear terrorism must be increasingly likely. The proliferation of nuclear technology and the increase in the amounts and movements of fissionable material will provide additional opportunities. If this thesis is correct, it points again to the necessity for national and international efforts to eradicate terrorist groups through a comprehensive strategy geared to the development of political solutions for, or amelioration of, the underlying causes.

* * *

Bertram Brown

A brief word on the unique perspective of a psychiatrist: There are a group of us you see on TV frequently, almost always on the issue of hostages and their families and their mental health. It is a hearty public band. There's a smaller, private band who have been involved in the psychology of crisis managers of terrorist incidents. The smallest band deals with the psychology of the terrorists themselves. This area is the least substantial in terms of our collective knowledge and experience, but we have some.

We on this panel are asked to judge between two extremes. One is that reported by George Gallup, who found that many people view a disastrous incident involving terrorists in this country as the most imminent danger, and the view expressed by Brian Jenkins in the final paragraph of his paper, so low-key that I'll repeat it: "Going nuclear still represents a quantum jump for terrorists, one that is not impossible but by no means imminent or inevitable."

Because of the seriousness of this issue, I will start by reflecting on a 1980 conference at the Rand Corporation, at which a group of specialists, probably similar to those here today, were broken up into groups to discuss government response, the terrorist mindset and so on. I was in the group on the future of terrorism, where I had the bold, bad luck to predict accurately the forthcoming assassination of the Pope. The analysis at that time had to do with the two structures most vulnerable to those interested in instability: the multinational corporations and the church. And to do the preacher's thing today and tell you my conclusion, I reluctantly conclude that we will see a nuclear incident before the end of this decade.

Let me briefly highlight how I came to such a troubling opinion. From 1961 to 1963 I was a special assistant to President John F. Kennedy in the White House and had access as a psychiatrist to that setting. I just want to bring up two incidents. Because I was the house "shrink," all the kooks, troubles, weird letters, everything you can imagine, came my way. A telegram came my way, hard to decipher, but essentially relating that a submarine would sink in a couple of months. Two months later, the *Thresher* sank. It is still unclear whether the author of that telegram was an insider making a prediction based on manufacturing difficulties, or someone more sinister.

More dramatically, in 1962, a very high government official brought his brother to see me privately. He had been railroaded out of an important job in the Department of the Interior. His position related to the licensing of land for oil shale exploration. From a psychiatric point of view, he was clearly diagnosable as a paranoid schizophrenic, bordering on the rare diagnosis of pure paranoia.

The papers he brought were both luminous and frightening. They included not only geological maps and findings, but a complete analysis and bibliography of his Rorshach tests, which by guile and sheer brainpower he had hoodwinked an experienced psychologist into diagnosing as showing pathology. There is no limit to the intelligence of a paranoid schizophrenic. His musings included not only the clear desire of someone to make billions of dollars, but he had also developed technological plans to create an artificial earthquake. He wanted to do that to prove a scientific point in contention on the relationship of natural gas to oil. I have no doubt that if he had had the support structure to bring off the earthquake, he would have done just that or been a pawn in the hands of those who wanted to see it done.

The point of this story is to illustrate the outer limits of how far an intelligent insider might go to prove a point, to wreak vengeance on his enemies, or to catharsize his feelings of anger or powerlessness. The insider story, and the implication of the outer limits of behavior and motivation, apply even more strongly to outsiders vis-à-vis nuclear power, I think. The question I would like to deal with is whether there is a basic difference, from a psychiatric or psychological point of view, in the use of fist, knife, gun, bomb, chemical, biological agent and nuclear power. Is there something different in motivation and psychological structures at these different levels? After careful reflection, my answer is a crisp "no." There is no essential difference.

The second question is whether there is any incompatability between being a person scientifically and technologically skilled, and being psychologically able to carry out a dreadful act of nuclear terror. The point I want to make is that, while statistically rare, such a combination of scientific competence and motivation is a distinct possibility and, I think, will increase.

Finally, I want to look at the question of whether the current driving force of religious fundamentalism, that is, theological motivation, makes it more or less likely that the psychological fusion of motivation and technical competence will occur. A nuclear Carlos is rare, but realistic. My answer is that the very nature of life and death of man, its great meaning and meaningless, the power of the afterworld, heaven, nirvana and paradise, all make it a more likely possibility that the combination that I mention—of scientific and technical competence and adequate motivation—will combine.

After all, be it fascism, communism or capitalism, all political systems want a world to run, whereas those motivated by theology do not care whether or not there is a real world. It's the afterworld that counts. Add to this mix state sponsorship—more important, religious fundamentalist state inspiration—and I've concluded we will see a major nuclear disaster before the 1980s are over.

* * *

Louis René Beres

The guiding question for this panel is easy to answer. There is little doubt that the essential requirements for nuclear terrorism[1]—capability and intention—can be met by a variety of insurgent groups. Indeed, such experts as Brian Jenkins, Theodore Taylor and Mason Willrich have been telling us this authoritatively for some time.

The critical question, of course, is what should be done to prevent nuclear terrorism. We do need a plan. But it must not be limited to the sorts of "quick fix" physical security measures that are now in fashion. Rather, it must rest upon a greatly improved understanding of terrorism generally, especially the motives behind those groups that seek to harm the United States. In this connection, particular attention must be directed toward those aspects of American foreign policy that may elicit hostile insurgent action against this country.

A certain number of insurgent groups lie beyond the pale of U.S. foreign policy changes. For all intents and purposes, their motives are fixed and irrevocable. Regarding the danger of nuclear terrorism posed by these groups, the only viable strategy of prevention lies in high-quality intelligence gathering and in efficient police and/or military operations. I will leave the details of this strategy to others at this conference who are much more knowledgeable on such matters.

There are, however, several groups of prospective nuclear terrorists that draw their anti-American orientations from specific aspects of current U.S. foreign policy. These are the groups that feel threatened by U.S./NATO Euromissile deployments and by the Reagan administration's indifference to human rights in anti-Soviet states. They might also include agents or supporters of allegedly pro-Soviet governments (e.g., Nicaragua) who resent U.S. intervention, or even U.S.-backed terrorists (e.g., contras) who feel that their American support has been pulled out from under them.

Consider the Euromissiles. If they really do serve a deterrent function, then we must deploy them whatever the risk of terrorism. But, contrary to what Washington would have us believe, these missiles can only *degrade* deterrence. Since these weapons could never actually be used in retaliation for conventional attacks by a sane president of the United States (because such use would probably elicit all-out nuclear war with the Soviet Union), they are perceived by Moscow as instruments of American preemption.

This perception is not lost upon millions of Europeans who oppose the stationing of cruise and Pershing II missiles on their territories. In response to what they see as American plans for "sanctuary nuclear war"—a strategy whereby Soviet nuclear reprisals would be confined to European targets—some of these threatened populations may embark upon a full-scale assault on U.S. and NATO military installations. Although it would be misguided for the United States to reverse Euromissile deployments solely out of fear of terrorist intimidation, the fact that these deployments undermine deterrence makes such reversal imperative.

Let us also consider human rights. Nurtured by the sterile clairvoyance of the Cold War, the Reagan administration will tolerate virtually any breach of human rights in pursuit of anti-Soviet advantage. As a result, certain of the oppressed peoples of Latin America and South Africa are now increasingly hostile to the United States. Recognizing the alliance between their oppressors and U.S. policy, they may target Americans as well as oligarchs.

There has been no learning from the lessons of the past. What can the Reagan administration hope to accomplish by standing alongside such pariah states as Chile and South Africa while unleashing attacks against less repressive regimes? If we are really interested in protecting ourselves against terrorism, why do we persist in support of governments that make terrorism inevitable? If we fear that Chile will become "another Nicaragua," why did we install the Pinochet regime in the first place?

Current policies that spawn terrorism against the United States also ensure the opposition of governments-in-the-making. During the next few years, insurgents fighting against regime terror in places such as Chile, Haiti, Paraguay and South Africa will likely prevail. Installed with authority, these former rebels will, in the fashion of Cuba, Nicaragua and Iran, become enemies of the United States. Sadly, this development would have been avoidable if only this country had remained true to its doctrinal foundations, opposing not only "leftist thugs" (President Reagan's characterization of the regime overthrown in Grenada), but also all tyrannical regimes (that is, rightist thugs as well).

What will happen when the opponents of U.S.-supported repression in Latin America and South Africa mount successful insurgencies, creating successor governments with strongly anti-American leanings? The answer is entirely predictable. This country will begin the next phase of geopolitical competition, mounting its own insurgencies to topple regimes that are now left-wing. Resembling the administration's current war against Nicaragua, these insurgencies, conducted by "freedom fighters," will seek to bring down a black majority government in South Africa that will be denounced as a "Soviet pawn." By this reasoning, the present condition of apartheid (as with Somoza's rule in Nicaragua) will be described as the "lesser evil."

The conclusion is unambiguous. To be effective, U.S. measures to combat terrorism will require disengagement from support of authoritarian regimes. They will also require an end to our support of counter-revolutionary forces in Nicaragua and to our Euromissile deployments.

The true danger of terrorism lies not in the guerrilla camps of Central America and southern Africa or in the strategems of Europe's anti-nuclear forces. The enemy lies in ourselves. By supporting invidious regimes in pursuit of anti-Soviet advantage, we spark and sustain a worldwide insurgency against the United States. And by endangering our European allies with provocative and useless nuclear deployments on their territories, we spawn a continuing and possibly escalating wave of anti-American violence.

Who Are the Terrorists?

Before the United States can reduce the risk of nuclear terrorism, its leaders must understand the difference between lawful and unlawful insurgencies. And this understanding must be based upon more than the desolate intuitions of geopolitics. Specifically, it must rest upon well-established jurisprudential standards that reflect not only international law but also the most cherished elements of the American political tradition.

The imperative is clear! To meet the requirements of effective counter-nuclear terrorism, the United States must oppose repressive regimes and movements whatever their ideological stripe. It must also support those insurgencies that spring from genuinely "just cause" and that are carried out with due regard for humanitarian rules governing the use of force.

Today, the Reagan administration embraces only one standard of judgment concerning American foreign policy: anti-Sovietism. Human rights have nothing to do with this standard. It follows that efforts to overthrow allegedly pro-Soviet regimes are always conducted by "freedom fighters" (even where these efforts— as in the case of the contras—involve rape, pillage, and mass murder),[2] while efforts to oppose anti-Soviet regimes (even where these efforts are undertaken by the most oppressed and downtrodden peoples under genocidal regimes) are always conducted by "terrorists."

Consider President Reagan's press conference of March 21, 1985, where he stated that the 17 blacks recently shot by South African police were not "simply killed," but were the excusable casualties of "rioting." Moments later, reacting to a question about Nicaragua, the President defended the use of force against a "communist tyranny." In other words, rebellion against apartheid must always be peaceful, but opposition to Sandinista rule must always be violent.

With this view, black South Africans, although understandably unhappy to be the victims of a uniquely repressive regime, are instructed to be "patient" as the United States continues with its policy of "constructive engagement." At the same time, contra rebels—widely and authoritatively associated with the execution of non-combatants in Nicaragua and with death-squad activities in El Salvador and Honduras—are embraced by the president as "our brothers." These "freedom fighters," said the president on March 1, "are the moral equal of our Founding Fathers."

The Reagan administration bases its selective regard for human rights on pure bravado. As a result, a majority of the world's peoples now see this country as an *affliction*. It follows that insurgent groups throughout the world are likely to accelerate their activities against the United States. In other words, by its failure to recognize the connection between regime terror and insurgent terror, this country will render itself increasingly vulnerable to terrorism in general and to nuclear terrorism in particular.

This increasing vulnerability is the result not only of the Reagan administration's tolerance of repression in "authoritarian" regimes. It is also the result of its active opposition to certain "totalitarian" governments. In Nicaragua, for example, it is obvious that the contras, even with significant levels of U.S. aid, will be defeated. An expected consequence of this defeat, in addition to hardened anti-American resolve by the Sandinista regime, may well be terrorism directed against the United States and/or its interests and personnel abroad. The origins of this terrorism might lie not only with the Sandinistas, who will have been pushed into the arms of the Soviet Union by self-defeating U.S. policies, but also with the remnants of an embittered contra force.

Recently, Secretary of State Shultz, in an address on "Terrorism and the Modern World," said the following: "I can assure you that in this Administration, our actions will be governed by the rule of law; and the rule of law is congenial to action against terrorists. . . . "[3] In fact, of course, the Reagan administration has been guided not by law but by the banal syntax of geopolitics. Although the rule of law is indeed congenial to action against terrorists, it does not permit the subordination of settled jurisprudential standards to the presumed requirements of Cold War competition.

The United States can't have it both ways. There is little point to our condemnations of state terrorism against American interests in the Middle East if we support our own terrorists in Central America. Moreover, there is little point in bemoaning terrorist indifference to the humanitarian rules of armed conflict—an indifference that occasions particular concern for nuclear terrorism—when contra rebels display total disregard for these rules.[4]

Preventing Nuclear Terrorism Through Nonproliferation

The recommended changes in U.S. foreign policy would reduce the threat of terrorism against this country. They would not, however, remove the threat altogether. To reduce the threat still further, it is essential that we also act to prevent terrorist access to nuclear weapons, nuclear power plants, and nuclear waste storage facilities.[5] Among other measures, this means that we act to control nuclear proliferation.[6]

The present nonproliferation regime is based upon a series of multilateral agreements, statutes, and safeguards. The principal elements of this series are the Atomic Energy Act of 1954; the Statute of the International Atomic Energy Agency, which came into force in 1957; the Nuclear Test Ban Treaty, which entered into force on October 10, 1963; the Outer Space Treaty, which entered into force on October 10, 1967; the Treaty Prohibiting Nuclear Weapons in Latin America, which entered into force on April 22, 1968; the Seabeds Arms Control Treaty, which entered into force on May 18, 1972; and the 1978 Nuclear Nonproliferation Act.

The single most important element of the nonproliferation regime, however, is the Treaty on the Nonproliferation of Nuclear Weapons, which entered into force on March 5, 1970. Since Article VI of this treaty calls for an end to the nuclear arms race between the superpowers,[7] the current U.S.-U.S.S.R. negotiations on arms control must also be counted as part of the nonproliferation regime. Before the world's non-nuclear powers can begin to take nonproliferation seriously, the United States and the Soviet Union will have to take prompt steps to limit their own nuclear armaments.

In the view of the non-nuclear weapon states, a "bargain" has been struck between the superpowers and themselves. Unless the Soviet Union and the United States begin to take more ambitious steps toward implementation of the Article VI pledge, they, too, will move in the direction of nuclear capability. The non-nuclear powers consider this bargain the most prudent path to safety.

From the standpoint of controlling nuclear proliferation and preventing nuclear terrorism, this suggests that the superpowers must restructure their central strategic relationship. Such restructuring must be oriented toward a return to strategies of "minimum deterrence"; a comprehensive nuclear test ban; a joint renunciation of first-use of nuclear weapons; and a joint effort toward creating additional nuclear-weapon-free zones.[8]

Additional incentives, however, would also be needed. Of these, the most important would be an understanding that nuclear weapons do not enhance the security of those states that still do not possess them. While such a view would prove difficult to understand in a world committed to the principles of "realism," its essential truthfulness suggests some cause for optimism. This cause might be heightened by maintaining the burdensome costs associated with a military nuclear program and by offering superpower security assurances to non-nuclear allies.

In conjunction with these measures, the IAEA must be granted greater authority to inspect nuclear facilities, search for clandestine stockpiles, and pursue stolen nuclear materials. Ultimately, such authority must be extended to all nuclear facilities of all non-nuclear weapons states. Without such a tightening of IAEA safeguards, a number of non-nuclear weapon states can be expected to calculate that the benefits of non-proliferation are exceeded by the costs.

The strengthening and expanding of IAEA safeguards and functions are essential to nonproliferation and the avoidance of nuclear terrorism. These goals can also be served by an improved international capability for gathering covert intelligence. In the future, many of the intelligence capabilities that now rest entirely with national governments will need to be pooled and coordinated.

A final arena in which the nonproliferation regime can be improved is nuclear export policy. This is the case because access to a nuclear weapons capability now depends largely on the policies of a small group of supplier states. In the years ahead, these states, which carry on international commerce in nuclear facilities, nuclear technology, and nuclear materials, will have to improve and coordinate their export policies.

The crux of the problem is the duality of nuclear exports. Although they contribute to the spread of nuclear weapons, they ar also an exceptionally lucrative market for the supplier states. Therefore, unless every supplier state can be convinced that its own commitment to restraint in the export of sensitive technologies will be paralleled by every other supplier state, the hazards of a worldwide plutonium economy will be irrepressible.

To avert these hazards, two systems are required: (1) a system for verification of compliance with common nuclear export policies; and (2) a system of sanctions for noncompliance in which the costs of departure from such policies are so great as to outweigh the anticipated benefits of export revenues. Without such systems, the obligations on nuclear exports now imposed by IAEA, Euratom, and the NPT will have no meaningful effect.

In control of nuclear exports, sanctions can play a vital part in affecting the decisions of recipient states. Since nonproliferation is an integral part of the plan to prevent nuclear terrorism, such sanctions must be considered to be targeted against states that support or at least tolerate the prospect of such terrorism. In this connection, such sanctions are already a part of this country's legal statutes and its agreements with other countries.

Ultimately, the effectiveness of nonproliferation as a means to prevent nuclear terrorism will depend upon a cooperative effort by the United States and the Soviet Union to control limited aspects of their respective alliance systems. Moreover, it will depend upon an extension of such superpower control to all prospective proliferator states that fall under the orbit of American or Soviet influence. While such a statement seems to exhibit characteristics of a new elitism, the effect of such control would be to bolster world order rather than primacy. Rather than reassert an earlier form of duopolistic domination, a selective tightening of bipolarity in world power processes could significantly enhance the promise of nonproliferation. This is the case because a tightening of superpower control over allies and other states would limit the freedom of action these states have to "go nuclear." The "tighter" the dualism of power, the greater the ability of the superpowers to assure broad compliance with nonproliferation goals and thereby prevent nuclear terrorism.

An important part of the nonproliferation/nuclear terrorism problem, therefore, is the control of too large a number of independent national wills. Such control is an instance of the more general problem of decision that arises when the benefits of common action are contingent upon the expectation that all parties will cooperate. Nonproliferation efforts will always be problematic to the extent that they rely upon volitional compliance. They may, however, be successful if the superpowers move with determination to assure the compliance of other states with the NPT and its associated norms and restrictions.9

Conclusion

In the final analysis, there can be no fully effective strategy of counternuclear terrorism. There can only be a carefully worked out configuration of physical security/behavioral measures and appropriate revisions of current foreign policy processes. Taken together, these steps can reduce our terrible vulnerability to a unique hazard of world affairs.

Given both the memory and the expectation of holocaust, the specter of nuclear terrorism is particularly insidious. Aware of an unprecedented vastness of infamy, we residents of a beleaguered planet are already witnesses to events that have defiled our whole species. Today, however, even the unimaginable has become possible. With the atomic secret torn from nature, *individuals* can threaten and destroy entire societies.

The situation *is* fraught with disquieting possibilities. But it is also too soon to despair. There are steps that can be taken, things that can and must be done, to prevent a new paradigm of violence. We need a plan, one that joins the elements of sound scholarship with the calling forth and mastery of visions of atomic annihilation. With such a plan, we can begin to take the first critical steps back from a future that glows as a numbing hallucination.

Before we are able to implement our plan, we must understand its critical dependence upon a strengthened tapestry of international treaties and agreements directed at nonproliferation and superpower arms control. Moreover, because the success of counternuclear terrorism will require a major rededication to the international legal order, we must explore the prospects for far-reaching transformations of foreign policy processes.

Lenin once observed: "Without a revolutionary theory, there is no revolutionary practice." The same relationship obtains between the theory of counternuclear terrorism and effective counternuclear terrorism in practice. Without the former, the latter is impossible. Recognizing this, we must construct a theory of counternuclear terrorism from which viable strategies, should they ever be needed, can be systematically derived.

NOTES

1. Nuclear terrorism could take the form of nuclear explosives, radiological weapons, or nuclear reactor sabotage. For more information, see Louis René Beres, *Terrorism and Global Security: The Nuclear Threat* (Boulder, CO.: Westview Press, 1979).
2. Ironically, Secretary of State George Shultz has often stated his commitment to the laws of war under international law, and his understanding that these humanitarian rules of armed conflict apply to insurgent forces. According to Shultz: "The grievances that terrorists supposedly seek to redress through acts of violence may or may not be legitimate. The terrorist acts themselves, however, can never be legitimate. And legitimate causes can never justify or excuse terrorism. Terrorist means discredit their ends." See "Terrorism and the Modern World," Current Policy No. 629, U.S. Department of State, Bureau of Public Affairs, Washington D.C., October 25, 1984, p. 3.
3. See "Terrorism and the Modern World," p. 1.
4. For documentation of such disregard, see, for example, *With Friends Like These,* The Americas Watch Report on Human Rights & U.S. Policy in Latin America, Cynthia Brown, ed. (New York: Pantheon Books, 1985), especially p. 175. See also the CIA manual for the contras, "Psychological Operations in Guerrilla Warfare," which calls for the extrajudicial execution of civilians and prisoners and for the hiring of paid criminals to murder both Nicaraguan government officials and contra sympathizers (to create martyrs).
5. Terrorist access to weapons of mass destruction represents the most substantial threat of nuclear terrorism. Such access, however, assumes serious dimensions only when it is coupled with four additional conditions: (1) terrorist orientation to nuclear violence; (2) terrorist insensitivity to traditional threats of deterrence; (3) cooperation between terrorist groups; and (4) tolerance and support of terrorism. For an in-depth treatment of these additional factors, see Louis René Beres, *Terrorism and Global Security: The Nuclear Threat* (Boulder, CO: Westview Press, 1979).
6. Nuclear proliferation refers not only to the actual production of nuclear weapons by states not yet members of the nuclear "club," but also to the further spread of the capability to make nuclear weapons. Since a very close relationship exists between civilian nuclear power programs and the capacity to develop nuclear weapons (such programs may provide access to weapons-usable materials, facilities, and expertise), the spread of these programs is an integral part of the proliferation problem. A state, of course, might also seek entry into the nuclear club with a research reactor to make weapons-grade plutonium or through the enrichment of uranium-235 to weapons-grade levels. In comparison with the plutonium that is made from power reactors, the plutonium from research reactors is cheaper and faster and of higher weapons-making quality. For information on the relevance of civilian nuclear power programs to

the proliferation of nuclear weapons, see, especially, Albert Wohlstetter, et al., *Swords from Plowshares: The Military Potential of Civilian Nuclear Energy* (Chicago and London: University of Chicago Press, 1979); and *Nuclear Proliferation and Civilian Nuclear Power,* 9 vol., A Report of the Non-proliferation Alternative Systems Assessment Program, DOE/NE-0001, U.S. Department of Energy, Washington, D.C., December 1979.
7. According to Article VI of the Treaty on the Non-Proliferation of Nuclear Weapons, "Each of the Parties to the Treaty undertakes to pursue negotiations in good faith on effective measures relating to cessation of the nuclear arms race at an early date and to nuclear disarmament, and on a treaty on general and complete disarmament under strict and effective international control."
8. For a detailed examination of these steps, see Louis René Beres, *Mimicking Sisyphus: America's Countervailing Nuclear Strategy* (Lexington, MA: Lexington Books, 1983); and Louis René Beres, *Reason and Realpolitik: U.S. Foreign Policy and World Order* (Lexington, MA: Lexington Books, 1984).
9. For extensive and authoritative information on nuclear proliferation and its connection to nuclear terrorism, see *Nuclear Proliferation: Studies and Strategies for Stopping the Spread of the Bomb,* a series of special reports by the Nuclear Control Institute of Washington, D.C.

Chapter Two

What Nuclear Means and Targets Might Terrorists Find Attractive?

Thomas D. Davies

INTRODUCTION

There is no lack of evidence that terrorism has entered the political culture on an unprecedented and international scale. Nor is there any question that there is the potential, at least, for the adoption by terrorists of the nuclear tool, whether for extortion, or sabotage, or just plain large-scale violence. Terrorism is an effective political weapon. While terrorists are extortionists, hijackers, thieves, and kidnappers for ransom, their true forte is destruction on a shocking scale: the car bomb driven into Marine headquarters, the plastique tossed into a crowded cafe, the passenger plane blown up on the runway. It is this aspect of terrorist activity, and the increasing sophistication of methods and equipment, that turns our minds, inevitably, to the vulnerability of our nuclear facilities—even of our nuclear weapons.

Since the 1983 terrorist assault on U.S. Marines in Beirut, the United States government has at last ceased to regard terrorism as something of a Middle East or European leftist aberration.[1] The secretary of state is fed up and determined to find ways to retaliate; the question of how to defend against and punish terrorism is hotly debated in the Congress. The talk is about punitive retaliation. But against whom? The target is uncertain, shadowy and elusive. The alternative to Draconian methods, it would seem, is to tighten up physical security—cement barricades around the White House and State Department, exclusion of citizens from areas, even in the halls of Congress, formerly free to public access.

In this atmosphere, we ask ourselves: will international terrorists try for a nuclear target or otherwise engage in nuclear violence? We know some of them have played around with the idea, and when we examine the various possibilities—the potential targets and their relative vulnerabilities—we have to acknowledge we have a problem.[2] And the problem lies beyond protection of nuclear weapons and facilities. Any industry may be fair game to terrorists in possession of nuclear explosives: strategically important industries; remotely sited pipelines, oil fields and oil rigs may be particularly attractive targets; military or civilian storage depots holding liquid natural gas; the Panama Canal; and so on.

SCOPE OF THE PROBLEM

In 1984, some 35 percent of terrorist incidents worldwide originated in the Middle East. Another third took place in Europe, and about 20 percent in Latin America.[3] If you want to know why the secretary of state is upset, it is because a third of all these attacks were directed against U.S. citizens and U.S. interests. It is interesting that the director of the State Department's Office of Counter Terrorism and Emergency Planning thinks "the problem for the United States is likely to continue to be external to the United States, not internal."[4] Why this is true, or why the director believes it to be true, is not clear. Perhaps the nuclear equation has not yet been factored into official thinking on the subject. In any case, the worldwide shock and publicity over the accident at Three Mile Island suggest that the reverberations of any nuclear terrorism anywhere will be felt everywhere.

There is an enormous quantity of nuclear explosive material out there. There are thousands of nuclear weapons deployed all over the world. There are hundreds of commercial power reactors, nearly as many research reactors, dozens of industries supporting their manufacture and operation, and an ever-extending, vulnerable transportation chain binding it all together.

Military and civilian nuclear facilities vary in their vulnerability to terrorist acts. When we look at the terrorist record of the past few years, it is safe to conclude that sabotage of such facilities is at the top of the danger list.[5] The risk of theft of special nuclear materials and of weapons or their components is also very real. But the spectrum of targets for sabotage at mines, enrichment and reprocessing plants, reactors, storage facilities, and waste sites is very broad, and the consequences of destruction or damage range from unpleasant to cataclysmic.[6]

Nevertheless, theft of nuclear explosive materials has to be considered a serious threat. In attempting to gauge its likelihood, we must first acknowledge that we don't know how much, if any, may already have been stolen. There is too much of it unaccounted for; in the U.S. alone, at least nine thousand pounds were missing from the books through 1981.[7] And if some part of this was stolen, to what use has it been put? Will terrorists try to make a bomb? Will they claim they *have* made a bomb? Was it stolen on commission for Gaddafi? If stolen secretly for terrorist purposes, some demonstration will be needed to prove possession; if stolen publicly some time in the future from, say, a transport vehicle, it may not be necessary to demonstrate anything. If terror is the objective, that will have been accomplished by the very act of theft. But whether the first nuclear terrorist action goes the route of sabotage or of theft, the targets are there.

The number of nuclear weapons throughout the world now approaches 50,000, spread through hundreds of storage areas and in a wide variety of political and geographic ambients.[8] Their service custodians can be Army, Navy, Marines or Air Force. There are undeployed stockpile weapons, forward deployed tactical warheads, and demolition mines, weapons stored *without* anti-theft disabling devices, by the way, on ships deployed from the Mediterranean to the western Pacific.[9] At European storage depots, in addition, armed nationals are used to guard outer and inner perimeters, while American soldiers protect the depot's inner core.[10]

In theory, nuclear weapons should be consistently secured by the highest quality systems and personnel. One suspects, however, that the military community includes a normal spectrum of good and bad, some ineptitude, and the vagaries of administration characteristic of an excessively large bureaucracy. How well does military security protect against terrorism? The Beirut attacks confirm that it was not then designed with terrorism in mind.

Targets in the civilian nuclear power complex are abundant, and even more vulnerable to theft and sabotage. The vast network of manufacturing, enrichment, and reprocessing plants that supports the weapons program is more than matched by similar facilities on the civilian side, except that the military treats bombs as bombs, and the civilian sector tends to treat plutonium and highly enriched uranium (which are, in effect, bombs) like commercial products.

Some 260 commercial nuclear power plants are operating in the non-communist world today.[11] Each has the capacity to produce bomb-capable plutonium, some up to 300 kilograms a year—altogether a total of about 45 metric tons a year, the equivalent of at least 6,000 nuclear weapons.[12] Approximately 20 plants, in 17 countries, can now process plutonium from reactor spent fuel.[13] Current economic and political problems with the plutonium fuel cycle and breeders make it difficult to estimate accurately how much plutonium will be in circulation by the year 2000. Earlier estimates have been scaled down to about 400 tons—still an awesome quantity: nearly twice the combined weapon stockpiles of plutonium held by the superpowers today. It is projected that the amount of civilian plutonium in the world will exceed the superpowers' military stocks within the next decade.[14]

The once super-secret technology of uranium enrichment, which produces fuel for reactors and material for weapons, is also proliferating. Worldwide, at least 12 countries are known to have enrichment facilities.[15]

As the quantities of nuclear materials follow a constant upward curve, they are always traveling, moving by air, sea, truck, and railway from the mines to the enrichment plants, the fabricators, bomb assembly depots, power reactors, processing plants, and storage. Transport of so much dangerous material in open commerce may well turn out to be the Achilles' heel of the nuclear industry, a prime target for terrorist theft.

NUCLEAR WEAPONS

Is there any profit in imagining the successful theft of a nuclear weapon? What about this scenario—a *hypothetical* set of events in a setting taken from real life?

A nuclear weapons storage depot, located on 40 acres of pine forest near Wesel, West Germany. The weapons stored here are taken in and out by truck or helicopter. Barbed concertina wire lies at the base of three 7 foot concentric fences topped by barbed and razor wire. There is a 60 foot watch tower and bright floodlighting at night. A sign posted on the outer fence reads "Restricted Area: Use of Deadly Force Permitted."

German guards patrol between the inner fences, American soldiers, the inner core. There is nothing to do. The guards, although rotated weekly, are bored. A dozen heavily armed men lie concealed in the forest, 50 yards from the perimeter. They know where to come because the site has been under surveillance by sympathizers—one of them is a former guard from this site—and the locations of depots throughout Europe have been publicized. They attack with mortars and automatic weapons. If the alarm is raised and the emergency response team arrives in time, as prescribed in the regulations, the attackers won't get their bomb.

A 1978 CIA report identified Western Europe's nuclear storage depots as "the most vulnerable and therefore most likely targets for future terrorist activity."[16] There have been no attempts yet, so far as we know, but it is still possible to get close enough for a good look at the site I have just described.

The most attractive target for nuclear terrorists might be to buy or steal a ready-made bomb. It certainly has been considered. Libya's Colonel Gaddafi, who once described the atomic bomb as a "means of terrorizing humanity," is known to have been shopping around for one for some time; it has been reported that he is most likely to hire terrorists to steal one.[17]

Claire Sterling reports that a raid on an Italian Red Brigade group two years ago turned up documentary evidence that the possibilities of stealing a tactical nuclear weapon were being discussed. The judge in the case, long experienced in terrorist trials, was seriously alarmed, and still is.[18] The terrorists who kidnapped General James Dozier in Italy questioned him extensively about the location of nuclear weapons in Europe.[19]

Does the Italian judge really have anything to worry about? There have been questions about the security of nuclear weapons and the degree of protection accorded them. Nuclear sites have spent untold millions over the past 40 years to prevent the spread of these weapons to national or sub-national or terrorist groups. Yet today there is a danger that long familiarity may have bred complacency. Many of those responsible for protection come from a generation born long after Hiroshima. Some may tend to regard nuclear weapons as no more than standard military hardware.

A security specialist in the Department of Energy's Office of Safeguards and Security told a congressional committee he found persistent failure in the department to comprehend "the true seriousness of security problems" and a "widespread attitude that nothing was ever going to happen—a sort of 'it can't happen here' approach to security."[20] Last year, Chairman Dingell of the House Energy and Commerce Committee reported that in exercises at the Los Alamos National Laboratory "mock terrorists would have been able to steal plutonium [and] in another test a band of terrorists would have easily stolen a nuclear test device."[21] These devices will no longer be kept at the laboratory.

Congressional investigations have also uncovered "major deficiencies" in the management structure underlying the Energy Department's physical security programs. Chairman Dingell has gone so far as to say "certain key officials . . . put this nation's national security and public health in serious jeopardy."[22] Definite progress has been made in tightening up security in consequence of the fuss kicked up in Congress. But the underlying problem of how to achieve a high degree of physical security in an open society and a free competitive economy is extremely difficult to resolve.

There are ways other than simple malfeasance that nuclear weapons may fall into unauthorized hands. Thomas Schelling, who knows the subject well, does not rule out gifts, blackmail, purchase, or defection of civilian or military custodial officials. Had nuclear weapons been in the hands of French forces in Algeria in 1958, he wonders whether "the paratroopers and Secret Army Organizations that challenged the Paris government might have made threatening use of such weapons or arranged their disappearance for use on some later occasion."[23] Given the relative instability of governments in many parts of the world, the security of weapons stockpiles and materials deployed in any of these countries is something to ponder.

A recent issue of *Time* magazine reminds us that technology may be the terrorist's friend. Pictured there is a nuclear weapon so well refined that a 58-pound backpack bomb with a yield of 250 tons TNT equivalent can be delivered by a two-man commando team.[24] However one views the efficacy of such a weapon, it is guaranteed to whet the appetite of any terrorist who yearns after the ultimate explosion.

SPECIAL NUCLEAR MATERIALS

Here is another scenario, true except for the hijacking. This one is set on a ferry crossing from West Germany to Sweden.

> Two guards on the ferry are accompanying a shipment by truck of highly enriched uranium, fabricated for use in a research reactor. One guard sleeps while the other keeps watch. (Both guards used to sleep, but the order is now out that one must keep awake.) Near the end of the journey both guards have been put to sleep by three travelers, who then drive the truck carrying the shipment off the ferry when it docks.

Highly enriched uranium and separated plutonium are the two explosives used in atomic weapons. Handling, storing, and transporting these substances should receive the same degree of security treatment as bombs. Would you put an atomic bomb on a ferry with two guards and send it off to another country?

HEU is used in research reactors. There are 137 such reactors in 34 countries.[25] Plutonium is a by-product of reactor operation, both power and research. There are tremendous amounts of these materials now moving in international commerce. Five to 8 kilograms of plutonium or 15 to 25 kilograms of highly enriched uranium are needed for the core of a multi-kiloton atomic bomb.[26] Enough of the latter is in circulation at any one time to manufacture a minimum of 160 nuclear weapons. According to one source, some 6,500 nuclear weapons could be made from the 44 metric tons of plutonium already separated from spent reactor fuel; if we add to this the plutonium remaining unprocessed, there would be enough for more than 25,000 weapons.[27]

There is no conceivable need for that much plutonium anywhere, and its transport poses serious problems of security. The same is true of highly enriched uranium moving in commercial channels to fuel research reactors. It is ironic that the world takes such tremendous risks for the sake of using nuclear explosive materials not needed for the purposes to which they are being put.

Most transport of these dangerous materials is undertaken by commercial carriers, and this brings into play the "bill of lading syndrome." When a certified carrier agrees to transport a shipment, the carrier agrees to provide whatever physical security of the cargo is warranted, using civilian guards who are not allowed to use deadly force unless their lives are endangered. Upon signing the bill of lading, the carrier assumes full legal and financial responsibility for the cargo. The carrier, naturally, takes out insurance for the value of the cargo. In the event of any attempted theft or sabotage of the cargo, the carrier is responsible only for the monetary value of the shipment. How likely is it that guards are going to put their lives on the line for cargo which is insured, particularly when the government and the owners are so casual about the cargo's national security significance?

Most of the commercial output of separated plutonium comes from the French, who might be termed "reprocessors to the world," providing these services for six European countries and Japan. Britain as of now is storing more spent fuel than it is processing, but plans to become a major commercial reprocessor soon.[28] As the amounts of plutonium being returned to their owners increase, so does the risk of hijacking in transit. The risk is multiplied by the fact that retransfers from country to country are now being made.

Countries with big commercial power programs, like Japan, have the choice of storing spent reactor fuel at home or shipping it abroad to reprocessors. Even if the separated elements—reusable uranium and plutonium—are not needed, it is considered desirable (and in some countries required by law) to move spent fuel out because of political objections to national storage. This means that a country with several operating reactors will have to get rid of hundreds of tons of spent fuel yearly. So it is shipped in bulky containers by truck, air or sea to France and

England, and in this unprocessed form is of no interest to hijackers. The return journey is another matter.

When plutonium and uranium are separated for reuse, a residue of highly toxic nuclear wastes is left. Part of this—the so-called high level liquid waste—is highly volatile and is placed in temporary storage 10 feet underground. If sabotaged, the resulting explosions would cause untold long-term damage to populations and the environment. Descriptions of these storage facilities, along with detailed drawings, are available in the Public Document Room of the Nuclear Regulatory Commission in Washington. Nevertheless, such sabotage would appear less likely than the theft of special nuclear materials in transit.

Outside the United States, transport of nuclear explosives has been treated in a somewhat cavalier manner. In 1982, for example, Japan proposed the following arrangement for shipping enough plutonium for 30 nuclear weapons from France to Japan.[29] The French were to package the material and transport it to Britain, where it was to be repackaged and transferred to a British container ship. The proposed route of travel was either through the Suez Canal or around South Africa, through the Straits of Malacca (where piracy is still common), and up through the China Sea to Japan. Security was to be provided by one or two armed men on deck.

The U.S. Department of Energy, which had issued Japan a permit to return plutonium derived from fuel of U.S. origin, was appalled. American intervention resulted, finally, in security precautions that culminated in what might be called "The Curious Voyage of the *Seishin Maru*."

By the time the shipment finally left France in October 1984, extraordinary security measures were in place. A Japanese cargo ship, the *Seishin Maru*, dedicated especially for the shipment, sailed without stop for Japan through the Panama Canal. Sophisticated communications measures, complete with satellite relay systems for position and status reporting, were sent along with the escort force. The ship's captain and the escort force had separate and independent reporting responsibilities and capabilities. All members of the crew and the escort force were given special background checks.

During the *Seishin Maru's* 40-day, 13,600-mile journey from France to Japan, it was continuously tracked by American military satellites and escorted by French naval ships and later by American warships and Japanese patrol boats. The ship arrived secretly in Tokyo harbor under heavy police security. After unloading, a convoy of 6 tractor trailers, escorted by 10 security vehicles, including 3 police patrol cars, carried the 6 special containers of plutonium oxide powder to their final destination 60 miles northwest of Tokyo. Security costs to the Japanese are understood to have reached $5 million.

The moral of this story would seem to be that the United States views the transport of nuclear explosives as a dangerous business. It once turned down proposed security arrangements for a shipment of highly enriched uranium to Germany, with the result that the material travelled on a Luftwaffe plane. What is troubling is that HEU fuel, once fabricated in Germany, can complete its journey by ferry to Sweden.

There are International Atomic Energy Agency guidelines—incorporated in an international convention not yet in force, covering physical security for nuclear materials, including transport.[30] But security is handled country by country: We say the transfer to Germany must be in a military plane, the Germans say the retransfer can be by ferry. The IAEA safeguards system does not oversee safe international transport of nuclear material and has no authority to pursue or retrieve missing shipments.

The fact is that a lot of what we have to protect should never have been produced in the first place; there is no way to traffic safely in nuclear explosive materials. In August 1982, the U.S. General Accounting Office found that the U.S. had trouble tracking and assuring the physical security of the highly enriched uranium (of which it is almost the sole supplier) for the world's research reactors.[31] The Department of State and the Arms Control and Disarmament Agency protested to GAO investigators about security measures accompanying the more than one metric ton of material being provided annually, pointing out the "profound repercussions on the security of all nations" should a significant quantity of highly enriched uranium be obtained by an irresponsible government or terrorist group.[32]

"They believed," reports the GAO,

> that the danger was not limited to materials located only in certain "problem" nations because an irresponsible nation or a sub-national group might seize materials from even the most responsible nation. They concluded that the danger existed regardless of the political orientation, social system, location, alliance relation, or current nuclear weapons status of the nations involved and that uranium with lower enrichment levels should be substituted for HEU to the extent possible.[33]

There is no technical reason for using bomb-capable material to fuel research reactors; it is just that it has always been done. The Nuclear Regulatory Commission's proposed rule lowering enrichment to non-explosive levels is being resisted in the academic community. In the meantime, regulations forbid possession of critical amounts of highly enriched uranium at campus-located reactors in the United States. The reasoning is that the five unirradiated kilos allowed make up only about a quarter of the amount needed for a bomb. Yet imagine five men synchronizing their watches by dark of night and hitting five campus reactors simultaneously.

A former FBI official, called in to review the highly enriched uranium-fueled research reactor at UCLA, told the House Science and Technology Committee it was one of the most undefended targets he had ever seen. "A terrorist intent on stealing the uranium," he said, "would have a field day, given the woefully inadequate security posture."[34] The UCLA reactor is no longer operating, but 23 other highly enriched uranium-fueled reactors are.

CIVILIAN NUCLEAR FACILITIES

In this scenario, we look at sabotage against civilian nuclear facilities:

The twin plants of the Calvert Cliffs Nuclear Power station are sited in a park-like setting overlooking a river in southern Maryland, 50 miles from Washington, D.C. There is a fence surrounding the plant area, and a guard at the gate. But immediately adjacent and slightly above the enclosed area are attractively landscaped parking and picnic facilities provided by the company for tourists who come to see the plants. There are 10 or 15 cars parked on this afternoon, plus a couple of school buses and a somewhat oversized van—apparently outsized to house both people and audio equipment of a roving rock band.

Members of the rock group leave their van and announce they are taking their picnic below the cliffs to the water's edge. Forty minutes later a tremendous explosion is heard at Solomon's Island, 20 miles down the road. One of the two reactors at the power station is operating at the time of the blast. The explosion is caused by a van bomb powerful enough to disable the control room and trigger a meltdown and a breach of the reactor's containment dome. The station is reduced to rubble. Radiation greater than that produced by a nuclear weapon is released on the countryside, and drifts toward Washington.

Here we have a classic terrorist incident. Because of the rash of car bombings worldwide, the Sandia National Laboratories recently conducted a study on this technique, postulating conventional explosives against nuclear facilities. The results of that study show that " . . . unacceptable damage to vital reactor systems could occur from a relatively small charge at close distances and also from larger but still reasonable size charges at large setback distances (greater than the protected area for most plants)."[35]

A light water nuclear power plant is inherently susceptible to sabotage. The public record is replete with recent testimony from demolition experts on how to enter and place charges at key points in civilian nuclear facilities. These plants are even more vulnerable if one or two insiders—knowledgeable in the design of the plant's safety systems—are determined to cause a core melt accident.

Every attempt to design an effective physical security system for an industrial facility runs head-on into the question of the use of deadly force. Reactor licensees see the possibility of seizure of a power plant by force as utterly remote. They argue that physical security arrangements against that kind of threat are expensive and disruptive in the work force: Perimeter fencing, armed guards, security clearances, and the like smack too much of military or police-like precautions in the civilian sector. But even if such measures were to be swallowed, plant owners choke at the thought of liability when the shooting starts.

Commercial nuclear plants are guarded by private security companies, and too often these guards are paid only slightly above the minimum wage. One large utility company pays for a guard force of 500 men, but this is unusual. Guards are not authorized to use deadly force except in self-defense (a situation in which authorization is not needed anyway).

There are an infinite number of scenarios for malevolent actions directed against commercial nuclear plants. Government officials responsible for drawing up regulations for physical security have never been able to decide what threat they want to protect against. No one can predict whether terrorists will mount a major assault with sophisticated weapons and explosives, or whether the problem will begin with a hijacked bus load of children, one of them the plant manager's.

Despite continual discussions and studies about plant security, the NRC and the nuclear industry continue to insist that protection against sabotage is a physical security function, unrelated to design of the plant itself. It all boils down to an inability to accept that nuclear facilities and materials are in a class apart, are inherently susceptible to sabotage and theft, and are a potential danger to the public. Once the uniqueness of these facilities is acknowledged, there are many elements of design that can be turned to physical protection.

THE MYSTIQUE OF NUCLEAR TECHNOLOGY

There is a mystique that attaches to all things nuclear. The initiates have encouraged the notion that you have to be a genius to understand the atom, that there is something inherently complicated about atomic bombs, or nuclear power generation, or the treatment of fissile materials. This notion persists, despite the fact that over the past 40 years literally hundreds of thousands of people have been involved in every aspect of the atom's exploitation. The secrecy generated by the weapons program has been the handmaiden of the nuclear insiders, and I suppose many of the 400,000 people in the Defense Department currently holding top secret clearances today share the illusion that nobody else knows what they know.[36]

Hans Bethe, a veteran of Los Alamos and the bomb, calculated a minimum of six well-trained people representing just the right specialties are needed to make an atomic bomb. This notion persists, although we now know that the design and manufacture of a usable nuclear weapon can be accomplished by those outside the inner circle—not a highly efficient bomb, perhaps, but one that will explode.

In this connection, the story of the mail order bomb is instructive. It was obtained for $150, according to a story in the *L.A. Weekly*.[37] The junk dealer in Ohio who advertised this item—a U.S. army surplus *Honest John* warhead that was disarmed and without fissile material—sold the three he had in his inventory. One went to the subject of the news story, a physicist who designs nuclear weapons. The dealer's records are so primitive that he says he doesn't know where the other two went. Challenged by this bizarre bit of Army surplus, the physicist got an electrical engineering student at Caltech to design a nuclear weapon (with no hints from his mentor) that could be built in a garage. It took the student 40 hours of work and research in the public record to come up with a design our physicist says will work. He plans to build it with only five moving parts salvaged from junkyards and the aid of the Edmond Scientific Catalog at a cost of $5,000. He is currently trying to figure out how to get the needed nuclear explosive legally.

Now, the nuclear experts will insist there is no way he can do this. But less knowledgeable, unawed people don't see why not. To the "outsider" with a little imagination, many things are possible. The American Society of International Law suggests that the technological difficulties of converting uranium or plutonium to a potentially explosive metallic form are on a par with something we do know about: the conversion of morphine base to heroin. Morphine base is toxic, it is explosive, it takes an expert to handle it; we can assume there are many technically skilled people plying this trade. The ASIL study noted: "These factors strongly suggest that criminal organizations could successfully design and operate clandestine nuclear material processing facilities if they wished to do so."[38] Well, maybe yes and maybe no: The point is that we show contempt for the ingenuity and skills of those outside the magic nuclear circle at our peril.

The experts who design our security systems tend to cast their adversaries in their own mold. They also *always* depend heavily on the myth of the "insider." Let me conclude by mentioning an episode in which this weakness accounted for the success of an unlikely band of seven men, dedicated only to getting rich, who pulled off the "robbery of the century" and walked away with something in the neighborhood of $2 million from Brinks' "absolutely burglar proof" vault in Boston. Planning for the robbery, which went on for six years, was carried out by a band of uneducated, professional thieves, most of whom had never worked for a living and from late childhood had never bought and paid for anything they could steal. Throughout this long period of preparation, secrecy was maintained, and they got away scot-free. It was only much later that one of their number talked to the police and brought them all down.[39]

As robberies go, this one went to the edge of plausibility. Where nuclear terrorism goes, we do not yet know what is plausible and what is not. We do know we are up against an international movement of ruthless and experienced destroyers. If they need "experts," they will find them. If they need opportunities, we will probably provide them.

Dealing with any form of terrorism presents exceedingly difficult problems; nuclear terrorism adds a dimension of complexity beyond the capabilities of traditional methods of physical security. The basic conclusion of this paper is that those responsible for both civilian and military programs need to break out of the framework of those traditional concepts of physical security and mirror-image treatment of the adversary. The audacity of the (to us) "fanatic" and the motivations of a counter-culture must be imputed to the "threat" to achieve a truly high degree of protection.

A further fundamental protection, of course, is to minimize and eventually eliminate nuclear explosive materials from civilian nuclear programs and commerce.

NOTES

1. See, for example, the speech on terrorism by Secretary of State George Shultz before the American Society for Industrial Security, Arlington, Virginia, February 4, 1985. In the speech, Secretary Shultz announced the formation of the Overseas Security Advisory Group, a joint venture between the State Department and the private sector. The goals of the Council are: "to establish a continuing liaison between officials in both the public and private sector in charge of security matters; to provide for regular exchanges of information on developments in the security fields; and to recommend plans for greater operational coordination between the government and the private sector overseas." On the same day, former Secretary of State Cyrus Vance urged the Senate Foreign Relations Committee "to increase our capability to cope with unconventional warfare." He suggested the improvement of intelligence gathering and the organization of more military anti-terrorist strike forces.
2. Earlier this month, Prime Minister Rajiv Gandhi complained of Federal Bureau of Investigation reluctance to inform him that arrested Sikh extremists had been planning to blow up installations in India, including a nuclear power plant. See the *New York Times,* June 5, 1985, p.1.
3. From a statement by Ambassador Robert B. Oakley, director, Office for Counter-Terrorism and Emergency Planning, before the Subcommittees on Arms Control, International Security, and Science, and on International Operations of the House Foreign Affairs Committee, Washington, D.C., March 5, 1985.
4. Ibid.
5. For an analysis of nuclear terror and potential targets, see J.F. Pilat, "Antinuclear Terrorism in the Advanced Industrial West," in Yonah Alexander and Charles K. Ebinger, eds., *Political Terrorism and Energy: The Threat and Response* (New York: Praeger Publishers, 1982), pp. 191-208.
6. An analysis of the vulnerability of nuclear installations to conventional attack and of the potential consequences is found in Bennett Ramberg, *Nuclear Power Plants as Weapons for the Enemy: An Unrecognized Military Peril* (Berkeley: University of California Press, 1980).
7. Data compiled by Bill Adler of the Nuclear Control Institute, as cited in Patrick O'Heffernan, Amory B. Lovins, and L. Hunter Lovins, *The First Nuclear World War* (New York: William Morrow and Company, Inc., 1983), pp. 159-161.
8. See William M. Arkin and Richard W. Fieldhouse, *Nuclear Battlefields* (Cambridge, MA: Ballinger, 1985).
9. "Who Could Start a Nuclear War?," *The Defense Monitor,* Vol. 14, No. 3 (Washington, D.C.: Center for Defense Information, 1985), pp. 4, 6.
10. Frank Greve, "Warhead Depots: A Weak Link in NATO's Security," *Philadelphia Inquirer,* March 13, 1983, p. F2.
11. By September 1, 1984, the total number of commercial nuclear power stations around the world that were operable, under construction, or on order was 531. The United States had 136; other nations accounted for 395. (Data obtained from a map produced by *Nuclear News,* copyright by the American Nuclear Society, 1984.)
12. David Albright, "World Inventories of Plutonium," draft paper, June 24, 1985. See also testimony by Albright before the Subcommittees on Arms Control, International Security and Science and on International Economic Policy and Trade of the House Foreign Affairs Committee, June 12, 1985.
13. See P.J. Mellinger, K.M. Harmon, and L.T. Lakey, "A Summary of Nuclear Fuel Reprocessing Activities Around the World," prepared for the U.S. Department of Energy under Contract DE-ACO6-76RLO 1830, by Pacific Northwest Laboratory,

November, 1984. According to the report, these 17 countries are known to be or have been engaged in fuel reprocessing activities. In addition to the 20 plants that are presently operating, at least 32 pilot, demonstration, or industrial reprocessing facilities are known to have been built, and 13 are proposed for operation prior to the year 2000. (Britain recently announced that it would help South Korea build a reprocessing plant when it is needed, apparently by the turn of the century. See *Nucleonics Week,* June 7, 1985, p. 11.) The countries with reprocessing technology are Argentina, Belgium, Brazil, Canada, China, France, the Federal Republic of Germany, India, Israel, Italy, Japan, Mexico, Pakistan, Spain, the Soviet Union, the United Kingdom, and the United States.
14. Op. cit., Albright, "World Inventories of Plutonium."
15. Countries that have or are known to have been engaged in uranium enrichment are Argentina, Canada, China, the Federal Republic of Germany, France, Japan, the Netherlands, Pakistan, South Africa, the Soviet Union, the United Kingdom, and the United States. In addition, four countries are partners in the French Eurodif enrichment consortium: Belgium, Italy, Iran, and Spain. Israel has been reported to be developing a laser enrichment capability. See *Nuclear Proliferation Factbook,* prepared for the Subcommittee on Energy, Nuclear Proliferation, and Federal Services of the Senate Committee on Governmental Affairs and the Subcommittee on International Economic Policy and Trade of the House Committee on Foreign Affairs, by the Environment and Natural Resources Policy Division, Congressional Research Service, Library of Congress, September, 1980, p. 180; SIPRI, *Uranium Enrichment and Nuclear Weapon Proliferation* (New York: Taylor and Francis, Inc., 1983), pp. 228-229; and Leonard S. Spector, *Nuclear Proliferation Today* (New York: Vintage Books, 1984), pp. 146-148.
16. Op. cit., Greve, "Warhead Depots."
17. "Who Has the Bomb," *Time,* p. 49.
18. Personal communication with Claire Sterling.
19. Letter from Rep. John D. Dingell (D-Mich.) to Department of Energy Secretary Donald P. Hodel, October 26, 1983, contained in *Nuclear Security Coverup,* Hearing before the Subcommittee on Oversight and Investigations of the Committee on Energy and Commerce, House of Representatives, 98th Cong., 2d sess., February 3, 1984, p. 181.
20. Ibid., p. 51.
21. Letter from Rep. Dingell to Secretary Hodel, May 7, 1984, in ibid., p. 337.
22. Letter from Rep. Dingell to Secretary Hodel, October 26, 1983, in ibid., p. 181.
23. Thomas C. Schelling, "Thinking about Nuclear Terrorism," *International Security,* Spring, 1982, p. 62.
24. *Time,* p. 52. See also Thomas B. Cochran, William M. Arkin, and Milton M. Hoenig, *Nuclear Weapons Databook,* Vol. 1: U.S. Nuclear Forces and Capabilities (Cambridge, MA: Ballinger, 1984), pp. 3, 8, 60, 91, 281.
25. "The Use of Atom Bomb Material in Civilian Research Reactors," Nuclear Control Institute, Washington, D.C., September, 1984, p. 1.
26. Op. cit., Spector, *Nuclear Proliferation Today,* p. 432. Eight kilograms of plutonium and 25 kilograms of highly enriched uranium are used by the IAEA as the minimum amounts of material necessary for nuclear weapons; the smaller figures of 5 and 15 kilograms, respectively, are conservative, widely accepted benchmarks according to Spector.
27. Albright testimony, June 12, 1985.
28. Roger Milne, "Reprocessing Plant Proposed for Dounreay," *New Scientist,* May 30, 1985, p. 6.

29. The story is in an unpublished paper by David Albright.
30. By December 31, 1984, 38 states and Euratom had signed the International Convention on the Physical Protection of Nuclear Material, but only 10 states had ratified it. The convention will enter into force after 21 ratifications. This would happen automatically once Euratom members ratified.
31. Comptroller General Report to Senator Gary Hart, *Obstacles to U.S. Ability to Control and Track Weapons-Grade Uranium Supplied Abroad,* GAO/ID-82-21 (Washington, D.C.: General Accounting Office, August 2, 1982).
32. Comptroller General Report to the Secretary of Energy, *The U.S. Nuclear Materials Information System Can Improve Service to Its User Agencies,* GAO/NSIAD-85-28 (Washington, D.C.: GAO, January 14, 1985), p. 7.
33. Ibid.
34. Statement of Richard D. Rogge, in *Conversion of Research and Test Reactors to Low-Enriched Uranium (LEU) Fuel,* Hearings before the Subcommittee on Energy Development and Applications and the Subcommittee on Energy Research and Production, Committee on Science and Technology, House of Representatives, 98th Cong., 2d sess., September 25, 1984, p. 507.
35. See references to the Sandia report in the Nuclear Regulatory Commission *Weekly Information Report to the Commissioners,* April 27, 1984, Enclosure E.
36. Chief of Naval Operations Admiral James Watkins remarked that 4.3 million U.S. military and civilian personnel are cleared to see secret information. See *Washington Post,* June 12, 1985, A-1.
37. Tim Evans, *L.A. Weekly,* March 7, 1985.
38. Mason Willrich, ed., *International Safeguards and Nuclear Industry,* published under the auspices of the American Society of International Law (Baltimore: The Johns Hopkins University Press, 1973) pp. 182–183.
39. Robert Considine, *The Brinks Robbery* (New York: Random House, 1964).

* * * * *

RESPONSES

Merrill Walters

It is difficult to discuss the subject of nuclear terrorism without considering the objectives and abilities of the terrorists. This morning we discussed capabilities. Admiral Davies' paper included a lengthy review of terrorist abilities and capabilities, and this information can provide us with some real clues as to what possible targets the terrorists might select.

We would be foolish to discount the possibility of nuclear violence. Moreover, the danger is growing. Terrorists are getting more technically expert every day, and the kind of things we see them doing now are things that we wouldn't have even dreamed about 5, or 6 or 10 years ago. International cooperation among terrorists has also increased, providing them with more technical expertise and more infrastructure support. We see a lot of money being driven into those organizations. They now have money to buy standoff missiles and standoff capability and high technology that they didn't have a few years ago. So certainly, it appears to me, terrorists have the capability for nuclear violence. It's up to us to plan for the future and see how we can counter that.

In looking at the problem of terrorists' targets, we need to ask some pertinent questions, such as where is the threat the greatest, what targets minimize the risks to the terrorists and maximize the political gain. We are still, after all, talking about a political gain, not a military one, from the terrorists' point of view.

Admiral Davies, in his paper, pointed out that transportation and reprocessing of nuclear materials are major weaknesses. Other speakers have spoken to that; I'm certainly not an expert, and I'm going to leave that issue to them. What I would like to talk about, though, is what threats and risks are involved in an attack on NATO's nuclear forces. Because of the strategic and national security implications, we just can't discount an attack, or the prospect of an attack, on our deployed nuclear forces or on some segment of them.

An attack on our nuclear forces could indeed have a very high public and political impact, even if unsuccessful. The nuclear sites are well known, and any event that is connected with nuclear weapons, even with the delivery system in which nuclear weapons are not involved, still raises a great deal of hysteria and concern all over the world, and in particular in NATO.

Any effort that reduces our ability to deploy and maintain nuclear forces is of value to the Soviets and certainly adds to their capabilities. If you are looking at small nations, or local terrorist organizations, even those that cooperate internationally have limited resources and capabilities. But if you are looking at the resources and nuclear capabilities of the Soviet Union as an exporter, that's an entirely different thing. It's a potential that we should recognize.

We should also note that a terrorist organization does not need a nuclear detonation or nuclear capability to succeed. All they have to do is establish some credibility through an incident or something involving our nuclear sites, which the media would then build up and which would cause mass hysteria. It's evident that the payoff could be very, very high for the terrorists if they are successful. The results could also be long-lasting for our security.

What I have done to this point is outline some possible objectives, assumptions and criteria. Now, if you accept these, I'd like to look at some of the targets that terrorists might address.

First, the storage sites. Everyone knows where the storage sites are; they are very visible. Since the mid-1970s, there has been a very large-scale effort to upgrade the security of all of these sites. A few years ago, there was a senior-level weapons protection group established under the chairmanship of the ATASD (AE) of the United States that included most of the NATO nations. They had the express task of upgrading the security of nuclear storage sites. There has been an awful lot done to date. Currently, the senior-level weapons protection group is looking at the future threat, 10, 15, 20, 25 years from now and is taking steps to protect the sites against these threats.

In our favor is the fact that the contents of the storage sites are unknown. That makes the payoff of any successful attack by the terrorists considerably uncertain. Weapons in those sites are stored to prevent easy removal, and there are a lot of systems that are designed into those storage sites to make the terrorist think twice, to reassess the risks involved in an attack on those sites.

For example, when a terrorist thinks about trying to attack a storage site, he must take into consideration a number of obstacles that will confront him. He has to overcome the fences, the cleared areas and the local security forces in place 24 hours a day. He must kill them to gain access to the storage areas and to gain control of a weapon that may or may not have inside devices designed to disable it. The weapon will be larger than men can carry, and so they will have to have some means of transporting it. He would have to have the outside support structure to enable him to move that weapon, to get that weapon over considerable distances to a sanctuary, under conditions of hot pursuit by security forces, and to do all of that before a reaction team could arrive. It would be a tremendous undertaking. A terrorist organization would have to be prepared to expend tremendous resources in order to do that. The risk in my mind makes that an unlikely option, though an attack on a storage site would certainly get everyone's attention and could give us grave problems whether or not it was successful.

An easier target could be the deployed forces that move on the roads. They are visible, and they are highly vulnerable to mines or sniper attack. They have a high signature and very high visibility. A terrorist might well gain his objectives from such an attack. If their main objective is to cause concern and hysteria among the public and within the governments about the basic safety of a nuclear delivery system, that is a possible, viable option.

Our dual-capable systems, such as aircraft, artillery, lance or so on, also are commonly visible. An attack on them would not necessarily be connected to their nuclear role, because warheads are normally not associated with them and not at risk. An attack on those systems is possible, but the concomitant reaction to an attack by the public and by local governments is difficult to gauge. Therefore the gain to terrorists would be considerably uncertain.

There are other kinds of nuclear-related incidents that terrorists might attempt. Smoke, fire, scattering of radioactive materials that terrorists have received by other means, accompanied with a media blitz to cause concern, are all possibilities that need to be considered now and in the future.

Those of you in the audience can see the mirror in back of me, as well as the mirror that I am facing. You can see that the reflections in the mirrors give you a sense of infinity because you keep looking at one reflection after another. It seems to me that's the kind of problem we've got. It's going to be with us a long time. And sometimes it is pretty hard to find where reality is.

But, in my opinion, the risk is currently high to terrorists who would attack our nuclear forces in NATO. It's uncertain what they would gain, and they would have to be prepared to commit a lot of resources if they would be successful. Our continuing task is to make sure that in the future, when any terrorist assesses any possible gain against the risks, he will decide that the chances of success are indeed uncertain and that the risks to him are very high.

* * *

Guenter Hildenbrand

We discussed this morning that nuclear terrorism is primarily a political, but nonetheless also a technical, issue. After a few comments on the first point, I want to address mainly the second one.

The Political Situation in the Federal Republic of Germany (FRG)

Because the German spent fuel management concept is for a number of reasons based on the closed fuel cycle, we will have, like other European countries, the so-called plutonium economy, and we will have to cope with it under the compulsory requirement not to contribute to nuclear terrorism. Let me first make some comments on the situation in my country in the early to mid-seventies and draw some conclusions related to the present situation. In that period, we faced campaigns of protest and opposition to nuclear energy by the antinuclear movement, whose rationale was: (1) Nuclear energy is a big technology with tremendous potential for danger and new dimensions of risk; and (2) Nuclear energy is a symbol of industrial development, unhampered economic growth and inhuman hard technology. The antinuclear movement undertook mass demonstrations against sites for nuclear power plants (Whyl, Brokford, Grohnde, Kalkar) and spent fuel management facilities (Gorleben), and also demonstrated in Bonn.

We also saw extremist and terrorist groups, in their fight against the political and social system and the state as such, using social, ecological or other concepts to try to take over the leadership of the antinuclear protest movements. Early on, the ecological movements, whose only actions were those free of force and violence, and the extremists and terrorists, who accepted force and violence as part of their basic strategy, were distinct. The ecologists knew they needed a broad public consensus if their efforts to prevent more nuclear power plants were to be successful. For its part, the population was against transgression and force. Therefore, the extreme left and terrorist groups could not influence the violence-free peoples' initiatives against nuclear energy.

At this time, the terrorist groups were also engaging in acts of sabotage against:

- The construction of nuclear power plants and supply industry facilities, through fire attacks; and
- High-tension poles next to nuclear power plants, through explosive attacks.

They made, however, *no attacks at all* of any kind against operating nuclear power plants or nuclear fuel manufacturing facilities or fissile material in transport. In their "handbooks," the terrorist groups recommend against sabotage of operating nuclear power plants leading to radiological hazards to the population. Given this experience, I conclude that:

1. None of the violence-free or terrorist actions jeopardized the peaceful use of nuclear energy in the FRG.
2. A strong revival of the antinuclear movement in the FRG is not very likely in the foreseeable future because of the good record for safe and environmentally harmless operation of our nuclear power plants—we have had no serious accidents.
3. Nonetheless, future acts of sabotage cannot be excluded, and terrorist actions—even by foreign groups—must be taken into account. This attitude is incorporated into the licensing procedures for nuclear power plants, nuclear fuel cycle facilities and transport of fissile material.

Physical Protection and Transport: The Legal Situation

I will review briefly the key relevant legislation governing the nuclear energy industry.

The Atomic Law of 1959 has as one of its aims to prevent the use or release of nuclear energy from jeopardizing the internal or external security of the FRG. Among the criteria for the licensing of nuclear facilities is physical protection against disturbing actions or other influences by third parties. The same is true for the storage, processing and other use, and transport of nuclear fuel, be it non-irradiated or irradiated material.

The goal of nuclear security is to prevent the violent release of radioactivity into the environment; the theft or robbery of radioactive or fissile material for misuse; and the use of the radiation potential of nuclear facilities as a threat. Measures for nuclear security are to be taken first by the operator of nuclear facilities and the transporter of fissile material, and second by the government via its response forces (police and military). The measures for which operators and transporters are responsible are spelled out in a governmental regulatory system called the "Security Measures Catalogue." It was established in 1977 and will be renewed from time to time, taking into account the state of the art and practical experience. These measures are in compliance with the international safeguards system for fissile material as an integrated concept for nuclear security. (Those nuclear activities—facilities and transport of fissile material—that must be protected by security measures are summarized in Annex 1.)

Integrated Concept for Nuclear Security of Facilities

Nuclear safety measures are designed to protect against outside influences and include design criteria for facilities and transport containers. They must be able to handle earthquakes, airplane crashes and gas cloud explosions. They must also be able to reduce the vulnerability of nuclear facilities to violent actions by third parties. They must protect sensitive nuclear facilities (nuclear power plants, highly enriched uranium and plutonium storage, processing and reprocessing plants) against attacks by explosives or conventional weapons. They have already proven effective.

The effectiveness of the above measures will be reinforced by:

- Safety-related systems that will be installed in greater numbers than required (redundancy) and in technically different configurations (diversification);
- Protective measures to guard against human failure; and
- Regular repeated function controls that prevent a step-wise putting-out-of-service of safety functions by "insider" perpetrators.

As to security measures listed in the catalogue, they include physical-technical barriers (Annex 2); technical detection and control systems; administrative measures; and personnel measures. The priority is construction-technical measures.

With respect to the physical-technical and technical detection and control systems, three areas of nuclear facilities (Annex 3) must be secured:

- The outer area with outer enclosure, by means of a safety fence; a NATO fence; a combination of detection systems (perimeter intrusion detection); an alarm control system (to differentiate between real and artificial or erroneous alarms), as a rule to consist of a TV and an illumination system; mechanical protection (a barrier against vehicles to prevent illegal passage by a heavy truck); an entrance system with vehicle and personnel locks; and a bullet-proof building, from which the technical systems for the outer area are operated. The outer system should remain unbreached for three minutes.
- Inner area with inner enclosure, by means of mechanical (physical) barriers against penetration by all kinds of projectiles, from portable firearms and explosives, and by intrusion by terrorists. The design has to afford at least a half-hour of security against intruders with tools and equipment. This requirement applies not only to the walls of the buildings, but also to all access points and openings (such as doors, etc.). A resistance time of half an hour (it applies to both facilities and transport as well) is enough at all sites in Germany to allow response forces to arrive at the point of attack.
- Specific areas with their enclosures, by means of physical barriers against internal perpetrators (intruders); and a central alarm station that contains all signals from the inner and from the specific areas, with a redundant communication system to the entrance system and to local response forces.

With respect to administrative measures, they include control of persons and vehicles, limited access to security areas and specific areas; and technical supervision of personnel locks in the inner security areas.

With respect to personnel measures, they include screening of operating personnel and of guards; a security guard service (armed with automatic handguns); and one person responsible for all physical protection (security) measures.

Transport of Fissile Material

A similar nuclear security concept applies to all transport of fissile material. That is, transport of such material has to be performed in accordance with principles that combine equivalent physical protection measures with corresponding control measures regarding personnel and the actual transportation (Annexes 4 and 5).

All plutonium, highly enriched uranium and mixed oxide fuel is transported in a special armored vehicle, accompanied by another car with armed watchmen. The vehicle is in continuous radio contact with a control station. In case of attack, the convoy is designed to withstand attack until the arrival of the governmental defense forces.

Since 1973, there have been between 12 and 20 shipments of plutonium-nitrate annually between the small German reprocessing plant, WAK, and the mixed oxide fuel manufacturing plant, ALKEM. There have been no problems. The total number of plutonium shipments—partly plutonium-nitrate from WAK to ALKEM, partly plutonium-oxide from the French reprocessing plant Cap la Hague to ALKEM, and partly mixed oxide fuel assemblies from ALKEM to nuclear power plants—was 40 in 1982 and 70 in 1983. (Actual and estimated shipments of fissile material and nuclear fuel assemblies in the FRG are found in Annex 6.)

Summary

The Atomic Law of the FRG aims, *inter alia,* to prevent violation of the internal or external security of the FRG by the use or release of nuclear energy. The licensing process requires protection against disruptive actions or other influences by third parties. The nuclear security measures are taken primarily by the operators of facilities and transporters of fissile material and secondly by governmental response forces. The law calls for an integrated concept for nuclear security that combines safety measures with security measures, in conjunction with the international safeguards system for fissile materials.

The nuclear safety measures are designed to protect against earthquakes, airplane crashes and gas cloud explosions and to reduce the vulnerability of nuclear facilities against violent actions of third parties. The security measures comprise physical barriers, technical and control systems, and administrative and personnel measures. They apply to three security areas at nuclear facilities. A corresponding nuclear security concept is applied to all transport of fissile material.

As long as the integrated concept for nuclear security of facilities and transport of fissile material is thoroughly observed, the chances for nuclear terrorism in the FRG are rather poor.

ANNEXES

Annex 1. Nuclear Activities Requiring Special Security Measures.

These activities include:

- Nuclear power plants (in the sense of being used by saboteurs to threaten major releases of radioactive material)
- Manufacturing facilities for HEU- and PU-processing
- Reprocessing plants
- Transport of HEU and PU.

As it is assumed that uranium enrichment plants produce only low enriched uranium, they are not mentioned here.

Annex 2. Design Criteria for Physical Barriers.

Barrier Type	Design Criteria	Wall Thickness (cm concrete)	Site of Application
I	Perforation by special explosives	250	Emergency feedwater system building
			Parts of reactor building
			Related cables and piping
II	Intrusion by use of mechanical and thermal tools and explosives	70	Reactor auxiliary building
			Switchgear building
III	Intrusion by use of mechanical tools	20	Central alarm station
IV	Intrusion by use of automatic handguns	24 Bulletproof brick wall	Main gate
V	Intrusion by use of physical force	12 Brick wall	Vital areas within the inner security area

Annex 3. Security Areas of Nuclear Facilities.

Nuclear Facility

Outer enclosure
(resistance time: 30 minutes)

Outer security area   Inner security area

Inner enclosure
(resistance time: 30 minutes)

Central alarm
station

Safety fence   NATO fence

Entrance
system

Governmental Action

Response
forces

Note: redundant communication.
Inner security area: Nuclear power plants—safety-related systems
Fuel facilities—fissile material.

Annex 4. Principles for Transport of Fissile Material.

The principles include:

- Security measures (see Annex 5)

- Screening of personnel

- Pre-planning of transport routes

- Control of actual transportation by communication with a control station.

- Transport of non-irradiated fuel: By road.

- Transport of irradiated fuel: By train, accompanied by two armed guards (railway police).

- Transport via plane or ship: Safety measures on departure and arrival of carrier, not during the trip (of plane or ship).

- Plutonium transport: No difference in risk potential between PuO_2 or PuNH.

- Transport of "sensitive" material ($U^{235} \geq 20\%$ and Pu): Category I of Annex 5.

Annex 5. Security Measures for Transport of Fissile Material.

Main goal: To prevent theft. Category	Valid for	Measures for street transport
Non-Irradiated Fuel		
I	>2 kg Pu	–Armored special vehicle, 3 men (2 armed)
	>5 kg U^{235} (>20% enr.)	–Accompanying car, with 2 armed guards
		–Radio contact with control station (of transporter)
II	>200 g Pu	–Special vehicle, 2 men
	>500 g U^{235} ($\geq$20% enr.) >1 kg U^{235} (10 to 20% enr.)	–Communication with control station (of transporter)
III	>15 g Pu >15 g U^{235} (>20% enr.) >100 g U^{235} (10 to 20% enr.)	–Normal vehicle, 2 men
S	U (1,5 to 10% enr.)	–Technical protection against theft
Irradiated fuel From power reactors		Transport containers meeting nuclear safety measures

Annex 6. Transport of Fissile Material in the FRG.

In 1982 and 1983

1,700 shipments of nuclear fuel, among them	1982	1983
Plutonium	40	70
Irradiated fuel	100	100

Assessment for 20,000 MWe installed nuclear generation capacity

From	To	Annual shipments
Nuclear fuel facilities	Nuclear power plants	120 500 t fuel assemblies
Nuclear power plants	• Intermediate storage facilities • Reprocessing plants	60 250 t irradiated fuel assemblies
Intermediate storage facilities	Reprocessing plants	
Pre-processing plants	Nuclear fuel factories	120 5 t Pu

Actual experience

One train accident in 1970: 2 UF^6-containers slumped from the railroad car but remained intact. Since 1973, there have been 12–20 shipments of WAK to ALKEM annually with no problems.

Annex 7. IAEA Safeguards Record.

In 1983, 520 nuclear facilities in 50 non-nuclear weapon states were under IAEA safeguards. They included: 147 nuclear power plants, 6 reprocessing plants, and 4 uranium enrichment plants. There were 1,840 inspections by 156 inspectors totaling 6,727 man-days.

Presently under IAEA safeguards are 93 t Pu in irradiated fuel assemblies; 7 t separated Pu; 11 t enriched U ($>20\%$ U^{235}); 18,590 t low enriched U; and 28,000 t natural U.

* * *

* * *

Theodore B. Taylor

Why worry about nuclear terrorism? Here are seven reasons:

1. Terrorism is on the rise, as we are all painfully aware this afternoon.
2. Tens of thousands of nuclear weapons now distributed worldwide are potential targets for theft for use by or sale to terrorists.
3. Given the needed nuclear materials, small groups of dedicated people could design and build easily transportable nuclear explosives with reasonably assured yields in the kiloton range, using information, skills, and non-nuclear materials that are accessible worldwide.
4. Inadequately secured nuclear weapon materials are spreading worldwide, along with technologies for making more. Among these materials is plutonium that has been extracted from spent fuel from nuclear power plants.
5. The stakes in nuclear blackmail by terrorists could be enormous compared to any that have yet been faced in acts of terrorism.
6. The threat of nuclear retaliation, which many believe has been the principal deterrent to military use of nuclear explosives since the early 1950s, would generally be ineffectual in dealing with nuclear terrorism.
7. It is possible to conceive ways that nuclear terrorism could trigger all-out nuclear war, whether or not this outcome were an initial objective of the terrorists.

Those who are trying to do something constructive about this danger face some frustrating problems and dilemmas that have to do with official secrecy and different perceptions of what best serves the public interest. I have wrestled with these issues for 20 years, without satisfactory resolution of any of them. Nevertheless, I am convinced that they are important parts of the reality that must be confronted in dealing constructively with the dangers of nuclear terrorism.

Many of the facts needed for thorough and realistic assessments of the threat of nuclear terrorism are still secret. How little plutonium or highly enriched uranium will suffice for crude or sophisticated nuclear explosives? Does the answer depend on the isotopic composition and chemical form of the materials? What are the minimum resources and skills needed to design and build nuclear explosives of various sizes, with various yields, with high or low reliability?

I have been asked these questions dozens of times and have been unable to give satisfactory answers because essential parts of the answers are still highly classified. Over and over again I hear or read statements that I know are wrong, that bear directly on how seriously we should consider possibilities of nuclear terrorism or what to do about them, but that cannot be thoroughly refuted publicly. I expect such statements to be made at this conference. I have to add that, more often than not, they are wrong in directions that seriously *underestimate* the dangers. I must emphasize, however, that secrecy does not prevent prospective nuclear terrorists from getting all the information *they* need from public sources.

Secrecy also surrounds the details concerning the physical security of nuclear weapons materials in military or civilian facilities or vehicles. I believe that this is as it should be; perhaps public access to such information should be even more restricted than it is. But the penalty for this secrecy is that the accountability of the people in charge of such matters is not subject to thorough public scrutiny. An especially insidious feature of this problem is the ease with which secret investigations of secret matters can often be thwarted by those being investigated.

Perceptions of just where to place the line of prudence between what the general public should and should not know about the possibilities of nuclear terrorism vary widely. I have been both severely criticized and warmly applauded, by people for whom I have deep respect, for going public with my concerns about nuclear terrorism. Yet I have no regrets about drawing the line where I have. One of the main reasons is the widespread ignorance of the relevant facts about nuclear weaponry among government officials and industrial managers charged with the handling of substantial quantities of nuclear weapons materials, not only in the United States, but internationally. To me, the general public includes these people, many of whom still believe the myth that designing and building atomic bombs is only credible for large organizations that have reached some sort of pinnacle of modern technological powers. Furthermore, without generally accepted international guarantees against theft of nuclear weapon materials or nuclear weapons— guarantees that cannot yet be substantiated—I have no doubts whatever about the rights of any individuals to know that nuclear terrorism is a real and growing danger, perhaps the greatest of our times.

* * *

William J. Dircks

Introduction

The Energy Reorganization Act of 1974, which dissolved the Atomic Energy Commission (AEC) and created the Nuclear Regulatory Commission (NRC), contains, among other things, specific provisions to assure adequate nuclear safeguards against threats, theft and sabotage involving the commercial licensed nuclear industry in this country. The NRC sees the threat of terrorism as real and important. Consequently, we require substantial safeguards systems to protect licensed nuclear activities that could be targets of terrorism with significant potential to harm the public health and safety. Among other things, we specifically require those safeguards systems to be designed to protect against determined violent assaults.

It is important to emphasize that the threats that are the NRC's design basis for nuclear theft and sabotage have been published for a number of years in Part 73 of the Code of Federal Regulations. These hypothetical "threats" should not be confused with real threats to licensed nuclear activities. They are more like design or performance specifications for use by licensees in designing their safeguards systems. And they unquestionably encompass potential threats from terrorism. I might add, the Commission is currently reviewing its safeguards design basis threats again, to make sure they are reasonable in light of the known threat environment.

Correcting Some Possible Misunderstandings about U.S. Nuclear Power Plants

This conference has raised some good questions and challenges for those of us charged with nuclear safeguards responsibilities. However, there have been some false concerns and factual errors in some of the papers and comments presented at the conference. It is wrong to associate together "nuclear explosive material," "nuclear weapons" and "commercial power reactors." It is wrong to talk of "explosive materials" moving from mines to "enrichment plants, the fabricators, bomb assembly depots, power reactors, processing plants and storage." These statements lump U.S. power reactors with strategic nuclear material and weapons as implied targets of nuclear theft.

I would like to dispel any such notions about nuclear theft and America's nuclear power industry. The low enriched uranium that fuels America's light water nuclear power plants is *not* an attractive target for nuclear theft, nor is the highly irradiated spent fuel at these plants. Moreover, spent fuel from U.S. commercial nuclear power plants is not being reprocessed. So statements linking U.S. light water reactors to nuclear proliferation or suggesting that they pose an atomic explosive threat to the American public in any way are simply incorrect.

U.S. Nonpower Test and Research Reactors

While on the subject of nuclear theft, I would also like to say a few words about nonpower reactors used for education, testing and research. Some of these use highly enriched uranium fuel, but it is in a form that cannot be used directly in a clandestine fission explosive device without first undergoing reprocessing to recover the uranium—a considerable undertaking. Moreover, because a typical nonpower reactor fuel element contains only 100-200 *grams* of U-235, one would successfully have to steal a large number of them to obtain a significant quantity of U-235. Nevertheless, in the interest of reducing or eliminating any potential targets of nuclear theft and terrorism in the licensed sector, the Commission recently decided to order all nonpower reactor licensees to remove any excess unirradiated highly enriched uranium fuel from their sites. The Commission also decided to issue a rule requiring these reactors to convert their cores to low enriched uranium—effectively reducing the risk of nuclear theft to "zero." Moreover, the Commission intends to seek direct funding and support from Congress and the executive branch to accomplish this fuel conversion.

Protecting Licensed Facilities Against Nuclear Theft

Licensed strategic special nuclear materials (highly enriched uranium and plutonium) that *must* be protected against theft are subject to very stringent NRC safeguards requirements. Depending upon the amounts and form of special nuclear material in their possession, the NRC requires licensees to develop various kinds of safeguards plans and programs that are carefully reviewed and approved by the NRC staff. Licensees that have very small amounts of special nuclear material of low strategic significance may only be required to develop and implement detailed NRC-approved plans for: material control and accounting; physical protection; and security force training and contingency response.

The NRC's *safety* principle of defense-in-depth also applies in *safeguards* planning. Thus, typical physical security plans for protecting nuclear materials against theft incorporate a number of elements such as perimeter protection, intrusion detection, security forces, multiple barriers, personnel screening and access controls. (I might add, these same features also typify the physical protection that the NRC requires against radiological sabotage at, for example, power reactors.)

Protecting Nuclear Materials in Transport

There has been the notion expressed today with regard to the transportation of nuclear materials that seems to imply that NRC transportation safeguards somehow rest upon bills of lading and undependable civilian guards. This notion is wrong. In fact, to transport a significant quantity of strategic special nuclear material over the road, the NRC requires the licensee to implement a number of safeguards such as the use of an armored vehicle or specially designed penetration-resistant truck with immobilization features, accompanied by armed escorts and separate escort vehicles—all backed by communications and law enforcement response arrangements. Moreover, if strategic special nuclear material is transported in less than significant amounts, so that individual shipments are not attractive targets of theft, NRC safeguards rules guard them against multiple thefts. We simply do not allow multiple shipments to be on the road at the same time, anywhere in the country, if they add up to a significant quantity of strategic special nuclear material. New shipments are delayed at the start, if necessary, until others have arrived at their destinations.

Protecting Nuclear Power Plants Against Radiological Sabotage

I was surprised to hear today the scenario about sabotage at one of the NRC's licensed power reactors in which a "van bomb" reduces the entire plant to rubble when detonated at a remote distance. We are not able to draw such drastic inferences from our own studies of explosives. To be sure, we are concerned about protecting licensed nuclear power plants from radiological sabotage and have highly sophisticated security in place at these plants, because the NRC is determined to protect them against terrorist attack. Again, I should point out that the NRC has a published design basis threat for radiological sabotage that includes terrorist-type violent assaults. However, the NRC's design basis for domestic safeguards must itself stand the test of reasonableness when judged in light of the current and anticipated threat environment of the United States.

The NRC regulates the licensed nuclear industry under a presumption of general civil order. If civil order were to be threatened in the U.S. by terrorist attacks or other occurrences, the licensed nuclear industry, along with all the other elements of the private sector, would seek protection and support from government. Existing NRC-approved contingency plans for power reactors already provide for local law enforcement support in the event of attack. Of course, each licensed facility has a formidable security system of its own to meet NRC requirements. There are, on average, about 55 armed security officers employed at each reactor, with an average annual operating budget for security of about $1.4 million per reactor unit. The average plant has about $8 million invested in its protection system, involving such things as perimeter protection, intrusion detection, multiple barriers and access controls. The size and equipment of these protective forces are comparable to the police force of some of our towns in the United States.

One must begin to wonder how much should be required of private industrial facilities to protect themselves. If we postulate threats to overcome these protective forces, then questions must be raised about vastly increasing publicly supported police forces and, more disturbing, moving much more aggressively to counter terrorism methods with all of their attendant impact on personal liberties.

Protecting Against Insider Threats at Nuclear Power Plants

Last year the Commission proposed a rule requiring an access authorization program for individuals seeking unescorted access to sensitive areas in nuclear power plants. The proposed rule, which will affect all nuclear power plant licensees, is intended to result in increased assurance of the trustworthiness of personnel at nuclear power plant sites. The Commission also supports legislation to provide licensee access to Federal Bureau of Investigation criminal data for the purpose of employee screening.

Verifying Safeguards

After NRC licensees implement their safeguards programs, they are subject to routine inspection and enforcement to assure continued compliance with NRC-approved plans. Independent of inspection and enforcement activities, NRC teams also conduct on-site effectiveness reviews to assure that the safeguards systems implemented by licensees actually provide intended levels of protection in relation to design basis threats. These effectiveness reviews involve the use of U.S. Army Special Forces under contract to us. Finally, the NRC staff analyzes data concerning safeguards-related events, domestic and foreign, and maintains contact with members of the intelligence community to assess the threat environment.

Terrorist Threat

At this point, I'd like to comment on some points about the nature and focus of the terrorist threat. To begin, we in the NRC do not see terrorism, as has been described, as "random and pointless." On the contrary, we generally credit terrorists with having focused agendas and goals. Second, attacks upon U.S. interests in strife-torn foreign environments do not necessarily translate into a domestic U.S. threat. For this reason, we tend to agree with the director of the State Department's Office of Counter Terrorism and Emergency Planning whom Admiral Davies quoted today as saying, "the problem for the United States is likely to continue to be external to the United States, not internal. . . . " We consider extreme forms of violence such as the Beirut truck bomb to be in this category. They are, in a sense, "acts of war" carried out in a chaotic environment that bears no resemblance whatsoever to the environment of general civil order upon which the U.S. domestic safeguards regulation is premised. Nevertheless, as a matter of prudence, the NRC is sponsoring research to obtain a clear and comprehensive understanding of the technical aspects of the "truck bomb" in case future changes in the threat environment were to indicate a need to protect U.S. domestic facilities against such a threat.

International Safeguards

Let me touch briefly on international aspects of nuclear safeguards. Although, as I have said, the NRC's principal safeguards mission involves the domestic licensed nuclear industry, we do have some involvement with international matters. For example, it is probably not widely known, but the NRC was certainly instrumental in helping bring about what Admiral Davies called the "extraordinary security measures" surrounding the big shipment of plutonium from France to Japan last year.

With regard to licensed exports, the NRC participates in reviews required by the Nuclear Non-Proliferation Act. In approving exports, the NRC and the executive branch must consider physical protection and international safeguards-related criteria; adequacy of physical security measures; application of IAEA safeguards; and maintenance of full-scope safeguards by recipient non-nuclear-weapons states.

Convention on Physical Protection

The NRC has developed a final rule to implement the Convention on the Physical Protection of Nuclear Material, a part of the IAEA agreements originally proposed by the secretary of state in 1974 and signed in 1980. The Convention, which provides for the security of international shipments of significant quantities of source or special nuclear material, was ratified by the Senate on July 30, 1981. The NRC rule will require a number of measures, including physical protection of transient shipments of special nuclear material and advance notifications about international movements of Convention-defined nuclear materials. By means of the NRC's rule, the United States will implement the Convention and help improve security for nuclear materials during international transport. As it stands now, the NRC's rule will take effect when the 21st nation ratifies the Convention.

Summary

To summarize, I would like to emphasize the importance of separating fiction from fact in considering terrorist threats and capabilities and the need to recognize that all things "nuclear" are not automatically targets of nuclear theft and sabotage. In particular, our licensed U.S. light water power reactors should not be lumped together with weapons-usable nuclear materials and nuclear weapons in our thinking or discussions.

Next, I would note that where safeguards are needed, we have them. We have significant levels of safeguards protection in place at NRC-licensed nuclear facilities and activities that are further assured through effectiveness reviews, inspection and enforcement as may be necessary.

Regarding terrorism, the NRC takes the threat very seriously and has incorporated terrorist characteristics in its published design basis threats for safeguards. These design threats are now being reviewed again by the Commission to assure their continued reasonableness in light of the actual threat environment.

Finally, the NRC's domestic safeguards regulations are premised upon an assumption of general civil order in this country. If that condition changes— because of terrorist or other activity—it will have a profound effect on the entire private sector within which the licensed nuclear industry is just one small part. Providing for adequate public protection under such circumstances is a challenge that should probably be met by federal contingency planning integrated at the highest levels of government.

* * *

D. A. V. Fischer

The discussion we have had about the risk and probability of nuclear terrorism has much in common with the debate on nuclear proliferation. In each case, today one can discern two schools of thought.

The first tends to assess risks on the basis of general trends and abstract scenarios. It observes with concern the proliferation of nuclear plants, fuel and technology. It reasons, in general terms, that spreading capability and multiplying opportunities coupled with political instability and insecurity are bound to mean more nuclear weapon nations or, in the context of terrorism, attempts to make or steal nuclear explosives or to apply nuclear blackmail.

The second, more pragmatic, school agrees that capability and opportunity are significant but considers that for both proliferation and terrorism, political factors are always paramount. It believes that it is possible to identify and narrow down the real danger spots, that each must be looked at individually, and that they are far fewer, at least in the short term, than one would conclude from generalized reasoning on the basis of spreading technology and human capacity for evil.

Let us look at international experience to date. As far as we know (and our knowledge is admittedly incomplete), there has so far been no serious purely *criminal* attempt to make a nuclear explosive or to blow up or threaten to blow up a nuclear plant or nuclear material. There have been several hoaxes and false alarms, but not even the Mafia has tried to exploit the nuclear connection. Why should a criminal engage in such a risky and difficult enterprise when it is so much easier to sell cocaine?

No *criminal* attempts so far, but quite a few *politically* inspired events. At this stage we need a working definition of nuclear terrorism in the political context. I propose "the violent misuse or destruction of nuclear hardware to gain a political objective." This would include attempted or threatened misuse (e.g., making a bomb or blackmail). It would cover nuclear plant and major components as well as nuclear material. It would not cover nuclear war.

The Potential Settings

From our very limited international experience, the most plausible settings for nuclear terrorism in this sense are civil war, civil insurrection or bitter regional tension between states.

Civil War. In the civil war scenario, territory on which a nuclear plant or material is located may change hands from one faction to another. The closest we have come to this so far was during the Vietnam war. A U.S.-supplied "TRIGA" reactor was operating at Dalat in what was then the Republic of Vietnam. When the Vietcong and North Vietnamese moved in, Dalat came under attack and eventually fell. No international safeguards or constraints applied any longer to the reactor. (The U.S. had already removed its very small fuel charge.) However, the North Vietnamese (People's Republic of Vietnam) eventually placed the reactor under IAEA safeguards again and later joined the Nuclear Non-Proliferation Treaty. (Incidentally, the chief of the Dalat center under the defunct Republic of Vietnam is again its chief today.)

In short, the new owners of the reactor have not sought to misuse it in any way. But there are obvious cases where one or more of the warring factions might prove less responsible. We should perhaps be thankful that, more by sheer chance than by prudent restraint, there is no significant nuclear installation of any kind in Lebanon.

Civil Insurrection. If we except violent demonstrations by enraged environmentalists, the only cases where civil insurrection has so far taken nuclear form have been the attacks (a) by the African National Congress (ANC) against the control room of the Koeberg nuclear power plant near Cape Town, South Africa; and (b) by Basque terrorists against the Lemoniz power plant in Spain. Both attacks took place before the reactors concerned were completed.

Regional Conflict. As we have seen in Lebanon, the distinction between civil war or insurrection and regional conflict can become very blurred. There have been reports (denied) that India has contemplated direct state action—a preemptive strike—against the Chasma enrichment plant in Pakistan, while Pakistan has been accused of planning to use Sikh extremists in India to blow up an Indian nuclear plant.

In the case of the Tammuz reactor in Iraq, we see, at first, state-inspired terrorism and, when that failed, a direct Israeli strike. The first terrorist act was the murder in a Parisian hotel room of the Egyptian who was working as chief engineer on the Tammuz project. Then terrorists blew up the (first) Tammuz reactor core while it was awaiting shipment at Marseilles. It was generally believed that Israeli agents "did the job," although the evidence left behind sought to implicate a French (Corsican?) terrorist group. Finally, Menachim Begin had the reactor destroyed by a pinpoint air attack. In the meantime, the Iranians may have made an unsuccessful attempt to do the same. And most recently Iran has accused Iraq of bombing the incomplete nuclear power plant at Bushire.

Analysis

What do these scattered incidents have in common?

1. In all cases except Lemoniz, the attacks or rumored plans of attack have involved countries where regional, religious and racial tensions are acute and whose governments are generally regarded as real or potential proliferators of nuclear weapons. Not surprisingly, proliferation and state-supported terrorism against the regional enemy often go hand in hand.
2. The record of success in gaining the political objective is uneven. The Koeberg and Lemoniz attacks achieved limited aims (the first demonstrated the ability of the ANC to penetrate a heavily guarded site, and the Lemoniz incident led to the cancellation of the plant and probably affected the Spanish government's nuclear power plans). The only completely successful operation in the sense of putting the target out of action for a long time—perhaps for good— was the air strike against Tammuz. But seen through terrorists' eyes, the record is not too bad.

3. In no case so far has the attacking group or country tried to use or threatened to use the target material or target plant as a bomb, or as a source for a bomb, or to release radioactivity. The object has been to destroy the target.
4. Lemoniz is the only case so far of serious nuclear terrorism in an industrialized country.

Possible Measures

We will not give up flying despite horrifying terrorist attacks, and we will not give up using nuclear energy (or making nuclear weapons) because of the risk of terrorism. What can we do to minimize the risk? Time and again we have seen that it is impossible to stamp out terrorism by retribution. But there is scope for both national and international action to combat nuclear terrorism.

First, what international action is possible? The 1980 International Convention for the Physical Protection of Nuclear Material is a useful agreement that binds the parties to observe certain rules regarding the transport of nuclear materials, to coordinate their actions to recover stolen material, to exchange information, to outlaw and punish terrorist and cognate activities, to extradite or promptly punish nuclear terrorists, etc. The Convention has been ratified by 14 nations; it needs 21 ratifications to enter into force. The 10 Common Market countries have signed the Convention; their joint action could bring it into force tomorrow.

The IAEA's recommendations about the steps that governments should take to protect nuclear material are a valuable set of minimum requirements. To some extent they are reflected in the International Convention. The IAEA issued them in 1977. As far as I know, the IAEA has taken no follow-up action; it has not sought to find out how many nations are applying the recommendations, what their experience has been and whether, 10 years later and after much more experience both of terrorism and of anti-terrorist measures, the recommendations need to be revised. I am sure the IAEA would be responsive to proposals by its member nations to follow through in this way. Its lack of action is chiefly the result of a shortage of qualified staff in this field.

The IAEA's own experience should be factored in. Although the IAEA does not have the right to apply or to verify the application of *physical protection measures* in its member countries, it is applying *safeguards* to 98 percent of the plants in the non-weapon countries and to some plants in the weapon countries. It must thus have some useful first-hand knowledge of how effective physical protection measures are in most countries operating nuclear plants.

Mason Willrich also mentioned this morning the need to strengthen IAEA safeguards themselves. Effective physical containment—essentially effective physical barriers to prevent the clandestine removal of material—is an important safeguards measure, particularly at reprocessing and enrichment plants where material accountancy may not be precise or prompt enough. The IAEA is also encouraging the development of real-time devices that would promptly signal the breach of a seal or other containment.

The time may also be ripe to have a look at the IAEA's safe transport regulations that are now applied by most countries. The chief aim of these regulations is to prescribe the measures that must be used to ensure radiation safety during transport, but this question is also obviously related to measures to combat hijacking or other terrorist action.

On a completely different note, I must point out that however sorely the United States may be tried by the injection of Middle East politics into the one-week General Conference of the IAEA (since the Israelis attacked the Tammuz reactor), the United States does not enhance the authority and effectiveness of the IAEA in matters of physical protection, safeguards or safety by withdrawing or threatening to withdraw from the IAEA.

International measures are an essential part of the anti-terrorist regime. But the key question is what should individual governments do?

- It is crucial to keep the number of potential targets in tense political areas as small as possible, and to "harden" those targets that are there.
- This implies extreme restraint in the export of any kind of nuclear plant to countries in regions like the Middle East, southern Africa and South Asia. And a total embargo on the export of any plant capable of making fissile material.
- The United States must, however, be aware that there are limits to what it can achieve single-handedly today and risks if it tries to go too far. The United States must bear in mind that it can no longer legislate worldwide anti-nuclear terrorist policies any more than it can legislate worldwide anti-proliferation policies. There is little prospect that the United States would be able to persuade the Western Europeans or Japanese to give up the production of civilian plutonium or to renounce their fast breeder programs. The fundamental justification of these programs, in their eyes, is energy independence rather than the expectation that the breeder (or the recycling of plutonium in thermal reactors) will be economically competitive. In any case, most of these programs are already slowing down under the weight of escalating costs and tighter budgets; it would probably be wisest to let nature take its course.
- What else could be done? Since the root causes of terrorism like the root causes of proliferation are political, the final answer is to heal or assuage the political sicknesses of the regions concerned. Since we obviously do not know how to do so, I think we have to accept the fact that terrorism, as well as nuclear installations and a certain amount of plutonium production, will be with us for a long time. There is nothing new about terrorism, only about the means it uses. Going back a little, on June 28, 1914, a young Serbian by the name of Princip, a member of a terrorist organization called the Black Hand,

intent on liberating Serbians from the Austrian yoke, was standing on a bridge at Sarajevo. As Archduke Franz Ferdinand of Austria and his wife, Archduchess Sophie, drove by in an open car, Princip fired twice. Those two shots are generally regarded as the proximate cause of the First World War.

We must of course ensure that no act of terrorism, even the worst conceivable nuclear terrorism, becomes the proximate cause of the third World War.

* * *

Peter Stockton

I couldn't agree with Ted Taylor more about overclassification and secrecy and the difficulties it causes in terms of accountability.

In mid-1982, Representative John D. Dingell wanted a review of the various safeguards at the Department of Energy facilities that manufacture nuclear weapons. The facilities contain complete nuclear weapons, plutonium, bomb-grade uranium and highly classified information, as well as test devices. There is a way of measuring the effectiveness of these safeguards. Since 1975, there has been a baseline threat level to be met by the Department of Energy. You can measure the safeguards, particularly the physical safeguards of these facilities, against that generic threat.

What the subcommittee found when it visited these facilities was a disaster waiting to happen. As Representative Dingell said, "They couldn't stop a group of Girl Scouts." There is ample documentation, or there was at that time, in DOE as well as in DOE field offices, to document these failures.

In 1980, an independent assessment program was put together by an extremely concerned assistant secretary, who brought in outside experts to look at these facilities. Two of the facilities that were most criticized were Savannah River and Los Alamos. The program was killed in 1981.

Let me read you a few of the subcommittee's findings. Since 1982, the subcommittee found that safeguards and security at our most sensitive nuclear facilities, weapons facilities, have been in a shambles: for example, guards that could not shoot, guards that were told not to shoot, emergency response vehicles that wouldn't start, an admitted burglar permitted to keep his Q-level security clearance to work in nuclear materials, sensors and alarms that would not work, guards that were not trained, vaults that weren't secure, nuclear test devices highly vulnerable to theft, and much more. I can cite a few examples, and we can talk about these weaknesses now because the facilities are no longer being used.

Let me tell you about a vault at Savannah River that was out in a field. As you know, Savannah River is a huge complex, with three strands of barbed wire around the perimeter. If you get within about 50 yards of this vault, there is an unalarmed fence that anyone could go over without being detected. You then come to a double fence, right outside the facility itself. From that point, it's 1.5 minutes on target. Normally the alarms weren't working at that point down there, and anyway, there was a force on force used with Miles equipment on that. The terrorists would have made off with plutonium that was sitting in the form of buttons in these nice tomato juice cans, ready to be shipped to Rocky Flats. The terrorists would have left the entire facility 16 minutes before a credible response was mounted. The next day, that vault was shut down.

At another facility, when you are inside the facility, they show you these marvelous vault doors that cost hundreds of thousands of dollars. We had a very smart fellow as a consultant on this program. We went around to the back of the facility, and there was a theater door that you could go through, which was 1.5 minutes on target from a public road.

Another problem was Los Alamos. In that first hearing, and this has been declassified now, we had as a witness the head of the international section of the defense programs group—the person in charge of traveling the world to make sure that safeguards were adequate in the various countries that were receiving special nuclear materials from the Department of Energy. He also had been the head of the independent assessment program that looked at Los Alamos. He was asked, if Los Alamos had been a sovereign nation, would he have advised the secretary of energy to send special nuclear materials to Los Alamos? After much stuttering, he admitted he would have to advise not sending it there. That says a lot.

The prime target at Los Alamos, and certainly the prime thing that the Department of Energy wants to protect in this program, is test devices, because as we understand it, it would take not terribly smart people a day or two to be able to explode a stolen test device. At Los Alamos, there was no way you could protect this particular facility—the S site. We went out there in the fall of 1983 and had a meeting with them. We suggested you couldn't protect it; the independent assessment program in 1980 said you couldn't protect it. Finally, Secretary Hodel sent his own inspection team out there, and in January 1984 ran an exercise against the facility and found that they would have made off with a test device.

About two weeks later, after the subcommittee was briefed on this report, we suggested that Representative Dingell was going to have apoplexy after learning of these results. Within an hour, the secretary shut down the facility. They don't assemble test devices any longer at Los Alamos.

Let me concur with Admiral Davies, who pointed out in his paper that there is an attitudinal problem throughout the system. There was a serious problem with DOE officials, top DOE officials, telling the truth to the subcommittee under oath. In the first hearing, the assistant secretary blatantly lied to the subcommittee. The manager of the Savannah River operations office did the same. It's enormously hard to move a bureaucracy, as you probably know, when you have to hold hearings in executive session and are not able to talk about the results.

The current assistant secretary had a little problem telling the truth before the Foreign Affairs Committee a few years ago, when he assured the committee that everything was fine, don't worry. Then the top nuclear person in the office of the secretary of defense came on and said, "Well, you know, the general said not to worry, but I think I'd worry, because the things he told you about aren't in place."

Most of the people who do tell the truth to the committee are harassed. They went after one particular fellow from the independent assessment program who testified before the subcommittee. They developed a bogus security clearance problem with him, which is being pursued by the committee.

Donald Hodel, the former secretary of the DOE, certainly gave some wrong signals, but he brought the facilities along significantly. John Harrington, the new secretary of energy whom we had little faith in when he started out, deserves high marks. He is instituting accountability in the system.

Chapter Three

How Can Government and Industry Effectively Respond?

Louis O. Giuffrida

First, some comments on which we can all agree: (1) Once terrorism starts, there is no guarantee that it can be satisfactorily stopped, even with massive use of security forces, e.g., Northern Ireland; and (2) it is impossible to protect everyone and everything from a terrorist attack.

Historically, every society has viewed force—which in this context is synonymous with violence—in relative terms, i.e., from its own peculiar perspective. Some use of violence is decreed as necessary to preserve that society and is ipso facto "legitimate." All other violence is declared "illegitimate." The society then assumes a monopoly on the use of violence and creates instrumentalities such as armies and police to apply that violence. Historically, too, societies have longed for an environment totally free of any illegitimate violence.

The harsh reality is that we cannot have it both ways! The only way a society can attempt totally to eliminate illegitimate violence by its own definition of "illegitimate" is to raise the level of *legitimate* violence to such a point that it completely obviates any semblance of individual freedom. Hitler's attempt to eliminate illegitimate violence, by his definition of "illegitimate," brought forth the Gestapo, which wielded its weapons of terror against non-Germans and Germans with equal vigor and brutality.

It seems to me we should stop trying to achieve the impossible and put our combined efforts into trying to define the *maximum* level of illegitimate violence we can tolerate and still remain a free society, even though there is no universal definition of when peaceful dissent ceases and unacceptable, deliberate violation of the law commences. In planning a defense for society against terror of various kinds, it is important to get a least a consensus definition of what we are trying to combat. There must be points of common agreement and a common vocabulary.

I accept, for this purpose, that terrorism can be generally and usefully defined as organized, illegitimate violence aimed to achieve some specific change, for example, a political change. I agree that the intended target is not necessarily the victim of the violence. This definition includes the "deliberate and systematic" elements of the definition used by Senator Henry Jackson in Jerusalem in 1979.

It seems to me that we in the United States have suffered uncertainty and lack of direction primarily because we have been unable to build a common vocabulary so that the terminology of terrorism is clearly understood throughout the entire country. Additionally, the United States seems to have been surprised by the growing frequency of terrorist acts in this country. For some years prior to 1974, one could sense throughout the United States a general attitude that "terrorism only happens in backward countries or in Europe or in Latin America, but certainly not here in the United States." What I am saying is that the general population was under the illusion that we Americans were immune from this problem.

Within the context of our freedoms, then, we must come up with a more specific definition of terrorism based on our laws and traditions. For example, we can agree that dissenters are not necessarily terrorists. Free people have the right to peaceful dissent, and we must all jealously guard that right. I believe that if any group is deprived of the right of lawful, peaceful dissent, then we are all deprived of that right. Social mechanisms for peaceful change must be preserved. This is one of our strengths. It makes terrorism less likely.

In arriving at this difficult balance, it is imperative that we understand what a terrorist is—and is not! The ability of the media to be both informed and objective will be a key factor in educating the public so that legal and acceptable governmental and societal actions can be carried out. There are those who have some reservations about the objectivity and depth of knowledge of some of the media, particularly when it comes to terrorists. For example, there were two Symbionese Liberation Armies (SLAs): one created by the media and the other, the real SLA. The media version was an actual army with a nationwide infrastructure, led by social and military experts who seemed to materialize from thin air! The entire world was inundated with almost hourly accounts of this so-called army. They were too frequently portrayed as an essentially benevolent group of humanists presumably driven to violent and desperate measures by an insensitive and oppressive government. They were portrayed as the "good guys" in far too many accounts. Then, there was the real SLA: a group of criminal misfits totally devoid of any semblance of legitimacy. They were bank robbers, car thieves, and shoplifters who "deliberately and systematically" set out menacing the innocent to gain their ill-defined political ends. Even today, there are those who eulogize the SLA as "folk heroes"!

Though domestically the United States appears relatively free of the international upward trend in terrorist acts so far, it is not because we have had organized programs to prevent it. There has, however, been an increase in the awareness of domestic terrorist incidents. Terrorist bombings are typical of the events that the United States has experienced so far. They are isolated, attention-getting, and make use of *conventional* technology.

We cannot, and should not, count on the current essentially uncoordinated terror methodology in the United States continuing indefinitely into the future. Realistically, the United States is extremely vulnerable to the conventional weapons and tactics of terrorism. Our highly interconnected infrastructure systems—power supply networks, natural gas and petroleum pipelines, nuclear power plants, water supply systems, the telephone network, and others—contain choke points that cannot all be defended simultaneously against site attacks by highly motivated and well-armed terrorists. The increasing reliance on high technology systems, designed more for efficiency than for ease of protection, simply increases America's vulnerability to economic, political, and social disruptions. This is clearly shown even by the frequent unintentional damaging of parts of these systems by peacetime disasters.

It is obvious that terrorism is not new; it has been with us all the time, and only the degrees of severity and of public awareness have varied. It is only inevitable that more and more terrorism will be state-supported because it is the cheapest and the least hazardous way to fight an undeclared war. How else could a sponsor nation provide money, training, and other support within the mantle of "normal diplomatic relations" almost totally free of the risk of military or economic reprisals from the target nation?

For a variety of reasons, the United States has not yet had to face at home highly organized, highly trained, state-supported terrorists. I would suggest that until now this could be explained at least in part by the existence of relatively easy targets in Europe and other parts of the world. This situation, however, is changing. Target countries like France, Italy, West Germany, and England have become tougher and better at dealing with terrorism; they can no longer be called "easy." It stands to reason, then, that terrorists will look for new targets that are not as well prepared to deal with them. The United States, unfortunately, automatically becomes a very attractive target.

The modern world has been fortunate that it has experienced no successful nuclear, biological, or chemical terrorist incident. Experts disagree on the extent to which a third-world country or private terrorist group might be able to construct a nuclear device that could be used convincingly to make demands. As a practical matter, however, responsible government officials have to assume a worst case situation in their planning.

The experts do agree that chemical or biological weapons are well within the technical capability of third-world countries or private terrorist groups. To give an idea of these threats, let me compare the weight of various agents needed to produce heavy casualties in a square mile area under idealized conditions. To produce about the same number of deaths in that square mile, it would take about 32 million grams of fragmentation cluster bomb material; 3,200,000 grams of mustard gas; 800,000 grams of nerve gas; 5,000 grams of material in a crude nuclear fission weapon; 80 grams of botulinal toxin Type A; and only 8 grams of anthrax spores.

A government facing a terrorist threat must find a solution that is not only effective but also acceptable. We in the United States are "instant problem-instant solution"-oriented. This national characteristic has always made us more inclined to be reactive rather than proactive. Virtually everything our government does is conceived and debated in conformance with "sunshine laws." When one factors in political opposition and fiercely protected domain, the development of a long-term, federally directed anti-terrorism strategic plan that is both effective and acceptable becomes difficult indeed!

Nevertheless, it is possible to identify the necessary components of a counter-terrorism program. The strategic plan must deal with every facet of combatting terrorism: legal, operational, budgetary, and administrative. It must consider not only government at every level, but also the public, the private sector, the media, and the academic community. Furthermore, the government cannot be perceived as dramatically changing its normal emergency response functions in order to deal with terrorism, else the terrorists' claimed ability to disrupt government will be given undeserved credibility.

The goals of counterterrorism must be: (1) to secure continuous intelligence on terrorists groups; (2) to identify and isolate terrorist groups and prevent terrorist actions by denying them food, money, shelter, weapons, medical treatment, etc.; and (3) to capture and bring to trial the terrorist leaders. Without leaders, terrorist groups are more likely to splinter and become less effective.

No counterterrorism program can hope to succeed without detailed, coordinated planning. The brunt of counteraction must fall on law enforcement and on the military, but many other agencies will also be involved, e.g., the border patrol, the coast guard, etc. There must be *one boss* with the power to impose an appropriate plan on all the agencies concerned. At the very minimum, there must be a common strategy and a clear delineation of agency responsibilities. There has to be a continuous, true dialogue among the agencies involved.

There is no question in my mind that we have the men, the materials, the skills, and the courage to assemble a special response force. Our biggest deficiency has been the lack of intelligence. I do not minimize the dangers implicit in re-assessing traditional legal safeguards or in restricting liberties. I am also very much aware of the difficulty in trying to get less glamorous or politicized reporting of terrorist acts. But fundamental to any chance for success is the necessity for us to recognize that all of our planning and all of our potential for anti-terrorism response that will be both effective and acceptable is *totally dependent* upon a continuum of intelligence information that can be clearly used by all the agencies that have the responsibility to plan for and to respond to acts of terrorism. Intelligence gathered by separate agencies must be centrally evaluated and must include a retrieval system so that the intelligence can be made readily available to those who need it in the performance of their duties. Intelligence has to include detailed knowledge of active terrorists and their supporters. The security forces must have valid intelligence to be able to identify command structures of terrorist groups. The computer sciences can greatly enhance the intelligence process and, properly and legally managed, can be utilized without flagrant disregard for personal liberties.

I am confident that we can handle acts of conventional terrorism such as bombs or disruptions of communications or power systems. I am not confident about our ability to deal with chemical or biological agents. It seems to me our best defense against this type of assault is the ability of our intelligence agencies to identify those terrorists who could and would use such techniques and to keep fully informed as to their whereabouts, intentions, affiliations, etc. Knowing who our potential enemies are and what they are doing is fundamental to our survival. Acquiring and using this essential intelligence and maintaining our free society need not be mutually exclusive.

No special reaction force or memorandum of understanding between agencies can replace reliable intelligence. In fact, the lack of good intelligence is what causes reliance on such things as baggage checks, roadblocks, body searches, etc. Any objective analysis would show that removing some of the restrictions on intelligence operations would be far more effective in terms of identifying terrorists. Not only is intelligence essential for any preventive measures, it is also required for successful rescue attempts or hostage situations.

At some point, we need to decide what concessions we would be prepared to make, if for no other reason than to measure what kind of emergency services we would need to survive the results of a terrorist action. This type of decision absolutely requires an understanding of the resources available to the government (and, incidentally, also to the terrorist) and a defensible, unemotional analysis of the physical results of a terrorist act. This is true whether we are considering conventional weapons or whether we're considering mass terrorism through the use of nuclear, biological, or chemical devices. The damage caused by terrorist weapons is directly related to the terrorist's selection of targets. For example, a heat-seeking rocket would do relatively little damage to a government building, but, the same rocket could completely destroy a loaded 747 aircraft.

We could do much better at controlling explosives and other death-dealing items. We do not require users of explosives to be careful enough in their storage of the items; they can be too easily stolen. We need to examine critically how far the government is entitled to go in lifting legal safeguards such as searches, detentions, etc.

Since the police will inevitably be involved, we should be looking hard at their readiness for counterterrorism actions. One could suggest that the specialized training, both technical and academic, that police have received might be more critical than the number of policemen who respond to terrorist incidents.

I think everyone will agree that there is a clearly identifiable ratio between the capabilities of terrorists and government's power to respond.

The list could go on, but really what I am saying is that we need to look hard at ourselves as nations. In the past, at the national and international levels, there has sometimes been an unfortunate amount of parochial bickering between and among the various agencies that should have been and could have been productively involved in addressing this type of emergency.

Let me now address some unique problems of nuclear terrorism that demand considerable thought and early resolution:

1. The National Atomic Energy Act makes the FBI responsible for managing the nuclear threat/incident.
2. How can local authorities be kept well-advised and still ensure that information is not prematurely released?
3. A credible hoax can cause almost as much social, emotional, and other problems as the real thing. Therefore, who should have control of the release of information (confirmations, denial, etc.)?
4. Are we talking about a potential federal criminal offense and a federal government's problem, or a state and local problem of health and public safety?
5. What takes precedence—conducting a clean, prosecutable investigation or eliminating potential danger to public safety—should there be a conflict?
6. Who makes public health/safety decisions during an incident, state officials or feds (FBI)?
7. Who pays for relocation, etc., if a disaster doesn't occur?

The Federal Emergency Management Agency (FEMA) has the general responsibility to coordinate federal responses to any emergency, irrespective of cause. In the United States, we had traditionally addressed emergencies by type rather than generically. The Congress would write a specific law to address, for example, earthquakes or floods, and then give the responsibility to separate agencies of the U.S. government for implementation. It was inevitable that this approach would be costly and less than fully effective. Finally, five years ago, FEMA was created essentially by lumping into one agency all of these previously autonomous functions and responsibilities.

Since governments have always had the responsibility of protecting their citizens, it follows that the citizens should have the right to demand from their government a predictable, effective, coordinated, and acceptable response to whatever imperils the population. If one were to list all the dangers, natural or manmade, facing the United States on a continuing basis and then go on to list what the government needs to have in place in order to fulfill its responsibility of protecting the citizens, he would list for each type of emergency—including war and terrorism—precisely the same requirements. The differences are not dynamic but only order of magnitude.

An Integrated Emergency Management System (IEMS) to address the entire spectrum is what we have been building for the past four years. Its development and implementation have involved the expenditure of millions of dollars to provide better communications systems, Emergency Operating Centers (EOCs), training programs, etc. We now have for the first time a National Emergency Management System (NEMS) in which we have been careful to include state and local governments in both the design and the execution of training programs, exercises, and conferences. At FEMA headquarters, we have a very large and sophisticated Emergency Information and Coordination Center (EICC) that is connected with all other agencies of the federal government and with state and local governments.

FEMA is not an intelligence-gathering agency and maintains no intelligence files. We depend upon those agencies that have a legal charter to collect and disseminate intelligence. However, FEMA does have the responsibility to plan for and coordinate the federal response to the *consequences* of terrorist incidents. If a terrorist act had major effects on the populace anywhere in the United States, FEMA would exercise its regular day-to-day channels to state and local emergency managers, and to other federal agencies, to assure a consistent and effective multi-jurisdictional response to the consequences of the incident.

It is important to note that FEMA's method of dealing with the consequences of terrorism is basically the same as the way it deals with any major emergency. It makes use of existing channels of communication to government and existing emergency managers, whom it has helped support and train on the best methods to manage any large emergency. When necessary, FEMA headquarters is prepared to send out trained coordinating teams to assist in the response at the scene. The same doctrine underlies our recent publication of a "National Contingency Plan for Responding to Consequences of an Extraordinary Situation at Special Events." The most obvious special events are, of course, the Olympics, the World's Fair, and the political conventions, but the plan sets forth coordinating arrangements for any kind of major emergency, not just a terrorist incident. Preparedness for disasters is accomplished using the Integrated Emergency Management System (IEMS) process. The physical consequences and the response to the disaster are generic in nature, irrespective of the precipitating incident.

I believe that the way in which FEMA is addressing its responsibilities through its state-aid programs and at its National Emergency Training Center (NETC) is the most logical way for this nation to deal with the consequences of terrorism. Through our training programs, we are elevating the level of consciousness, imparting factual and theoretical knowledge to those whose responsibility it will be to actually deal with emergency situations once they arise.

Because very few state and local governments have had to deal with a credible terrorist threat, there are some people who look upon terrorism as a purely federal problem. While no part of the country is totally immune, it is possible to identify most of the probable target states and cities and include them in federal exercises. Properly implemented, this training will enable the various levels of government to exercise their authority, if required, with considerably less parochial difficulty. It has been our experience that programs and training that fit logically into our Integrated Emergency Management System are well received by Congress and by the general public.

While I am not suggesting that the United States is fully prepared to deal with the problem of terrorism, I am convinced that we are making measurable progress in getting our act together. The real challenge for us is to continue making progress while at the same time keeping the public informed and supportive.

* * * * *

RESPONSES
James K. Asselstine

Introduction

I listened with interest to General Giuffrida's opening comments and was impressed by his assurances regarding federal agency planning. It is comforting to know that FEMA has made considerable progress in concert with federal, state and local governments in preparing to respond to a wide range of emergencies and incidents including those that might arise from terrorist acts in this country. Many of his remarks, however, dealt with how we can stop terrorism in this country. In that regard, past history would suggest that we are not facing major problems from terrorism here in America, but events elsewhere should certainly serve as a warning to us of potential danger. I think it is important to emphasize the lack of an immediate identified terrorist threat here in America, because it gives us at least some time to think and plan without abandoning our institutions and liberties in the process. As General Giuffrida pointed out, this entire matter involves a "difficult balance."

I'd like to seize upon something else that General Giuffrida said with which I wholeheartedly agree, namely, "that if any group is deprived of the right of lawful, peaceful dissent then we are all deprived of that right"—that "social mechanisms for peaceful change must be preserved"—and that this *"makes terrorism less likely."* In America, where we have open and frank airings of differences and democratic mechanisms for resolving them, we have every reason to hope that we will not be a fertile ground for indigenous terrorism. This is not to say that we should neglect the matter.

Removing Potential Targets of Terrorism

In that regard, I can assure you that the Nuclear Regulatory Commission, of which I am a member, is taking terrorism very seriously. The safeguarding of licensed nuclear materials and facilities against threats, theft and sabotage, including terrorism, is one of the principal missions of the NRC. But because we are not facing imminent identified terrorist threats to the domestic nuclear industry, we have been able to deal with this matter in a more deliberate and reasonable fashion that involves the public through rule making to the maximum extent.

The NRC's approach is very straightforward. We simply want to reduce the attractiveness of licensed nuclear activities as potential targets of terrorism. In come cases, the Commission is acting literally to eliminate potential nuclear targets of terrorism. For example, the Commission recently decided to order the removal of excess highly enriched uranium from licensed research and test reactors throughout the country—effectively eliminating that material as a target of nuclear theft. The Commission has also decided to issue regulations that will cause non-power reactors to substitute low enriched uranium for the highly enriched uranium in their cores. To bring this about, the Commission intends to seek direct support and funding from Congress and the executive branch. We hope that these efforts will both reduce the potential risk of theft of this material in this country and aid in our efforts to reduce further the international commerce in highly enriched uranium.

This same prudent philosophy is reflected in the Commission's rules for safeguarding special nuclear material in transport. In some cases we have essentially no safeguards alternative other than to apply solid physical protection. For example, to transport a significant quantity of strategic special nuclear material over the road, NRC requires the licensee to implement a number of safeguards measures, such as the use of an armored car or a specially designed penetration-resistant truck with immobilization features, accompanied by seven armed escorts and separate escort vehicles—all backed by communications and law enforcement response arrangements. The concept of eliminating potential targets of nuclear terrorism is also reflected in NRC's safeguards rules for transporting lesser quantities of special nuclear material. NRC does not allow multiple shipments to be on the road at the same time anywhere in the country if they add up to a significant quantity of strategic special nuclear material. Shipments en route must reach their destination safely before new ones are permitted to depart.

Designing Nuclear Safeguards

Under NRC regulations, licensees are required to provide safeguards as appropriate for licensed nuclear fuel facilities, transportation, nuclear storage facilities and nuclear power plants. To provide a basis for designing safeguards systems, the NRC has published what it calls "design basis threats" in its regulations. These hypothetical threats are not a reflection of any imminent danger to licensed nuclear activities but are more like an engineering design specification against which safeguards systems to protect against theft and sabotage can be developed and their performance measured. The Commission works closely with its staff to assure the continued reasonableness of NRC's safeguards design basis threats in the context of a changing threat environment.

NRC Regulation Is Premised upon Civil Order

It is important to note that NRC regulates the licensed nuclear industry under a presumption of general civil order. If civil disorder were to break out in the United States—a situation that might include terrorist attacks—the licensed nuclear industry would expect to join with other elements of the private sector and citizenry in seeking protection and support from local, state and federal government. Initially, licensed nuclear facilities could expect support from local law enforcement agencies, as arranged in their NRC-approved safeguards contingency plans. Additional response forces or other support might be expected from state and federal sources, depending upon the severity and scope of the problem. And as General Giuffrida pointed out, we can expect FEMA and other emergency response agencies to organize recovery in the wake of any major successful terrorist acts.

Radiological Emergency Planning

Should a successful terrorist act occur at a commercial nuclear power plant, we would look to the applicable state and local radiological emergency response plans as one means for dealing with the consequences of such an act. Our capability for dealing with the consequences of radiological emergencies, whether caused by equipment breakdowns, human error or deliberate attack, has been improving steadily in recent years, since we, FEMA, our licensees, and state and local governments began giving greater attention to this area in the wake of the Three Mile Island accident. Our accomplishments in the emergency planning area have substantially improved our ability to deal with the consequences of a terrorist act should one occur at some of our licensed commercial nuclear facilities.

The Role of Intelligence

General Giuffrida noted that our best defense against a terrorist assault is the ability of our intelligence agencies to identify those terrorists who could and would use such techniques and to keep fully informed as to their whereabouts, intentions, affiliations, etc. I agree very much with his view, and I believe that the FBI and the intelligence community have been quite successful in the past in their efforts to identify domestic terrorist threats in the United States. But events in other countries in recent years, including the most recent events directed against Americans overseas, raise questions in my mind concerning the intelligence community's ability, despite its best efforts, to provide sufficient early warning of a specific terrorist threat. This may be a particular problem in the case of state-sponsored terrorism, given the demonstrated commitment, capability and resources of some of these groups. Indeed, the rapidly developing international environment for state-sponsored terrorism may well dictate additional prudent preventative measures at nuclear facilities even in the absence of a specific, identified terrorist threat against a U.S. nuclear facility.

Summary

In summary, the NRC views terrorism as a serious potential threat to licensed nuclear materials and facilities. We in the United States have been fortunate in the past in having the time to deal with it through deliberate planning and regulatory process. Hopefully NRC's safeguards systems will never be challenged by actual terrorist acts. Hopefully our free and open society and its domestic institutions and processes will prevent indigenous terrorism from taking root in America. But we must not be caught off guard, especially given the possibility that state-sponsored terrorism could be exported to this country from abroad rather quickly with little or no advance warning. Accordingly, NRC will continue to maintain a viable safeguards program for the licensed nuclear industry and will continue to cooperate with other agencies of government in contingency planning for effective incident response and recovery. But the Commission also believes that we need to pursue improved preparedness and contingency planning at the federal level to assure prompt integrated response actions involving all levels of government in the event that conditions change and we actually have to combat serious terrorism on our own soil.

* * *

Donald Devito

From the perspective of a state Emergency Management Office, and perhaps from the perspective of local government as well, counterterrorism is not our province. Whatever the source of a threat, anything that has the potential for impacting the public safety is our province. We are crisis managers. Crisis management under stress, assuring that government is in control—that's what we are about. When discussing the element of terrorism, we are not lead agencies; law enforcement generally has that role. Our responsibility is to be the focal point for the chief executive officer as regards population protection, whether that individual is the governor of a state, the mayor of a city or village, or the top official of a town or county.

It is important for anyone considering the potential impact of a terrorist act to understand that the bottom line, the final decision among alternatives, is not a scientific/technical nor a bureaucratic one. It is a political decision. It is a decision that must be based on credible information, and that is where the scientific-technological and bureaucratic communities play their most vital role.

There are a number of issues that are of concern to those in the emergency management business at the state and local levels of government. They have to do with the issue of "turf"; they have to do with matters of fixed centralized authority; they have to do with such things as differentiating between a federal problem of investigation and a state and local problem of public safety; they have to do with fiscal and social issues; they have to do with the complex aftermath of "perceived threat" and "credible hoax," as well as the potential legacy of the "cry wolf" syndrome.

In addressing these concerns and in meeting all of our responsibilities for public safety, we work under a principle called Comprehensive Emergency Management. Simply put, it is the use of all of the resources available at every level of government to cope with all hazards, whether manmade or natural, in peace or in war. We address them in what I refer to as the "3 Rs" of emergency management. They are the three essential components of the emergency management problem: readiness, response, and recovery.

Essentially, readiness has several components. Whatever the threat to the public safety, emergency managers must turn their attention to the establishment of a system that will provide for centralized direction and control involving a multitude of agencies, representing both the public and private sectors. The development and maintenance of a suitable communications network are vital to that effort. Part of this infrastructure must include the pre-positioning of the proper instrumentality for determining and monitoring the threat to the public. Here we must rely on the scientific-technological community to tell us what we ought to make available at the state and local level, for example, radiological monitoring devices and of what type, what kinds of chemical testing kits, and so on. Basically, what ought our "tool kit" contain? Infrastructure building is a key part of readiness.

Then we must plan. Often, in the emergency business, we find that the process of planning is significantly more important than the product we produce. Frequently, it is the first time that the diverse elements of state and local governments sit down "eyeball-to-eyeball" to resolve many of the issues that can manifest themselves during a crisis: resolution of turf; the response process; and the development of requisite guidance and/or policy, procedures and methodologies. This planning process can produce broad, flexible guidelines as to how we deal with any potential catastrophe. Then we have to train.

The training process must take us through a variety of exercises that give us the chance to experience crisis management under stress—although obviously in any testing environment, there can never be the level of stress that would exist in an actual situation.

Infrastructure building, planning and training—these are the readiness components of the emergency management problem. If we do them well, we will be better prepared to cope with a response. In the response mode, the scientific-technological and bureaucratic communities play a major role in the assessment and evaluation of the threat, from its credibility to its probability. It is here their advice is critical.

As the probability of the event increases, we move to a more subjective arena, one in which political decisions are going to have to be made among competing alternatives. In reaction to a nuclear threat, evacuation is the principal, perhaps the only major, response. It is fraught with all kinds of problems. There are those who are placed at serious risk if we evacuate. There are requirements for the congregate care of those who are evacuated—in effect, a post-relocation support infrastructure. Certainly, there must be a coordinated multi-agency effort.

During a major emergency, there must be a fixed point that clearly constitutes the seat of government. Normally referred to as emergency operation centers (EOCs), they are where the representatives of all the agencies and the executive decision-makers must gather; where information (intelligence, if you will) can flow to them for analysis; and from which their subsequent decisions can funnel out in a clear and concise manner to all the responders in the field. It is here that information must be controlled. The EOC should be the single place for the media to obtain information as to what is going on, rather than their trying to ferret it out from the uninformed. Similarly, there should be provisions for rumor control at the EOC. When there is a threat to public safety and it is an emotional situation, as is always the case when nuclear materials are involved, there must be some way of assuaging those concerns and of conveying accurate information when a public response is underway. Absent such provisions, confusion and, perhaps, panic could result, thereby complicating an already troublesome situation.

The final component of the emergency management problem, the recovery phase, involves the task of restoring the community, and government, back to normalcy as quickly as possible. It may involve the coordination of a multi-government and volunteer agency relief effort for those who have been impacted by the event, if we are unfortunate enough to have probability become reality. The recovery phase is usually where we pay later for the insufficient readiness that contributes to an inadequate response.

I want to assure you that a system does exist. There is an infrastructure to respond to the nuclear dimension of terrorism. It is the same infrastructure that responds to hurricanes, to tornadoes and flooding, and to hazardous materials incidents. It is an overtaxed system because events occur everyday. Regrettably, it is an underfunded system. We must make adequate resources available to provide a system that will maximize public safety. However, we live in a society where there are many competing demands for rather limited resources. We must leave the decisions as to the proper allocation of these resources to those whom we elect to make them. But the reality is, in this nuclear dimension of terrorism, as in all of the emergency business, we either pay now or we pay later. In this case, God help us if we are forced to pay later.

Jacques Meurant

In his remarkable book, *Terrorism and Global Security*, Louis René Beres comments on the prevention of nuclear terrorism as follows: "We must decide between the doctor and the locksmith, between changing the condition of the terrorist pathology or placing new 'locks' on the terrorist potential for violence."[1] We are tempted to add that the prevention of nuclear terrorism also needs a "wizard" in order to tackle the consequences of the acts of terrorists, if by any chance they gained access to such things as nuclear weapons, materials or facilities. It would have to be a wizard able not only to limit the effects of nuclear terrorist acts, but also to foresee the unexpected. Is this mere fiction? Is it possible to prepare oneself for the serious consequences of what would be a nuclear disaster, even of a limited nature, caused by terrorists, or should we not rather believe in miracles? As President Lyndon Johnson said, "Today the problem is not making miracles—but managing them"! How to manage miracles could be the title of our exposé, as we try to find what kind of response governments are able in our time to produce to mitigate the consequences of a nuclear terrorist act.

Plausibility of Nuclear Terrorist Acts

As Professor Yonah Alexander states, "Modern terrorism has introduced a new breed of warfare in terms of technology, victimization, threat and response. And the most alarming possibilities are situations where terrorists could obtain and use nuclear devices to intimidate, blackmail and even devastate entire cities and countries."[2]

The threat of nuclear terrorism grows from the concurrence of two conditions: the growth of the civil nuclear power industry, and the vulnerability to theft or attack by small groups. We are aware that certain experts think it most unlikely for several reasons, to wit, safeguards against terrorist access to appropriate nuclear materials should prevent such incidents, biological and chemical agents have long been available but have remained unused, and the use of mass destruction weapons would be counter-productive to terrorists. For instance, it would be most difficult to imagine the use of nuclear devices in defense of the interest of workers or in compelling major social reforms.

Is this a realistic opinion? Certainly less than it was 20 years ago. Even the best protected nuclear installations are subject to attack. There have been some examples of low-level nuclear hoaxes, low-level sabotage of nuclear facilities, of seizure of hostages at nuclear facilities. Furthermore, security in nuclear energy plants all over the world may not always be of a high degree, and there is a possibility of terrorists holding a nuclear plant in a hostage-barricade situation and threatening leakage or other sabotage unless demands are met. Moreover, the most important characteristic of the potential nuclear terrorist is a willingness to take high risks. The means of terrorism are closely related to ends, and, given the goals and methods of nuclear terrorism, they would fall into two types: destructive acts serving primarily strategic goals, and complicated bargaining moves implementing both general as well as specific aims. Destructive terrorism would mean the theft and detonation of nuclear weapons, and/or materials, the sabotage of nuclear facilities, the theft and dispersal of radioactive substances.[3]

Radical factions of terrorist movements do not necessarily fear the alienation of world opinion and may be attracted to mass destruction in the pursuit of their disruptive aims. The irrational can occur. There is the possible use of nuclear weapons or sabotage of nuclear facilities with *limited effect* to create political disruption, while leveling radical demands at the authorities. As Robert Kupperman and Darrell Trent state, "Even if mass destruction terrorism were highly improbable, its potential consequences cannot be ignored."[4] For this reason, exhaustive efforts have to be made to minimize the hazards associated with nuclear power, especially with respect to protecting nuclear material, weapons, power plants and other nuclear facilities from terrorists. In other words, we have to rely less on a wizard's power and more on a manager's capacity. That means a real mobilization of government forces, assisted by other institutions, in order to plan any measures to prevent, but also to face, disruptive acts of terrorism.

Possible Government Responses: Prevention

Management and technology are the key factors for a government to be able to tackle any threat or act by terrorists, as well as to handle its consequences. However, they are not the only elements to be considered, i.e., counter-terrorism must necessarily use intelligence and police and military operations, as well as psychological, medical and behavioral science techniques before, during and after threatened or actual incidents.[5] This parade can be divided into four stages: prevention, control, containment and restoration.

Technological Prevention. This means the avoidance of terrorist incidents by preventing access to appropriate instruments where possible, by successful protection of critical targets or by deterring incidents through a combination of deterrence and protection. What is called "hardening the target" includes the use of sensors at focal points of transportation and at barriers such as airport gates; closed circuit television; metal detectors; the erection of fences and barriers against intruders; armored cars; etc. We must also include measures to guard against the attempted diversion of nuclear material and methods to "corrupt" or despoil special nuclear material so that during transport it would become unsuitable for the manufacture of nuclear weapons.[6]

Psychological Prevention. We are, however, aware that the most sophisticated physical security measures are not enough. We must also act on terrorists through behavioral strategies. "Softening the adversary," as Beres states, "is based on a sound understanding of the risk calculation of terrorists."[7] We shall not elaborate on this point, as the subject is covered by eminent experts, but merely recall that counter-terrorist strategies have to be adapted to the various categories of risk calculations involved. To put it in a nutshell, let us say that this strategy would aim at convincing terrorists that higher order violence would be counter-productive to their objectives.[8]

Possible Government Responses: Control, Containment, Restoration

According to Robert A. Friedlünder, "The problem of terrorism is one of control, not one of elimination."[9]

Kupperman and Trent define *control* as "the timely establishment of mechanisms for command and control of governmental resources to assure an efficient response to any incident, with adequate informational and decision-making provisions, designed to seize the initiative from the terrorists."[10]

Prevention of the terrorist act is the first priority. However, in spite of safeguard measures, terrorists may attack. To retaliate, governments must manage their diverse assets, limit damage, and provide emergency health care to contain the incident and restore the target.

- *Containment* comprises the emergency measures taken to delimit the terrorist act in a physical sense and to decouple it in a psychological sense from the intended political consequences. Actions to limit damage and provide emergency health care are included.
- *Restoration* means deliberate actions to conclude the incident and restore the situation, lasting until the situation is returned to normal and routine services are again available.

To illustrate these various methods, we give three examples.

A hostage-barricade case. Government *control* means securing radio and telephone communications, isolating the terrorists, identifying them, entering into contact with them, keeping research intelligence files on known terrorists, employing hostage-negotiation techniques.

Containment in this case means gaining time to arrange for a careful and methodical rescue operation, to include specially selected and trained police assault teams who have to be marshaled, briefed and prepared for a forceful rescue operation.

The desired outcome is the terrorists' surrender, resulting from their isolation, loss of initiative, and consequent feelings of helplessness. If they do not surrender and appear unlikely to do so, at some point the decision must be made to rescue the hostages and terminate the incident. In this case, *restoration* implies taking action to conclude a terrorist incident, reinstate routine services and return to the normal state.

Attacks on nuclear power sites. Government *control* of a threatened attack on nuclear power plants entails enhancement of security at threatened installations and intensified search for the terrorists and their instruments (firearms, explosives, incendiaries).

Containment of terrorist action against a nuclear installation has a structural similarity to containment of many other types of attacks. If terrorists were to occupy a nuclear reactor site and threaten its destruction unless their demands (ransom or political concessions, for example) were met, then the situation would be similar to the hostage-barricade situation that occurs frequently. Law enforcement authorities now use some psychological techniques, communications equipment, night vision devices, body armor and long-range accurate weapons to contain such threats. Considerable technological improvement in these methods is possible and necessary. Because such situations might occur at nuclear sites, development and acquisition of countermeasure technology would be extremely useful. In the case of an attack against a nuclear reactor site, specialized radiation-detecting equipment would also be needed.

If the postulated terrorist attack took the form of a "hit-and-run" attempt at destruction, *containment* of the incident would take a different form. In the nuclear case, the potential release of radioactivity is the most unusual feature and the one that may cause the most widespread actual or psychological damage. Technology can help by determining in a convincing way the location and intensity of any radioactivity that might have spread. Instruments for this are available at nuclear power sites and could be obtained from the damaged installation if the terrorists did not destroy or take them.

Restoration of the situation after an attack on a nuclear reactor could entail decontamination measures.

Use of a nuclear weapon. If a terrorist group were to use a nuclear weapon, we would face a very serious civil emergency, in which case concern about martial law, evacuation, logistical arrangements, housing, food and health care would all be dominant.

With the use of a radiological agent and in case of the dispersal of radioactive elements, the contributions of technology to the task of *control* are limited to the use of specialized detectors, decontamination equipment, and managerial tools such as information systems to allocate emergency resources and mathematical models to estimate the extent of damage and the duration of danger. It would also be quite useful to develop technical means to perform rapid diagnosis and to identify specific pathogens.

Were a weapon of mass destruction used, there are a few technological means for *containment* that would prove useful. Here, the problem may be divided into two functions: first, to prevent further attacks, and, second, to contain or limit the physical effects of the initial attack. If there were no communications between the authorities and the terrorists, the first goal could be achieved only through intelligence and police means. On the other hand, if the terrorists and the authorities were in regular contact, behavioral techniques could prove valuable as well.

To meet the second goal, the public must be informed about decontamination and antiseptic procedures, as well as suitable sheltering. Further, if the attack unleashed a highly contagious disease, such as pneumonic plague, containment would crucially depend on early detection and diagnosis as well as on quarantine procedures.

Restoration entails a massive clean-up, a great decontamination effort and the feeding, sheltering and logistical support of thousands of people.

For an Adapted National Disaster Relief Plan
National Pre-Disaster Planning and Preparedness

After explaining the various stages of what could be the government's response to threats or acts by terrorists, we must be conscious of the necessity of carefully planned measures in order to limit the potential physical, institutional and psychological damage that terrorists can inflict. On this point, it can be said that the havoc wrought by terrorists closely resembles the effects of natural calamaties and accidents.[11]

What is a Disaster? A disaster is a catastrophic situation in which the day-to-day patterns of life are, in many instances, suddenly disrupted. People are plunged into helplessness and suffering and, as a result, need protection, food, clothing, shelter, medical and social care and other necessities of life. Suffering may be the result of any of the following: (1) extreme or violent acts of nature, such as floods, volcanic eruptions, earthquakes, tropical storms, tidal abnormalities and land and snowslides; (2) sudden catastrophes, such as fires, explosions, transportation wrecks and contamination from escaped gases, chemicals or other harmful elements such as radioactive agents; (3) illness or disease of epidemic proportions; (4) famine and resultant malnutrition and related illnesses; (5) acts of hostility or armed conflicts, both internal and international, in which the civilian population is threatened or affected.

From the above, it can be seen that former definitions of disaster may have been rather restricted and may even have been detrimental in prompting effective action in prevention and relief. It must be kept in mind that plans developed by the government must include not only the emergency period, but also the post-emergency period—or temporary recovery period—plus the long-term period of rehabilitation and reconstruction. Measures, therefore, should be planned in such a way as to provide the foundation for recovery, rehabilitation and reconstruction.

Government Responsibility. In times of disaster, government responsibility remains the same as in normal times and includes the protection and safeguarding of life, property, public health and welfare. Disaster increases but in general does not change the responsibility of the government.

The Effects of Disaster. While the characteristics of a disaster may vary, there are certain effects that are common to most disasters which must be considered in the national relief plan. These effects can be basically divided into three groups: effects on people, on the community and on systems and services.

People may be killed, injured or become ill. All will be affected by grief and shock. They may be made homeless or become separated from their families, with many reported missing. There are heavy personal losses, including food, clothing, medicines and medical supplies, household goods, dwellings, outbuildings and land, employment and income, livestock, crops and farm equipment, etc.

Communities suffer extensively from destruction or severe damage to public buildings, including schools, hospitals, factories and other places of employment, apartment buildings, religious centers, etc. Transportation is disrupted because of destruction and damage to streets, highways, bridges, railways, harbor and airport facilities, public transportation systems, river embankments and dikes, etc. Communications and other public services are interrupted by the destruction of and damage to electrical and gas, telephone, radio and television, water and sanitation facilities, etc. The accumulation of debris hampers all community activities.

Systems and services suffer greatly from the closing of schools and religious centers, the disruption of health and welfare services, the loss of revenue, dislocation of transport and communications, etc.

The Needs Created. The needs created are virtually the same in every disaster and include the four basic human needs of food, clothing, shelter and medical care (first-aid, nursing or hospital care). There is frequently a need to trace missing persons and to reunite families, to provide information on the types and kinds of assistance available, to provide social and welfare services, and to assist in the re-establishment of households and the restoration of incomes. The needs of the community include the normal responsibilities of the government, which will be greatly increased by the disaster. This is why the government must become operational as quickly as possible so that it can carry out its functions.

Differences Between Natural Disasters and Nuclear Terrorist-Inspired Disasters. What distinguishes "classic" natural catastrophes and those that terrorists could cause is *frequency* and *intent*. What terrorists can do is to increase the frequency with which we have to endure such catastrophes, thereby making preparations against them more urgent. Moreover, terrorists hold out the threat of repeatedly induced catastrophes that accident and nature do not.

In order to limit damage, government should mobilize its resources to accomplish the functional tasks of control, containment and restoration. Unfortunately, damage-limiting actions cannot always be easily put into effect. But because maintaining public confidence in the government is of supreme importance, appearance may often be more important than reality. During a terrorist crisis, one of a government's foremost responsibilities and challenges is *to maintain public confidence* in its ability to cope with all contingencies. As long as a government can convince its citizens that it has the ability to govern, despite whatever concessions are made or physical damage is inflicted, the terrorists will be denied a major objective, and government's leadership will remain unshaken.

An emergency preparedness plan is therefore necessary for all governments, and most planned measures should be adapted to terrorist-inspired disasters.

Developing a National Disaster Relief Plan

The basis of a national disaster relief plan is a legally constituted act, law or executive order establishing a central body for the planning and implementation of any national disaster relief action. In setting up such a central disaster relief body, consideration should be given to placing authority and responsibility with that ministry, department and/or branch of government whose day-to-day services and activities relate closely to the needs created by disasters and whose structure will, on a national basis, provide proper administrative links to regional and local levels throughout the country. The central disaster relief body should also be given the authority to call upon any branch of government whose services and resources can appropriately be used in disaster prevention and preparedness and in relief and rehabilitation.

The chief representative of this body, together with a responsible representative of other branches of government, would normally constitute a National Coordinating Committee dealing with all disaster-related problems. The suggested membership could include representatives from the key sectors of the community, public works, food and agriculture, telecommunications, public information, relief and rehabilitation, public health, social welfare, civil defense, police, fire brigade and Red Cross Society. Among the functions of the National Co-ordinating Committee would be the following:

Prior to a Disaster

1. Analyze records of past major disasters of the same type and evaluate potential hazards and their effects.
2. Foresee the scope of the disaster relief and rehabilitation plans, as well as establish the basic policies governing such plans.
3. Establish a method of screening the eligibility of victims for different types of assistance programs.
4. Legislate or obtain judicial authorization for certain disaster-related measures that are not covered under the legally constituted national disaster plan, such as:
    (a) Enforced evacuation of the endangered population
    (b) River control
    (c) Land-use control
    (d) Requisitioning of services, supplies, labor, etc., for relief operations.
  Here should be mentioned the possible incompatibility between an effective safeguards system and civil liberties policy.
5. Develop a clearcut chain of command and alert system. This is most important in the case of hostage-barricade situations or an attack on a nuclear plant.
6. Establish operational plans for handling various types of disasters.
7. Collect and maintain current data on the various resources available for use in disasters.

8. Promote a widespread understanding of the national disaster relief plan.
9. Ensure that regular tests or training exercises are conducted.
10. Ensure that all organizations to which specific responsibilities have been delegated are fully prepared to carry out these responsibilities (including civil defense agencies, the National Red Cross Society, etc.).

During the Disaster

1. Establish a disaster relief control center or headquarters.
2. Put operational plans into effect.
3. Coordinate the aid and relief work of all governmental and private organizations, both national and international.
4. Allocate available relief supplies to disaster areas.
5. Control and coordinate the use of transport and communication facilities.

After the Disaster

1. Put into effect various rehabilitation programs. Here the restoration measures to be taken by governments have already been mentioned.
2. Evaluate the effectiveness of relief following the operation.
3. Ensure that relevant experiences from the disaster are included in future national development planning.

Resource data

In order to deal effectively with a disaster that threatens a country, or with a disaster that has actually occurred, it is essential that the information on the existing national resources be kept up-to-date and be maintained nationally/regionally/locally according to their use.

(1) *Manpower—General*
   (a) A directory showing the names, addresses and telephone numbers of all national government department heads, state or provincial governors, and municipal mayors or their counterparts. (It is assumed that the representative of the armed forces and the civil defense will have data readily available on the location and strength of the various units.)
   (b) A directory showing names, addresses and telephone numbers of all organizations with delegated responsibilities.
   (c) A record of the location of educational institutions, with the name and telephone number of the head of each institution.
   (d) A record of the location of all employers of large numbers of people.
   (e) A record of all medical and social welfare personnel, including doctors, nurses, paramedics, midwives, social workers, etc.

(2) *Equipment*
   Records should be maintained of the location, availability and plans for obtaining equipment such as:

(a) Transport, including four-wheel drive vehicles and trucks, speed and cargo boats, helicopters and aircraft, and ambulances that could be used for warning, rescue, evacuation, movement of supplies and personnel, and fuel and lubricants.
(b) Heavy equipment such as bulldozers, cranes and earth-moving equipment for rescue or for protective work, and for the removal of debris.
(c) Portable and fixed communication equipment.
(d) Location of relief stocks, including food, clothing, tents, blankets, medicaments, etc.
(e) Tanks for transporting drinking water.
(f) Generators and power units for auxiliary power.
(g) The location and equipment of all firefighting and rescue units.
(h) Means of water purification.

(3) *Facilities*

Records (including contact person and telephone numbers or other contact means) should include the following:
(a) Location, type and bed capacity of all hospitals and clinics, and their operational capacity.
(b) The location and size of all schools and other facilities, such as hotels, religious centers, public halls, etc., that could be used as shelters or emergency hospitals (appropriate arrangements should be made in advance for their use).
(c) Location and runway capacity of all airports and airstrips.
(d) Location, depth, tonnage capacity and storage facilities of all seaports, and their loading and unloading capacity.
(e) Location and storage capacity of warehouses or buildings, etc., that could be used for temporary storage (appropriate arrangements should be made in advance for their use).

These details should be annexed to a written plan and made available to all interested individuals and organizations. The information should be updated at regular intervals.

(4) *Financial Arrangements*

To facilitate the speedy intervention and effectiveness of relief action by governmental organizations, adequate financial arrangements should be made in advance. These should include:
(a) Contingency funds and ordinary and extraordinary budgets, to cover government relief operation expenses.
(b) Financial aid to victims, such as:
    (i) Loans or grants
    (ii) Special credits
    (iii) Extension of the terms of payments on indebtedness.
(c) Compensation for the requisition of services, supplies, labor and equipment.

(d) Compensation for the loss of, or damage, to properties requisitioned and used for relief operations.
(e) Assistance for general rehabilitation, reconstruction and repair purposes.
(f) The regulation of prices in disaster areas.
(g) Special funds through which contributions must be channeled and administered.
(h) The provision of foreign currencies to procure relief supplies and equipment.
(i) Arrangements for expediting administrative procedures.
(j) Legislation authorizing appropriate bodies to put these measures into effect.

The "Nuclear" Dimension

Such a national relief plan, to be applied before, during and after a disaster, may constitute a credible basis to ensure protection and relief measures in case of a nuclear terrorist threat or act. It is, however, insufficient for the following reasons:

1. Damage-limiting actions cannot always be easily put into effect. What is the threshold of applicability of such a national plan? Can we measure all the consequences of a nuclear terrorist attack, even a limited one?
2. Such a plan might be useless in case of a mass-destruction attack by surprise.
3. Nuclear terrorism entails the development of highly specialized technical resources and highly trained experts to deal with the wide variety of terrorist incidents.
4. A disaster relief plan also requires a system of identification of high-risk groups.
5. Governments at the local, regional and national levels may not be able to implement their plans, especially in case of the use of nuclear weapons.

In any case, special emphasis should be put on medical rescue in the case of terrorist attacks. It needs more attention at the national level than is often the case with "traditional" types of disasters. As Kupperman and Trent say:

> The citizens of each nation have a right to protection of life and limbs, whether the etiological agent be a terrorist, an industrial accident, or a natural disaster. Technology has grown too complicated, populations too congested, and the incidents of regional medical emergencies too frequent to place sole reliance on the local community or the neighbourly volunteer approach. Disaster planning for large events has been largely unsuccessful because it has been partitioned from the successful emergency medical systems that operate daily. The personnel disappear and become untrained, and rehearsals tend to be unrealistic. Perhaps the necessity of counterterrorism will bolster the need for national emergency medical systems.

The topic of emergency health care delivery is not strange to government. It is receiving considerable attention, but possibly not enough. It is a complicated matter involving logistical and other management problems, resource allocation, communications, training programs for paramedical personnel, stockpiling of equipment and drugs, and clinical research and evaluation objectives. Considerable technological development is needed to make a national system truly efficient.[12]

We cannot but approve what Martin E. Silverstein states: "An antiterrorist rescue system will require intelligence, education and reeducation of medical personnel, preparatory planning, resource deployment and a nation-wide management system."[13]

The Role of Other Institutions

Whether at the national, regional or local level, governmental authorities cannot master all impending situations; they need the contribution of other institutions, either public or private, to assist them. On this point, we would like to emphasize the role of civil defense authorities and of voluntary institutions, such as the Red Cross.

Civil Defense. In many countries, civil defense plans are drawn up in peacetime as an essential part of any national defense posture aimed at deterring aggression. We might also say that if a nation is seen in time of peace to have taken positive civil defense measures in anticipation of attack, then the credibility of its deterrent posture will be enhanced, and its power to deter will be increased accordingly.[14]

It is the responsibility first and foremost of civil defense to inform the public that usually does not believe or does not want to believe in nuclear war or accident. "Taking the public along is not only one of the most important, but also one of the most sensitive areas in civil defense."[15]

Risk does, however, exist. It implies looking at civil defense as a demonstration of the humanitarian wish and social obligation to care for people, to care for them consistently with no regard to themselves, to save lives in a contingency that we are absolutely powerless to prevent.

What can civil defense do in case of a nuclear accident or terrorist act? In some countries, civil defense foresees short-term, medium-term and long-term measures. In the short-term phase, civil defense is designed to foresee major hazards that people may have to face; it is also designed to contribute to the protection against fallout radiation. And this shows the importance of having well-trained radioactive monitoring personnel in communities, as well as scientific advisers to local authorities to be used to warn people when it is safe to leave a shelter. Civil defense action also entails provision of shelters and of basic supplies and equipment.

Here, however, what is important, and more especially in case of a surprise nuclear attack, is that communities should draw up their own local emergency plans (medical aid, home nursing, first aid, emergency feeding, food distribution, water supplies, etc.). In fact, people must be prepared to be their own policemen, firemen and doctors.

In the medium-term phase, civil defense can assist authorities with environmental health plans, and in the long-term period, they can contribute to the restoration and regeneration program.

Red Cross Plan. It is the duty of the National Red Cross and Red Crescent Societies, as auxiliaries to the public authorities in time of peace and in time of armed conflict, to assist the governments of their respective countries in case of emergencies or serious crises. In order to face these situations, they must have a disaster relief plan ready.

The objective of the Red Cross disaster relief program is to mitigate the suffering caused by disaster. The program and policies of the National Society will depend on the responsibilities delegated to it by its government or by its role as recognized through past performance in disaster relief in the country. Since no two disaster situations are alike, special adjustments and improvisations may be necessary to deal with certain conditions. Experience has proved that a well-planned organization and trained personnel are essential to successful relief operations.

The disaster relief plan of a National Society should be so developed that the role of the National Society in disaster relief, the relationship of the National Society to its government and the operational plans for carrying out the Red Cross responsibilities are clearly and concisely stated and understandable. Therefore, the plan should focus on *how* the National Society will carry out its role in meeting the emergency needs of disaster victims. Plans must be made for handling such responsibilities as:

1. Establishing a chain of command for relief personnel and a reliable alert system.
2. Surveying and assessing the disaster.
3. Disseminating warnings of approaching dangers.
4. Evacuating the population from the areas of danger.
5. Rescuing disaster victims.
6. Recruiting and training volunteers.
7. Providing food, clothing, temporary shelter and basic comfort items.
8. Providing first-aid, medical and nursing services.
9. Providing emergency social welfare services.
10. Making arrangements for replying to inquiries about the well-being and safety of persons in affected areas.
11. Making arrangements for the receipt, storage, transport and distribution of relief supplies.
12. Establishing reporting procedures throughout the chain of command.
13. Keeping disaster victims and the public informed.
14. Maintaining continuous liaison with the government at different levels.

15. Making an appeal for funds and relief supplies.
16. Coordinating Red Cross relief activities with those of the government and of voluntary organizations.
17. Maintaining liaison with the League of Red Cross and Red Crescent Societies.

There are many similarities between the government relief disaster plan and that of the Red Cross, which also deals with warning, evacuation, rescue, food supplies, clothing, shelter, health services, social welfare services, communications, transport and public information. Such a plan must be complementary to the government one, but it would be difficult to know how far it can be applied in case of a nuclear incident. Here we find the same restrictions as mentioned above regarding the government plan, and the same uncertainties as to possible interventions in the case of a surprise attack.

Conclusion

As previously noted, damage done by terrorists has many things in common with industrial accidents and natural disasters except frequency and intent. Only a strengthening of the system required for such calamities and a shortening of the time required for the system to operate appear to be indicated.

As an incident develops and the nature of the threat becomes manifest, highly specific and sophisticated technology may be applicable to control the outcome or contain the damage done. It may prove well worthwhile to develop highly specialized technical resources to deal with certain types of likely terrorist incidents. In an emergency, rapid access to a wide variety of experts and equipment rather than ubiquity is the crucial factor determining the usefulness of such resources. The technical means of organizing such availability by various pre-arrangements and by the use of management information systems is an important technological aspect of combatting terrorism. In some countries we know that emergency preparedness focuses on the management of an emergency incident, but far less on the management of the consequences of such an incident, especially of a nuclear terrorist nature.

As has already been said: "The international community is not integrated into preplanned modes of response. Research on terrorist behaviour, target hardening and the problem of restoration after attack, is only in its infancy."[16]

The challenge for governments in the future will be to combine crisis management and the management of the consequences of such a crisis, and to integrate the nuclear factor and its consequences into the national relief disaster plan.

All this will require a vigorous research and development program and, above all, conviction by governments, implying care as to the importance of their task to prevent and to face nuclear terrorist acts, conviction by the society of its own endurance and in the resilience of democratic institutions. Some thought and courage are all that lie between the usual perils of civilization and the specter of self-inflicted carnage.

NOTES

1. Louis René Beres, *Terrorism and Global Security* (Boulder, CO: Westview Press, 1979), p. 65 (hereafter Beres).
2. Yonah Alexander, ed., *International Terrorism—National, Regional and Global Perspectives* (New York: Praeger Publishers, 1976), p. xv.
3. On this point, see *Terrorism—Interdisciplinary Perspectives* (New York: John Jay Press, 1977); and Martha Crewshaw Hutchinson, *Defining Future Threat—Terrorism and Nuclear Proliferation*, p. 302.
4. Robert Kupperman and Darrell Trent, *Terrorism, Threat, Reality, Response* (Stanford, CA: Hoover Institution, Stanford University, 1979), p. 52.
5. Ibid., p. 75.
6. Yonah Alexander, ed., *Political Terrorism and Energy—Threat and Response,* Praeger Special Studies (New York: Praeger Scientific, 1982), and N. Livingstone, *Megadeath—Radioactive Terrorism,* p. 171.
7. *Op. cit.* Beres, p. 79, et seq.
8. Ibid, pp. 88-93.
9. Robert A. Friedlünder, *Terror—Violence, Aspects of Social Control* (New York: Oceana Publications, 1983), p. 135.
10. *Op. cit.,* Kupperman and Trent, p. 75.
11. The content of this sub-chapter has been inspired by the *Handbook on Red Cross Disaster Relief,* published by the League of Red Cross and Red Crescent Societies and adopted and revised by the International Conference of the Red Cross in 1977.
12. *Op. cit.,* Kupperman and Trent, p. 138.
13. Ibid., and Martin E. Silverstein, *Medical Survival of Victims of Terrorism,* Selected readings, p. 349.
14. On this subject, see *Nuclear Attack—Civil Defense—Aspects of Civil Defense in the Nuclear Age,* London: Brasseys, 1982.
15. Ibid., p. 5.
16. *Op. cit.,* Kupperman and Trent, p. 177.

* * *

Steven Goldberg

I would like to focus on the legal implications of the likely responses of our government to nuclear terrorism. Whether you regard litigation as a safeguard of our fundamental values or as a nuisance, you cannot deny that legal issues are likely to be prominent in the aftermath of a terrorist incident, just as they have been in the crises of the past, ranging from the Kent State shootings to the Iranian hostage agreement. Moreover, a focus at the outset on likely legal concerns can facilitate the development of proper and effective action against terrorism that preserves our individual liberties.

Let's look at the legal aspects of government responses to terrorism sequentially, beginning with the gathering of intelligence on suspected terrorists. Broad intelligence-gathering procedures, ranging from the use of undercover agents to the use of wiretaps based on proper warrants, have long been upheld by the courts. The more difficult legal issues surround the gathering of extensive intelligence files in computers, raising the risk of unauthorized and damaging disclosures of information concerning individuals who have done nothing wrong. The current Supreme Court has recognized that the constitutional right to privacy may require that the government provide adequate procedures to assure that computerized files are kept private and used only for proper purposes. In the case of *Whalen v. Roe,* which concerned a New York State computer file of records involving drug prescriptions, Justice John Stevens wrote for the court that the right to assemble computer files for public purposes, including enforcement of criminal laws, is "typically accompanied by a concomitant statutory or regulatory duty to avoid unwarranted disclosures." The justice went on to say that this duty was arguably rooted in the Constitution. [429 U.S. 589,605] Now, in *Whalen v. Roe,* the court found that New York had provided adequate statutory protections, so it upheld the New York record-gathering system. Under the New York system, computer files were kept in secure rooms, and when the computer was in use to look at secure files, it was run "off line," which means that no terminal outside the computer room could gain access to the information. Surely, it would be desirable to be at least equally as sure that any intelligence files gathered for counter-terrorism be subject to adequate statutory and regulatory restrictions or release of information. Otherwise, private citizens might be harmed, and courts might be free to strike down the intelligence-gathering system.

The next stage where counter-terrorism might intersect with legal doctrine concerns the physical protection of nuclear materials. To what extent may those guarding such materials use deadly force against a thief? Of course, guards can use weapons to defend their own lives against armed attackers, but what about their ability to shoot at an escaping felon? It might be thought that this poses no legal problem, since, under common law rules, for many years deadly force was permissible against those who committed any felony, including burglary or theft. But just a few months ago the U.S. Supreme Court ruled, in the case of *Tennessee v. Garner,* that it was unconstitutional to use deadly force to prevent the escape of all felony suspects. The Court said that such force could be used only when the police officer "has probable cause to believe that the suspect poses a threat of serious physical harm, either to the officer or to others. . . . " [105 S.Ct. 1694, at 1701] Obviously, someone escaping with strategic nuclear material fits that definition, but that does not solve all of the problems a guard might face. If a guard, at night, shoots a teenager who is scaling down a fence in an attempt to leave a nuclear facility, that guard might be shooting a simple trespasser. That is a human tragedy, and it could expose the government to considerable liability. The safest way for the government to meet the probable cause approach of *Tennessee v. Garner* is to maintain a training and regulatory regime that assures that guards know which areas of a facility are sensitive and which are not, and under what circumstances deadly force is reasonably applied.

If nuclear material is stolen and terrorists are hiding it, of course it will be necessary to search for it. Time pressure might make it difficult to seek a warrant, and, in any event, a large area might have to be searched. While I do not mean to minimize the loss of privacy and social disruption that could result from such a search, it should be noted that the Supreme Court is likely to be sympathetic to the government in such a case. There is precedent under which the Court could uphold a search that is aimed at protecting the public, because of the emergency circumstances. We have all gotten used to airline searches; indeed, the Supreme Court itself makes those who would visit its courtroom pass through a metal detector. Perhaps the most suggestive recent precedent is a Supreme Court case, *New York v. Quarles,* decided in June of 1984. In *Quarles,* a fleeing suspect had hidden a handgun in a supermarket. The officers questioned him about the whereabouts of the gun without giving Miranda warnings. The Court allowed the suspect's statements concerning the location of the gun to be admitted in court, holding that there was a "public safety" exception to Miranda. The Court said that "[s]o long as the gun was concealed somewhere in the supermarket . . . it obviously posed . . . danger to the public safety." [104 S.Ct. 2626,2632] The danger posed by nuclear materials hidden in an urban area is even greater, and it is possible that in such a case the court might carve out a public safety exception to the Fourth Amendment to enable law enforcement officials to find such materials to protect the public.

But finding the location of the nuclear materials does not end the interaction between law and security in this field. What if measures taken by security officials to capture the terrorists result in damage to civilian property and lives? In wartime, it is well-established that the government can destroy civilian property without paying compensation. Indeed, the very first volume of the *United States Reports* contains a case from 1788, *Respublica v. Sparhawk,* which held that citizens could not recover for property taken by the Continental Army during the revolutionary war. [1 U.S. 357] There are similar cases for every war since. But in a counter-terrorist situation, there is unlikely to be a formal declaration of war, and public and judicial concern may be somewhat more heightened. It is, for example, an open question whether the city of Philadelphia could be required to pay damages for the destruction that took place when police bombed the headquarters of the MOVE organization a few weeks ago. Philadelphia has volunteered to make such payment, so the legal question remains unresolved. Under current precedent, it is likely that government action to root out terrorists would be judged under the general reasonableness standard of the Fourth Amendment. Government action that was negligent or inadequately thought out could expose the government to considerable liability. Careful advance planning, including consideration of appropriate tactics and material, is likely to lead to more publicly and legally acceptable government action.

In conclusion, it seems clear to me that thoughtful planning today, in areas ranging from the security of computer files through the training of guards to the planning of limited tactical assaults, can alleviate legal problems and protect individual rights in the future.

* * *

André Kleinman

Geopolitics of the Swiss Civil Defense

As you know, Switzerland has the reputation of having one of the best programs for civil defense in the world. However, before speaking about the program itself, we have to put it in perspective and develop an understanding of the particular conditions existing in Switzerland that have led to the creation of a strong civil defense.

Switzerland, a confederation of 23 cantons, has a population of 6.5 million people, about the same as the state of New Jersey, and an area of 41,000 square kilometers, which is double the surface of New Jersey, of which 60 percent is mountains. In 1815, Switzerland became a neutral state. It is fully armed to defend this neutrality; we have an army of 650,000 men organized into a militia system.

Switzerland has a very high gross national product (GNP) per capita— $15,000. Our defense budget is 2 percent of our GNP.

Our defense is based on dissuasion. We try to make a potential aggressor realize that there is an unacceptable disproportion between what he hopes to gain by attacking Switzerland and what costs he is going to have to pay to do it.

Switzerland is one of the oldest democracies in the world. We have three levels of executive power—the federal state, the cantons and the communes. The people in Switzerland express their democratic rights by voting on about 60 different subjects every year. We have the right to a referendum against a new law we do not like, and the right of initiative to foster new ideas. In 1959, we had a vote to establish our present civil defense system. The people of Switzerland expressed the need for it, thinking that Switzerland must defend its civilian population.

Philosophy of Civil Defense

The concept of civil defense originates from the idea that we in Switzerland cannot exclude the possibility of being affected directly or indirectly by war. Civil defense is part of our national defense. Its mission is, firstly, to reduce the possibility of an attack or attempt at blackmail against Switzerland. Secondly, if our country is involved in a war, civil defense assures the safety of the population and its survival.

Several different scenarios as to the potential war danger menacing our population can be summarized as follows:

- War operations in neighboring countries
- Blackmail
- The use of conventional arms
- Limited use of arms of massive destruction
- Strategic destruction.

In the same way, peacetime emergencies can also endanger the civilian population. These menaces include accidents, sabotage or terrorism in factories and depots of nuclear arms, crashes involving atomic weapon carriers, radioactive fall-out, accidents during transport of nuclear, chemical or bacteriological substances, and other technological disasters. Natural disasters, such as bursting of dams and dikes, storms, earthquakes, avalanches, floods, landslides and fires, can also occur.

In all these situations, the personnel, equipment and facilities of the civil defense are available as a means of assistance. The policy of the Swiss Civil Defense is to be ready for all possibilities since we cannot be sure which specific one may occur. Vertical evacuation in shelters is forced on us by the topography of the country.

The basic principles of Swiss Civil Defense are:

- A place in a shelter for each inhabitant of Switzerland.
- Preventive and gradual occupation of the shelters when political and military tension reach a critical stage.
- Ability to live autonomously in the shelters for two weeks in case of need.

The principal goal of our civil defense is the survival of the largest part of our population. We have attempted to use the most cost-effective means to attain this goal:

- We think that prevention is better than cure.
- Since we feel that there is no absolute protection, we build simple and resistant shelters. We aim at reasonably efficient protection to guarantee a high probability of survival.
- We make the best use of all possibilities of protection, incorporating into our system cellars, basements and parking garages that can be converted rapidly to shelters.
- We plan to be flexible and to adapt to different needs.

Since the preservation of our population is the central point of civil defense, we bear in mind the following psychological factors:

- Equal chance for all is a necessity.
- We know that men and women can adapt to the "life-boat" conditions in shelters.
- We keep community groups together and maintain individual family units.
- We provide for guidance, assistance and organization in shelters.

Organization of Civil Defense

Civil defense shelters are the most important elements of our program. Broadly speaking, there are three types of shelters: (a) private home shelters; (b) public shelters; and (c) organizational shelters such as command posts, preparation facilities and medical facilities.

Civil defense is primarily a commune activity. The commune is responsible for enforcement of the federal or cantonal laws and regulations. After first working on general civil defense planning, we have now completed the second phase or allocation plan, a detailed assignment of population to shelters. In each commune, a local civil defense chief has a staff composed of the chiefs of the different civil defense services, including intelligence, communications, atomic and chemical protection, engineering, fire fighting, medical service, supplies, transportation and so on. The local chief has at his disposal three protective organizations: first, the local organization that gets the civil defense facilities ready for occupation, supervises shelter occupation, takes measures against atomic and chemical effects, rescues persons and goods, fights fire, takes care of the homeless and refugees and provides medical care; second, the industrial defense organization; and third, the population shelters organization. Let's all hope we won't have to use our civil defense, but in case of necessity, we in Switzerland are ready, "or almost."

Chapter Four

How Can Nuclear Violence Be Prevented?

Bernard O'Keefe

There is very little that can be done to prevent a skilled, determined, well-organized terrorist organization from setting off a nuclear detonation on United States territory. Nuclear explosives exist in the tens of thousands, scattered all over the earth. Six nations—the United States, the Soviet Union, China, France, Great Britain and India—admit to having developed and tested nuclear devices. Israel almost certainly has them but won't admit it. Such countries as Argentina, Brazil, Pakistan, Saudi Arabia and South Africa have refused to sign the nuclear non-proliferation treaty, for whatever reason. Any modern, industrial nation, acting within the security of its own borders, has the capacity to fabricate a quantity of nuclear explosives. Hundreds of kilograms of fissionable material have been lost, stolen or misdirected in international commerce; I have heard it said that fissionable material sells on the international black market for about the same price per kilogram as cocaine.

Nor is it difficult to smuggle nuclear explosives across international borders. A very powerful device will fit into a small trunk and, properly disguised, would be much easier to handle than a bale of marijuana, to which our borders are virtually transparent.

Given such vulnerability, the best policy would be to ensure that skilled, determined, well-organized terrorist organizations do not exist. If that is not practical, the next best policy would be to dissuade such organizations from making the attempt and to demonstrate that even if the attempt is made and succeeds, it will be counterproductive to the organization's goals and objectives.

Nuclear weapons are not tinkertoys. Their design and fabrication or theft require a degree of skill, determination and sense of purpose far removed from the concept of the ordinary wooden pistol-wielding wacko. Even their handling and detonation, although quite straightforward, are extremely intimidating to the uninitiated. Experience in weapons testing shows that there is a great fear of radiation exposure and accidental detonation on the part of those who are not expert in their use.

Non-nuclear terrorism is a spectator sport. It is meant to be a media event designed to accomplish a short-term, transient advantage not achievable by other means. Objectives are generally such things as transportation to safety, release of prisoners or recognition of the terrorists for their self-perceived religious and moral superiority. Ordinary terrorism is a strategy of the weak, those without the skills or talents to achieve their purposes by any other means.

Nuclear terrorism must perforce be a strategy of the strong, those with skills and prowess sufficient to have alternate choices for the accomplishment of their objectives. This must be the basic concept for the prevention of nuclear terrorism. It is, unfortunately, the only available concept. If the traditional mad scientist manages to get possession of a nuclear weapon and decides to detonate it for whatever purpose exists in his unstable mind, there is nothing we can do about it. We must then fall back to a different problem, the prevention of the annihilation of civilization.

We must also consider the intermediate condition, the non-nuclear terrorist group that claims to have a nuclear device but does not have one. This condition has existed for years, exists today and will certainly continue in the future. There have been more than a hundred threats to use nuclear weapons, usually from urban areas, including such large cities as Los Angeles and Boston. Fortunately, none of these threats has had substance, but has been dealt with crisply and expertly by existing government organizations.

The visible arm of these organizations is the United States Nuclear Emergency Search Team (NEST), which is in continuous readiness to respond to such threats anywhere around the globe. The NEST group has available background radiation data for most populated areas, with detailed maps delineating radiation levels in the vicinity of nuclear power plants, nuclear research laboratories and weapons installations. These teams respond almost instantly to any threats, searching for radiation emissions and other classified indicators of nuclear weapons in the threatened area.

The task is not a simple one, since weapons emanations are fairly easy to shield. It is a tribute to the NEST organization that these many investigations have been carried out with no alarm to the populace. One incident handled by the NEST organization, although not a weapons threat, deserves mention here as an excellent example of international cooperation. In November, 1977, U.S. observers noted that Cosmos 954, a Russian satellite thought to be nuclear-powered, was in trouble. A hotline communication at the highest level between U.S. and Soviet officials established that the satellite was indeed nuclear-powered and would come to earth somewhere about January 22, 1978. In order to forestall a "Chicken Little" syndrome throughout the world, the problem was classified at the highest classification by both nations for almost three months. When it was determined that the satellite would land in the Canadian Northwest Territories, the Canadian government was informed, and a joint Canadian-U.S. NEST organization was formed to search a 1,500-square mile area in which the debris was to fall. The radioactive fragments were collected and removed with no injuries or alarm to the populace in the sparsely settled area.

Since 1945, nuclear weapons have proven to be too powerful for use as instruments of international political policy. During the decades of United States nuclear supremacy, with the single possible exception of the Cuban missile crisis, the threat of nuclear annihilation has had virtually no effect on the aggressive international policies of the Soviet Union, China, North Korea, Cambodia, North Vietnam or even Cuba. They are blunt instruments, too catastrophic to be credible.

If nuclear terrorism is truly a strategy of the strong, it must be connected with an ongoing, at least semi-stable, organization with long-term objectives. Whether that organization is an established government, an opposition party or a multi-nation movement, nuclear weapons are again too catastrophic to be credible. Their supply to a semi-independent terrorist movement could easily backfire. The Soviet practice is instructive. They never let fissionable materials out of their hands, even to their allies in the Warsaw Pact. The missiles are located on satellite soil, but the nuclear material remains in Soviet possession. The message can be brought to the Palestine Liberation Organizations, the Qaddafis and the Khomenis of this world that they succor nuclear terrorist groups at their own peril.

But suppose they don't listen. Suppose these organizations persist in setting up terrorist groups of their own or furnish assistance to semi-independent groups. If they furnish assistance to semi-independent groups, it can be called terrorism. If they set up groups of their own, it can be called preparation for nuclear welfare. Then we must ferret out such groups and warn them of the dire and counterproductive effects of their projected actions, while remaining alert to detect any preparations on our own soil. To accomplish these purposes we must have two advantages: intelligence and international cooperation. Intelligence we can accumulate by our own actions; for international cooperation we must stimulate actions on the part of others, particularly the Soviet Union. For my own part, I am more sanguine about the Soviet Union than I am about ourselves.

If a terrorist nuclear device is detonated anywhere in the world, retribution must be swift and decisive. For swift and decisive action, there must be existing international policy and agreement. If the action is carried out under the auspices of the government of any existing nation, nuclear retaliation must be agreed upon and authorized in advance. If the action is carried out by a semi-autonomous group, swift non-nuclear military action against the host country must be authorized. If the identity of the terrorist group is not revealed or the detonation executed without warning, the full weight of international intelligence gathering must be brought to bear immediately. Any and all of these cooperative actions must be authorized and well-publicized in advance so as to have the maximum deterrent effect. The stronger and more specific the authorized retaliation, the more powerful the deterrent. Such authorizations are difficult and delicate to negotiate because they require an international enabling agency and an agreement with the strength of a treaty. Treaty agreements between nations are formidable in their complexity, since they encroach on sovereignty and, in the democracies, become entangled in domestic policies. They will be particularly difficult in the United States because in this country there is little appreciation among the citizenry of the imminence and catastrophic nature of the threat.

The key to international cooperation is the Soviet Union. I think that for all their intransigence, they will be easier to convince than will our own citizens. In the first place, the Soviets are most suspicious and more concerned with the actions of foreigners than we are. Secondly, they are not at all restrained by domestic politics in their handling of international affairs. Thirdly, they have a habit of abiding by international agreements, ratified or not, when it is in their own interest to do so. They abide by the 1963 Limited Nuclear Test Ban Treaty and the several treaties associated with it; they abide by the SALT agreements even though we have not ratified SALT II; they abide by the Anti-Ballistic Missile Treaty even though our "Star Wars" intentions will force us to abrogate it; they abide by the Incidents at Sea Agreement designed to prevent confrontations on the oceans; they cooperated completely in the 1978 nuclear-powered satellite disintegration; they scrupulously inform us of missile tests that might look hostile and of stray missiles coming in our direction. To be sure, they do irritating things like building phased-array radars in the wrong place and occasionally pushing the limit on underground nuclear test yields, but I don't know of a single substantive act on their part in violation of international nuclear-related agreements.

The Soviets have another advantage. They know that we will not strike first with nuclear weapons. They recognize that their greatest danger is in accidental or terrorist-inspired nuclear conflagration. They may be more willing than the U.S. to work out an anti-terrorist agreement. There are enormous advantages to our side. If we can put our intelligence on nuclear terrorist matters together with that of the KGB, the quality of the resulting information will not merely be doubled, it will be magnified to the *nth* power.

One further advantage. Soviet threats of retaliation will always be taken more seriously by terrorists because the Soviets will not be restrained by the shackles of domestic policies. If the Soviets say they will blast an offending nation off the face of the earth, they will be believed. The negotiations with the USSR will be long and difficult, as usual, but the prize of mutual cooperation will be worth the toil and trouble.

It is in the United States that I expect the struggle for a firm anti-nuclear terrorist policy to be most difficult. There is absolutely no perception of the probability of a terrorist nuclear attack in the United States today. We expend an appallingly large portion of our national resources on defense against a Soviet nuclear attack. We spend an appallingly large portion of our national resources on defense against a Soviet invasion of Western Europe. In my opinion, the chances of either event occurring are remote except if triggered by a terrorist-inspired nuclear detonation that would decapitate either of our command and control systems, such as well-timed explosions in Washington or Moscow. For all our plans and proposals for C^{3}I, the resultant confusion could easily escalate into full-scale thermonuclear warfare. This is our greatest danger, yet it receives our minimal attention.

To work against the terrorist threat, we need a vastly expanded intelligence-gathering system. Such a system invariably will lead to conflicts with our current constitutional concept of human rights. Terrorists do not play by Marquis of Queensbury rules. Where the stakes are the survival of civilization, it would certainly not be humane to permit the nuclear obliteration of this capital city of our nation while reading a suspected terrorist his Miranda rights. We should begin the debate now on the tradeoffs for intelligence gathering between civil liberties and the cessation of civilization. We can't have it both ways.

International cooperative agreements for retaliation against terrorism have grave constitutional impediments. Any substantive agreement between nations will certainly imply some loss of sovereignty to the signatories. I don't mean to suggest that we should turn Thomas Jefferson over in his grave, but I do recommend that we give formal attention to the constitutional and practical political limitations to meaningful international agreements.

With tens of thousands of nuclear weapons spread about the world and with the information for making new ones widely disseminated, I believe that the greatest threat to civilization today is the prospect of a terrorist-implemented nuclear explosion or explosions. Simultaneous explosions in Moscow and Washington would be duck soup for a skilled, determined, well-organized terrorist group— such groups are relatively easy to assemble.

I recommend wide dissemination in the press of the probability of such events and of the calamity they would cause. With popular support, legislation can be enacted to specify the intelligence-gathering capabilities needed for threat assessment and the degree of international agreement needed for discussion. The constitutional and political conflicts for assessment and prevention of terrorist-inspired nuclear attacks can be then laid before the citizenry for their choice. The debate will truly be dramatic; the stakes are the highest imaginable.

* * * * *

RESPONSES

Harold Agnew

I would agree with Dr. Bernard Feld that if we could combine the intelligence capabilities of the West and the East, and I include the United Kingdom, France, Israel, the Soviet Union, and Japan, we clearly would lessen the risk of terrorism across the board. Unfortunately, I share the worry that, for the most part, many of these terrorist actions give the Soviet Union some comfort. They disrupt our society, they cause psychological damage, they cause economic damage, and to date the Soviet Union has not been very cooperative in supplying information along this line. They clearly reneged on a U.N. Charter agreement: If you look back on the Egyptian-Israeli war, they knew what was going to go on, and they didn't tell anybody. They did alert us to a potential test in South Africa; whether it was going to take place or not one doesn't know, but I have a feeling they analyzed the situation and said perhaps it's in their best interest that we be alerted to that particular potential incident. So I would certainly agree that if one could have cooperation on intelligence across the board, it would certainly lessen the potential for terrorist acts.

Now, if we can't have that, what can we do? Many of the speakers have noted that you can't have a nuclear detonation unless you first have some material. Ted Taylor mentioned how simple it is, in his opinion, to make a crude bomb. In theory, I would subscribe to that, if you get your hands on the material. The materials are messy to deal with, and unless there is some form of government backing or organizational backing, even a few sophisticated terrorists would have a very difficult time putting together a crude nuclear weapon. But it is clearly a possibility, and I think the first line of defense is to guard against the unauthorized acquisition of nuclear material. In this respect, in the past at least, the Soviets have had a very good system. As was pointed out, they essentially lease the fissile material to their client states. In other words, they control the material going into the reactor, and they require that it be returned to them.

In an article published 8 or 10 years ago in the *Bulletin of Atomic Scientists* when Bernard Feld was editor, I suggested that leasing material was what the West should do. The main players in making reactor fuel available are nuclear power states. They have nuclear material, and I thought that the material should be made available worldwide to nations that have reactors. Afterwards, the material should be returned to the originators. Then they could determine whether or not it should be reprocessed or recycled, based on economic grounds. In fact, you could have a common pool for recycling among the suppliers.

Unfortunately, we don't do that. Material is out, and, as someone said, sometimes reactor deals are "sweetened" by throwing in a reprocessing plant. This is very dangerous. An argument has been given in some states that energy independence is the driving factor behind reprocessing, but today there are so many sources of uranium available that I think reprocessing is completely unwarranted.

Now, assuming I wanted a bicycle and I didn't have the money to buy it, I could understand the technology to build one. But I'm not going to build one; I'm going to steal one. It's much simpler to steal a bicycle or a car than to make one. And so I think that the most probable avenue for a terrorist group to obtain a weapon is through overt means, not through clandestine means. In this country, we have put into being systems that originally called for permissive action links (PALs), which have been developed by the Sandia Corporation under the Atomic Energy Commission, Department of Energy (ERDA). These are devices that are embedded in the bowels of almost all of our nuclear weapons and that, in my opinion, would preclude an individual from being able to detonate that weapon. Some of these systems even go so far that if you try to fool around with weapons, it is non-violently dudded so it's just completely useless.

In 1962, with Chet Hollofield's permission, I went to France to try to sell them this particular idea. Unfortunately, politics and the State Department screwed it all up. But I would like to suggest that we make this technology available to all nuclear powers, including the Soviets, with the provision that if we make it available, they have to agree to use it. Some of this technology is quite sophisticated, and we may be giving up something, but I am convinced that the technology is so good that even if a person understands it, they can't crack it. And that's a fact.

I think another thing we need to do is educate the press to get this concept across; otherwise the terrorist says he's got one, and everybody panics. There has to be credibility. The press, the media and even our own people have to be convinced that this technology is that good. The Sandia Corporation on some of the systems has actually brought in individuals, sometimes explained the whole damn system to them, and said, "Now you try to crack it." Knowing what it is, they've still been unable to do it, and of course individuals who do not understand the systems couldn't crack it either. I think non-violent penalty systems should be employed, especially on those weapons deployed overseas.

Now there are certain of our military services that have opposed this particular implementation in their particular weapons and warheads. I think that's wrong. My reason for this is, that in 1959, I got sent to NATO to convince the officers that we were going to put these systems into weapons. There was a tremendous hue and cry by the military against this, because essentially we were tying up their weapons. President Kennedy prevailed and ordered that it be done. But the thing that really sold me on it was a talk with some senior officers, who have the highest regard for our military. They said, "Harold, you're gonna lock these things up and we have to get the code numbers, it's either 6 or 8 digits, whatever it is, in a particular sequence, in order to use our weapons?" And I said, "That's right." And they said, "Well, what if we don't get the word?" And that's what sold me on the idea that we should have this, because as you're aware, we have weapons in lots of places, and this is a positive control. It is now incorporated as part of the "word." So this word can be the enabling feature. Again, I think this is something that we should offer to all nuclear power states, but I don't think it would be much good unless press and the media clearly understand these particular systems. And I think that they have to be educated on that.

On the subject of power plants, they have to be realized as being very rugged. And they are. Unfortunately, in contrast to nuclear weapons, where we're perhaps in our 10th generation of technology, present nuclear power plants are really in the first generation. And the reason for that is it's about 30 years per generation. It's not like a new car, where you bring out a new model every year; we're essentially stuck with it for a long time. But there are new technologies in reactor designs, where reactors can essentially be placed underground, or below ground level, reactors can be built so that independent of any human or mechanical failure, they are safe to the public, and also safe to the financiers. It's a walkaway safe design. This concept is being pursued in Germany; it's being pursued in this country under auspices of the Department of Energy. I think it has some distinct advantages, especially as we look down the road to those developing nations where nuclear power is going to be important. I think this particular technology will be extremely valuable to try to implement in the next generation. I should mention that this technology was also proven in our nuclear rocket program many years ago, where we intentionally destroyed the reactor explosively. The subsequent cleanup was very simple, because there were no liquids involved. It was just a matter of picking up pieces. Now, in the case of a reactor, this just couldn't happen. Essentially, they are like pyramids, and you can't blow up a pyramid through conventional means.

In conclusion, I would like to urge the press to educate people better as to the potential available to us in preventing nuclear terrorism, especially if terrorists should say that they had acquired one of our weapons. And I would urge the world at large to try to get other governments to implement the same type of controls that we have implemented in our nuclear weapons.

* * *

William O. Doub

The subject of the potential for nuclear terrorism is a highly charged, emotional subject at best. From the standpoint of a thoughtful, disciplined analysis of these complex issues, this conference could not occur at a worse time. The recent TWA skyjacking has overly sensitized all of us as to the reality and terrible consequences of terrorism generally. While many of the papers and comments of participants at this conference have been quite well-written and pertinent to the subject, there has been a perhaps understandable tendency of certain speakers to range far afield, focusing attention on issues of limited value or relevancy to the realism of terrorism.

For example, yesterday we heard from speakers addressing the subject in terms of attacking our nation's foreign policy. Certain speakers, in fact, suggested that our foreign policies are the primary contributing factor to the potential for nuclear terrorism, particularly our policies toward the Soviet Union, Israel and South Africa and in Central America. These speakers suggested that somehow the potential for nuclear terrorism would be alleviated, reduced or eliminated if we were only to change our foreign policy in these areas. While they may be correct in an immediate sense, a major industrial power's foreign policy will always be opposed by many, regardless of its content.

The contradictions contained in certain statements have revealed the frustrations obviously felt with regard to the current TWA affair. One speaker suggested that the cause of our problems in the Middle East is our unyielding support of Israel. Another speaker suggests that Israel is the key to preventing certain renegade Arab nations from obtaining nuclear weapons technology, using the Israeli bombing of an Iraqi reactor as an example.

I think I have made my point, and what I would like to try to do now is briefly put these issues of potential nuclear terrorism in some perspective and suggest some ideas to improve the civilian nuclear power program against terrorism, building on Bernard O'Keefe's paper.

While O'Keefe's discussion focuses on the larger question of possession of nuclear weapons by terrorists or threats to use or acquire such weapons, I will address a different topic. I will attempt to examine whether there is presently a credible threat that international terrorists could succeed in disrupting peaceful nuclear power activities in the United States or other countries. By nuclear power industry, I mean our nation's operating nuclear power reactors, those under construction, and portions of the civilian nuclear fuel cycle, such as transportation of nuclear materials, which support the production of power in nuclear reactors.

At present, commercial nuclear power in the United States generates about 14 percent of our total nation's demand for electric power. There are approximately 90 power reactors currently operating in the United States, with some 40 more under construction, of which more than one-half are near completion. Even most critics of nuclear power concede that, except for coal, there are no reasonable alternatives in the foreseeable future for generating large amounts of electric power. With increasing concerns about the environmental effects of burning coal, most of those who have been opposed to commercial nuclear power, for one reason or another, are now forced to reassess their beliefs. Without sufficient supplies of electricity, it will be impossible for the United States to maintain its role as an industrial and technological leader. If that leadership is lost, the fundamental structure of our society will change, challenging our very ability to survive as a democracy. Consequently, we cannot assess decisions affecting the supply of electricity on a casual basis or in a way that treats electricity as some kind of a luxury.

Despite almost three decades of commercial operation of nuclear power reactors, there has never been a fatality associated with such operations. In my view, the only failure of nuclear power to date concerns the complex economics of recent plants, not safety or environmental concerns and certainly not susceptibility to terrorism. The recent cancellations of nearly completed nuclear power units is a domestic spectacle that amazes government and industry officials throughout the world.

Although this conference addresses international nuclear terrorism, I might observe, in passing, that it is often misleading to single out particular kinds of threats without comparing them to related threats. For example, the introduction of ionizing radiation into medicine resulted in great saving of lives and lessening of suffering. However, the medical community readily acknowledges that certain critical mistakes in treatment were made in the early years that resulted in some thyroid nodules and cancers. If time allowed, we could compare notes on the paradox that nearly every industrial or scientific advance leads to associated problems. As I proceed to the substance of my discussion, I wish to emphasize my view that any residual risks from operation of nuclear power stations must be viewed against the countervailing risks of not operating those stations. These risks include the strong possibility that our nation will have an inadequate electricity supply or will be forced to rely on other forms of power generation that will not be ready in sufficient time or will carry unacceptable environmental and safety consequences of their own.

Risks of Terrorism Directed at Nuclear Power Facilities

As O'Keefe pointed out in his paper, the principal risk of nuclear terrorism is that terrorists will seek to acquire nuclear explosives and threaten their use. However, his paper may cause some people to conclude that terrorists will be equally interested in threatening civilian nuclear power facilities and stealing plutonium from the U.S. weapons program. The risks are very different. The civilian nuclear power industry in the United States is neither an attractive nor even logical target for terrorists whose objective is to acquire nuclear weapons or the means or technology to make them. First and foremost, the nuclear power industry in the United States does not employ separated plutonium. It is true, of course, that when the low-enriched uranium fuel elements used in all except one nuclear power reactor in the United States are used to produce power, plutonium is created in an unseparated state in the fuel rods, along with other fission products.

As almost every one agrees, however, these irradiated fuel elements are not attractive targets for terrorists bent upon acquisition of plutonium as such or highly enriched uranium with which to fabricate nuclear devices. A scenario involving diversion of irradiated fuel elements by a terrorist group verges on the ludicrous. First, the terrorist would need to acquire a suitable shipping cask in which the fuel elements could be loaded (or possibly capture such casks in transit). They would then need to escape to a remote location with a cask weighing many tons that must be transported on a large tractor-trailer truck. The spent fuel elements would then need to be reprocessed to extract the plutonium. Assuming that the terrorists had assembled a team of technical experts, had acquired complex remote handling and other essential equipment, and included competent professionals from a range of technical and professional disciplines, reprocessing might be possible. The difficulties and risks of capture, detection or failure at each step of this long sequence of events necessary to separate plutonium from spent reactor fuel elements should by itself convince even the most extreme (or stupid) terrorists to abandon any thought of this route. Since the U.S. nuclear power industry does not employ separated plutonium and has no present plans to do so, it is simply not a credible target for attack by terrorists bent on acquiring nuclear weapons, and can be disposed of as such for the purposes of this conference.

The Regulatory Aspects of Physical Protection of Nuclear Power Plants and Associated Facilities

Although the panel this afternoon must deal with the topic of "what can be done to prevent terrorist nuclear violence," some assessment of the relative risks of such violence is essential. As I mentioned, there is little credible risk in the case of the nuclear power industry. I must briefly address, however, the argument that terrorists might attempt to damage a civilian nuclear reactor, in an attempt to cause it to disperse some of its radioactive contents. As long as there are terrorists, we must always consider such possibilities as these. During my tenure as a commissioner of the Atomic Energy Commission and to this date, these possibilities have been exhaustively considered. The list of studies directed to these precise topics is extremely long, but I will mention a few.

The regulatory aspects of physical protection of nuclear power plants and associated facilities could easily be the subject of an entire treatise. Therefore, I have time to touch only briefly on the single most pertinent Nuclear Regulatory Commission (NRC) provision regarding the matter of possible terrorist actions directed against power plants. Part 73 of the NRC's regulations deals with "Physical Protection of Plants and Materials." Part 73, which has been amended many times since its original promulgation in 1969, sets forth the conservative assumption that radiological sabotage might be attempted by a "determined violent external assault" by "well-trained and dedicated individuals or with inside assistance which may include a knowledgeable individual who attempts to participate in a passive role or an active role." The regulations further assume that the attackers will possess automatic weapons, explosives and other sophisticated capabilities. To guard against the postulated threats, Part 73 specifies myriad protections. These include guards, physical barriers, alarm systems, requirements for screening applicants for employment, communication systems, contingency and response plans, and a host of other safeguards too numerous to mention here. Moreover, the NRC is constantly studying the need for further measures, as is demonstrated by numerous amendments to Part 73 over the years.

Intelligence Gathering and Civil Liberties

I would like to address O'Keefe's view that, to work against the terrorist threat, "we need a vastly expanded intelligence gathering system." He mentioned the possibility that such a system will lead to conflicts with our current constitutional concepts of human rights. In my view, there is no serious legal argument that can be raised against the constitutionality of the type of regulations presently in place in this country regarding physical security of nuclear material and nuclear facilities, such as Part 73 of the NRC's regulations. As the Supreme Court has long recognized, both the states and the federal government have broad authority to formulate regulations and pass laws protecting the public safety and health. One modern-day example is the federal regulations subjecting air travelers in the United States to inspection of baggage and even body searches. Various search techniques, including metal detectors and other measures, undeniably infringe upon certain personal freedoms that air travelers possessed before the age of airline hijackings. It is also true that individuals wishing to gain employment with NRC-licensed facilities must undergo background checks and other measures intended to exclude individuals with certain types of criminal records or whose background presents clear evidence of a potential security risk. These same standards are applied to hundreds of thousands of individuals who work for state and federal agencies (and even certain private industries) throughout the United States. Security measures taken at U.S. military installations and applied to armed forces personnel and contractor employees have been in place for many decades and have survived constitutional challenge in a wide variety of circumstances.

As free people, Americans generally wish to be subject to as little regulation as possible. However, there is a clear need for certain regulation in the public interest, whether it be safety in coal mines, speed limits to reduce highway fatalities or the many other regulatory measures that are now part of the fabric of our society.

The Need for Additional International Cooperation

In one important respect, I strongly agree with O'Keefe. He calls for greater international cooperation to combat nuclear terrorism. However, he does not mention the substantial record of existing international cooperation in this respect. I would like to give you a brief review.

The International Atomic Energy Agency (IAEA) and the Treaty on the Non-Proliferation of Nuclear Weapons (NPT) are both strong forces against nuclear terrorism, although they were not created to deal with that problem. If nations that are members of the IAEA are shown to be involved in fostering the activities of a nuclear terrorist group, the membership status of such nations could be called into question through the suspension mechanisms set forth in the IAEA statute in Article XIX. Most countries that are parties to the NPT and members of the IAEA must at least consider the international stigma of expulsion from these organizations if they are shown to have contributed to the work of terrorists.

More directly in point is the Convention on the Physical Protection of Nuclear Material. Its purpose is to provide for the establishment of physical security with respect to international shipment of significant quantities of source or special nuclear material. The United States signed the Convention in March 1980, and Congress enacted legislation implementing the Convention in 1982. Although the Convention has not yet achieved the necessary number of ratifications to enter into force, that will probably occur within the next year or two. The parties to the Convention recognize that "offenses related to nuclear material are a matter of grave concern that there is an urgent need to adopt appropriate and effective measures to ensure the prevention, detection and punishment of such offenses." In Article VII, the Convention sets forth various acts, including theft or robbery of nuclear material and nuclear threats, that must be made punishable offenses by each state party to the Convention under its national law. The Convention is a substantial step forward toward the ultimate goal of comprehensive international agreements which ensure that terrorists find no safe haven in the world and that nations cooperate in every way possible to ensure that terrorist acts are deterred.

Nuclear Terrorism and Plutonium in the Civilian Fuel Cycle

At present, the U.S. nuclear industry is not pursuing the use of plutonium, following decisions by Presidents Gerald Ford and Jimmy Carter to delay and establish a moratorium on such activity. However, the international reality is that other nations, including France, Britain, West Germany and Japan, are proceeding with their own national plans to close the fuel cycle, which will involve the presence of separated plutonium at certain stages. Fortunately, the excellent non-proliferation credentials of these nations are undisputed, as is their commitment to ensuring adequate physical security of separated plutonium. We must bear in mind that the United States recently attempted to persuade other nations to abandon reliance on plutonium. Although other nations noted with surprise the U.S. voluntary decision to forego plutonium in the civilian fuel cycle, none was persuaded to follow the U.S. example. The nations simply feel that the rewards are great in the long term and that an acceptable level of risk can be achieved. One of the lessons learned from the Nuclear Non-Proliferation Act of 1978 (NNPA) is that the United States cannot dictate to other nations non-proliferation measures that other nations may feel are unnecessary, unwise or contrary to their national self-interest.

The United States still exercises legal controls over substantial amounts of plutonium generated from nuclear fuel of U.S. origin. However, the amount of plutonium subject to United States controls is steadily shrinking, as other nations find non-U.S. sources or turn to producing plutonium indigenously.

Since the United States cannot and should not necessarily stop other nations from pursuing their energy independence by completing the nuclear fuel cycle, the essential question is how the United States can work with other nations to thwart possible nuclear terrorism directed at facilities where plutonium in separated form is stored or used.

In his paper, O'Keefe concentrated on the need to cooperate with the Soviet Union, and I agree. I am not sure, however, as to the degree to which we need to share U.S. intelligence on nuclear terrorist matters with the KGB. I would prefer to concentrate on achieving multinational agreements rather than to concentrate on a regime of collaboration with the KGB. Incidentally, the United States and the Soviet Union have cooperated to a considerable degree in multinational efforts to stop the spread of nuclear weapons. The Soviets recently announced their intent voluntarily to submit their civilian nuclear facilities to IAEA safeguards.

As I mentioned previously, the IAEA is a good forum for addressing concerns about nuclear terrorism directed against plutonium. Its statutory mandate includes measures to help insure the safe use of plutonium, and it has already served as a forum for negotiation of the Physical Security Convention as well as international discussions concerning an international plutonium storage regime. In my view, the IAEA should build upon its previous accomplishments by promulgating new guidelines regarding measures for ensuring the physical security of plutonium while in transit and during its existence in a separated form at reprocessing facilities, mixed oxide fuel facilities and other installations. With our far-reaching communication capabilities, plutonium can and should be tracked during every second of its separated existence through a worldwide monitoring system, with communication satellite links to ensure instantaneous communication of data. While the IAEA cannot supply the police force to react to diversion attempts, it can sound the alarm.

The primary responsibility for physical protection of plutonium must, of course, rest with the nations that elect to use it in their civilian fuel cycles. These nations should promptly negotiate and ratify a multinational agreement to ensure that physical security measures for plutonium are so formidable as to deter even the most determined terrorist. Nations using plutonium in their civilian fuel cycles must protect it with the same degree of vigilance as nuclear weapons states protect their military stockpile of plutonium.

Some solutions can probably be found in technology. Physical barriers to plutonium must be of the highest order and redundant to the point where plutonium stocks would be unmovable even if terrorists gained access to the facility where they are kept. Guard forces and security controls regarding access and other matters should be at the same level as is present at military installations where nuclear weapons are stored. Moreover, the time during which plutonium is present in separated form should be reduced to the absolute minimum.

Conclusion

While the United States cannot dictate nuclear policy to other nations, it can urge other nations to refrain from actions that jeopardize our common security. Although nations may disagree about certain matters, such as the wisdom of using plutonium in the civilian fuel cycle, they share the need to ensure that terrorists do not divert national supplies of nuclear material or attack nuclear facilities. This common interest can serve to ensure that our institutions and technology allow the use of nuclear power without credible risks of diversion or disruption by terrorists.

* * *

Bernard T. Feld

The threat that a terrorist group may be able to come into possession of a nuclear explosive device is indeed uncomfortably great and, what is more alarming, growing. On a time scale of the next decade or two, unless drastic changes are made in the procedures employed in the non-communist world for handling fissionable materials, I believe that this possibility is bound to become a certainty.

The existence of large arsenals of nuclear weapons in at least six nations is, in my view, a secondary aspect of the problem. Such weapons can be and, in the main, are being guarded with the care necessary to prevent their falling into unauthorized hands. (They are dangerous enough in the hands of legitimate military establishments, especially in times of crises and confrontations.) The major source of my concerns lies in the growing dependence on and commerce in nuclear power reactors based on the reactor-produced element, plutonium. While, for a variety of reasons—in part technological, in part political and in larger part economic—the plutonium power economy has not come about as rapidly as had been expected some 20 to 30 years ago, it is nevertheless a fact that the world, both the developed and the developing regions thereof, continues to move inexorably in this direction. Nuclear reactors and, more important from the point of view of weapons proliferation, fuel fabrication and reprocessing facilities are rapidly being exported from the nuclear "haves" to the "have-nots." Plutonium (and, to a lesser degree, highly enriched uranium) is increasingly becoming an item of international traffic, being transported within countries and across international boundaries aboard all sorts of conveyances—trucks, trains, aircraft, barges and boats—and with a wholly inadequate degree of protection.

As noted by O'Keefe, this is not so within the Soviet sphere. The Soviet Union, while an enthusiastic booster of fission power and a generous supplier of power reactors to its allies, treats the fissionable components with the respect they require. The fuel elements are only fabricated in the Soviet Union, transported under guard to the reactors that require them, and installed by Soviet technicians, who also remove the spent fuel elements and arrange for their transportation, again under adequate guard, to reprocessing facilities in the Soviet Union.

Sooner or later, and the sooner the safer, the nations of the West must adopt a similar procedure. They should agree on a limited (preferably small) number of reprocessing and storage facilities in a few key supplier nations, and adopt the same sort of procedures as are used by the Soviets for the transport, reprocessing and storage of weapons-usable materials.

I refer to this as the "Fort Knox solution," in view of its similarity to the procedures used in our country for the transport and storage of gold. Plutonium is more valuable than gold, and much, much more lethal. Surely, it deserves at least as much care in its handling.

* * *

Paul Warnke

I read Bernard O'Keefe's paper with great interest. I think his prescription for preventing nuclear terrorism is a sound one. He calls for the world community to organize with respect to intelligence gathering and deterrence to deal with the threat of nuclear violence. Now, I know that deterrence has a pejorative meaning for a lot of people, but that's basically what our criminal code is based on. And I think that deterrence is a necessary part of any kind of a scheme for preventing terrorist nuclear violence.

I disagree somewhat with Harold Agnew as to the lack of receptivity of the Soviet Union to this kind of an approach. My own feeling is that the Soviet Union regards itself as public enemy number one and as the most likely target for a nuclear attack, whether by another government or by terrorist groups. It is probably a sound judgement on its part. As a result, I would agree with O'Keefe that the Soviets may be motivated to cooperate in international efforts to prevent terrorism from acquiring a nuclear dimension.

On the question of deterrence, I do have a couple of reservations about O'Keefe's paper. He suggests, as I understand it, that if nuclear terrorism is carried on under the auspices of a government, there ought to be nuclear retaliation. If a semi-autonomous group is the perpetrator, the non-nuclear retaliation against the host country would be in order. I wonder whether we can really make that sort of a distinction.

It seems to me that the distinction instead is between action by a government and action by a terrorist organization. If a government uses a nuclear device against another country, that is a nuclear attack. The doctrinal response is, of course, nuclear retaliation.

In the case of terrorist use of a nuclear device, I wonder whether non-nuclear retaliation isn't always the more appropriate response. Whether the terrorist organization has been abetted by a host country or acted under its auspices, that country is going to be a Third World nation. It is not going to be the Soviet Union; it is not going to be France or Britain, not even the People's Republic of China. It thus will have a very limited nuclear capability. Therefore, it is perhaps disproportionate, and perhaps ineffective and a further erosion of the barriers against the use of nuclear weapons, to respond with a nuclear attack. What really ought to be developed is the certainty of the response, rather than to attempt to decide whether a nuclear or a non-nuclear response is appropriate. I think it's the certainty of the response, the fact that the international community will react and react strongly, that constitutes the best deterrent.

I think we are, of course, fortunate that we need to be dealing only with international terrorism. I don't believe there is any likelihood that a domestic terrorist group would use nuclear devices within the United States. The nature of our society is such, the homogeneity is such, that we don't have the kind of internal dissidence that could lead to this sort of aggravated action. It is, I suppose, conceivable, but to me it is of a high order of unlikelihood. So we are dealing with an international problem, a problem of foreign terrorist groups, and I think it calls for an international response.

I'm not as concerned, perhaps, as I should be about the inevitability of a conflict between our traditional constitutional civil liberties and the kinds of actions we should take to prevent terrorists from using nuclear weapons. I don't think that conflict is inevitable or even likely. Basically, I think what we're dealing with is whether the international community can organize itself to deal with a problem that is going to affect other countries at least as much as it does the United States. I would think that the risks of a terrorist group using a nuclear device are much greater in some of the impacted multi-national continents than they are in the U.S. Our physical separation from the rest of the world gives us a better chance of dealing with the problem of international terrorism, whether nuclear or non-nuclear.

And then I think one other note ought to be struck. My own view is that unless the United States and the Soviet Union begin to do something really constructive, really quite drastic, about putting an end to the runaway race to develop more and more nuclear weapons, then the problem of international nuclear terrorism is going to increase.

Article VI of the Non-Proliferation Treaty makes a very good point. It calls upon the nuclear powers to bring their own arsenals under control, to rein in what is sometimes referred to as vertical proliferation. We have not been doing a very good job in that regard. We are adding thousands and thousands of nuclear weapons to our stockpiles. And I think that that threatens world peace, not only in terms of a nuclear exchange between the Soviet Union and the United States, but also as these weapons become more and more accepted, more and more countries will get into the nuclear weapons business.

We can't count on all of these countries, or perhaps on any of them, to be as careful as we have become and as we hope the Soviet Union is becoming. I believe, therefore, that something has to be done to implement Article VI of the Non-Proliferation Treaty, or else the problem will continue to increase, and the risk of the use of nuclear devices by third countries or sub-national groups will become graver.

* * *

Amiram Nir

Allow me to open by saying that I speak here not in any official capacity, but as a private interested observer.

We Israelis know from our experience—and we know it only too well—that combatting terrorism is not a battle that can be won decisively. At the most, one can score points. Any tool, any means that can serve the purpose, even if not very promising at first sight, should be tried. In that respect, I think all the ideas and the proposals of Bernard O'Keefe's paper are very good. I think, on principle, these are the guidelines to follow in trying to deal with nuclear terrorism, on which, fortunately, I can only speak academically, since Israel is not subject to nuclear terrorist threats.

However, guidelines must be translated into actual policy and everyday deeds. When I was trying to analyze the different ideas in this paper, and to put them into a wider perspective, it became clear that what is involved here are the three classic aspects of combatting terrorism: defensive, offensive, and intelligence.

Defensive strategies will always have their limitations. You can defend the targets, you can defend the arsenal, you can defend the materials and prevent their unauthorized possession, but only up to a point. Beyond that, if you want to invest more—and there are practically no limits to what one can invest in defense—you sometimes limit the use of a very important potential tool. This might be called a "blind" defensive strategy. You know where the targets might be, you know where the arsenal might be, you know where the materials might be stolen from, and therefore you try to defend them as well as you can. Beyond this, you must supplement your defense with intelligence information. In order to invest your efforts in the right order, in the right priority, you have to have intelligence. In order to know which target is more likely than others to be hit, or which material is more likely than others to be stolen, you must have intelligence information.

An offensive strategy, a strategy of retaliation, also has its limitations. How do you retaliate against terrorists? Usually, the advantage of a terrorist organization is that it offers hardly any targets. It is very difficult to find targets that can be hit with the means or the tools that a country has available to it. In this respect, prospective nuclear terrorist organizations are very much like any other terrorist groups, relatively unexposed to retaliation.

So an offensive strategy also must depend, to a very great extent, on intelligence. If you don't know who the terrorists are, where they are located, what is their vulnerability, you don't know where to hit. There can be no retaliation and, to a large extent, no offense.

Thus, the importance of intelligence. With respect to nuclear terrorism, there are two different types of intelligence that should concern you. One is basic intelligence, the information about those terrorist organizations that are likely to go into the nuclear field, or that have already gone into the nuclear field; information about a black market in nuclear materials; information about links between organizations and states, links that can serve to supply nuclear material from a country to a terrorist organization or group.

This is basic information. It is extremely important. It will serve all three purposes. Once you begin to look for the materials and look for the organizations, you will have a much better picture than you have today about the potential danger. The international community should have sufficient intelligence resources to do this. Once you do this, a defensive strategy can be directed to vulnerable targets, and the offensive can be both effective and a deterrent.

The second type of intelligence is what I will call real-time field intelligence. Once a threat is made, an immediate real-time intelligence operation has to be organized in order to identify the threat, to analyze it, to evaluate whether it is a serious threat, what kind of material is involved, where it is located, how it can be defused or how it can be taken or found, what kind of group we are talking about, whether it is likely this group would be involved in such an operation, whether it is likely for them to have something in hand, and eventually to provide operational units with the necessary intelligence for them to be effective. I'm not referring to threats where the event is a detonation, but to the more common nuclear blackmail threats that the United States has faced in the last ten years.

This is the second phase of intelligence that you need, a very efficient, very quick, real-time field intelligence, in order to handle a threat when it appears. Such a capability will also, once in effect, serve to deter, to a certain extent, groups from going into this field.

Now, the second point that I want to elaborate on is the need for international cooperation, which several panelists have mentioned. First of all, cooperation with whom? Among whom? Are we talking about nuclear states only? I think that would be a great mistake, and it seems to me that at least some of the panelists have referred mainly to those states.

The second question concerning cooperation is whether agreements, treaties, and things of this sort are required to formalize cooperative arrangements. Our experience has been that a lot of energy is sometimes invested in trying to achieve very formal and binding treaties, only to find, later on, that the substance that should fill the framework is not there. A more practical approach is to try to figure out what one wants to accomplish and then decide if a treaty or an agreement is needed.

Why am I saying this? The amount of energy that is invested in formulating agreements and negotiating treaties is perhaps better used to start doing something. If you wait for agreements and treaties, you might just be too late.

The third point—what type of cooperation should you look for in the intelligence arena? To be realistic, I would say that the best you can hope for is not necessarily joint intelligence collection or gathering operations, but joint definition of the threat from the intelligence point of view. and then joint participation in analyzing the data collected. This is on the level of basic intelligence.

On the level of field intelligence, I don't believe you can count on international cooperation. Each nation should construct its own independent capability to deal with the threat of nuclear terrorism. I cannot imagine for a minute one country letting another country operate inside one's own sovereign land, once a real threat emerges. This is inconceivable.

These are not modest goals. Perhaps they seem a little more modest than the ambitious framework that was put forward in the beginning of this panel.

Many people ask, in relation to nuclear terrorism, why has it not yet occurred? If this danger exists, if it's so highly probable, why hasn't it occurred? This skepticism may explain why some countries have not invested the necessary effort to acquire the ability to combat nuclear terrorism. Nuclear terrorism is a probable threat. This subject receives a lot of media attention. The ideas that are discussed here in this panel, and in this conference, are not very far from the eyes and ears of those who might turn the idea into reality. So this is not a distant future threat, it is a real threat. Instead of trying to set unachievable goals, countries should go for practical terms, practical means, and push for practical achievements in the field.

Chapter Five

Two Congressional Perspectives

Richard A. Gephardt
Jeremiah Denton

THE NEW NIGHTMARE: NUCLEAR TERRORISM

U.S. Representative Richard A. Gephardt

Too often, we as policymakers are forced to react to crises rather than prepare for them. Yet we should have learned that we can best deal with terrorism before the terrorist strikes, not after. So I commend the Nuclear Control Institute and the State University of New York's Institute for Studies in International Terrorism for taking a hard look into the future and, through this conference, focusing national attention on preventing nuclear terrorism before it's too late.

I deeply regret, as I know you do, that the tragic events of this past week—from the killing of our brave Marines in El Salvador to the continuing sad saga in Beirut—make this conference so topical and timely. Once more our nation—all of us—watch as events play themselves out on a distant stage, beyond our control and often beyond our comprehension. Once more we see the yellow ribbons of an America held hostage, as our fellow citizens become lightning rods for crackling currents of hate and resentment from religious and political groups few Americans have heard of and even fewer understand. I am sure that we all stand behind the President today as he struggles with the difficult task of asserting our national interest and at the same time tries to extricate our hostages and return them to their families.

Make no mistake about it: *we are a nation at war*. We fight not uniformed soldiers but zealous barbarians who blend into the crowd, pop up when least expected, leave a bomb at an airport, and then call the local radio stations. President John F. Kennedy once described the cold war as a "long, twilight struggle" between the forces of democratic freedom and those of communist tyranny. While that struggle still tests our resolve, we must now—a quarter century later—steel ourselves for a second, dawning struggle, a struggle with the growing bands of fanatics who are willing to blow themselves into immortality as they kill innocent Americans.

It's tragically ironic that this week the House of Representatives is considering a nearly $300 billion defense bill to preserve our military strength and protect us from attack by our most dangerous adversary, the Soviet Union. Yet who is attacking us today? A puny gang of thugs within a puny faction within a leaderless, war-torn country that can barely hold together a standing army. That's who's taking America hostage. That's who's tying us down, like Gulliver. That's who's holding at bay—the mightiest military machine in the world. That, my friends, is a national security disaster.

If a puny gang of thugs within a puny faction within a leaderless country should ever acquire nuclear weapons, that, my friends, would be a national security nightmare. For the security of our own nation—indeed, the nations of the free world—we *must* prevent today's terrorist with an AK47 from becoming tomorrow's terrorist with an atomic bomb. We *must* prevent the terrorist's ultimate prize from becoming not only airline passengers to hold hostage, but separated plutonium to build an atomic bomb.

Anybody who thinks nuclear terrorism can't become a reality hasn't *faced* reality. Anybody who thinks terrorists can't acquire the technical knowledge to build an atom bomb hasn't picked up your average encyclopedia or talked to a college physics major. Anybody who thinks terrorists aren't cunning or ruthless enough to pull off a nuclear attack has forgotten the Munich Olympics, the showdown at Entebbe, or the shooting of the Pope. Anybody who thinks an outlaw country won't help terrorists "go nuclear" hasn't been to Teheran or Tripoli.

Our current vulnerability to terrorist attack only foreshadows how seriously a terrorist group, armed with an atomic bomb, could damage our national security. By attacking or blackmailing U.S. business operations overseas, for example, a terrorist group could severely hamper our ability to compete in the world market. The companies some of you represent couldn't open an office or build a factory without fearing a terrorist attack. Since our economic security at home depends increasingly on our ability to compete abroad, any disruption of trade—whether by a foreign import quota or, far graver, a terrorist's bomb—will dangerously erode our economic strength.

Even more critically, nuclear terrorists could cripple our ability to act freely on the world stage as we seek to protect our vital national interests and advance the cause of freedom around the globe. We have spent tens of billions of dollars on a Rapid Deployment Force (RDF) to secure a free flow of oil from the Persian gulf, for our allies and ourselves. Yet terrorists with well-placed bombs could destroy the very oil fields, pipelines, and refineries we seek to defend. And all the money spent on the RDF will avail us little. Now, the president wants to spend hundreds of billions of dollars on "Star Wars" to defend against Soviet missiles. That won't give us a dime's worth of security against a terrorist's nuclear bomb.

And what about our allies? If actual or threatened attacks by nuclear terrorists succeed in splitting apart NATO or our other alliances, we will suffer another chink in our security shield. Far-fetched? Maybe not. Several weeks ago, Direct-Action, a left-wing French terrorist group, and Germany's Red Army faction reportedly forged an alliance with the apparent intent of carrying out bombings and assassinations across Europe to disrupt the NATO alliance. And we've all heard the chilling scenarios describing how terrorist nuclear explosions could spark regional or even global nuclear conflict. While the risk may be remote, even the slightest chance of terrorist nuclear attack raises grave doubts about the security, if not the survival, of the free world.

I don't claim to be an expert either on terrorism or on nuclear technology. But as an elected official with a sworn duty under the Constitution to provide for the common defense, I care deeply about these issues. As a father with three young children, I fear for their future in a world riddled with terrorism. For two converging trends convince me nuclear terrorism is increasingly likely—if we don't act now to prevent it.

First, just as our world constantly changes, so the nature of terrorism is dangerously changing, in four respects:

- The amount of worldwide terrorist violence has increased dramatically—from a few deaths in 1970 to nearly 4,000 last year.
- American citizens, as well as their property, have become the targets of choice.
- The randomness and the brutality of terrorist attacks have increased.
- Finally, terrorists have advanced to more sophisticated weaponry and more cunning strategy.

Now, consider a *second*, equally disturbing trend—the accelerating spread, around the world, of nuclear explosives material and technology. Some 260 commercial nuclear power reactors operating today in the non-communist world can produce, each year, 45 metric tons of bomb-usable plutonium, the equivalent of 6,000 nuclear weapons. Fortunately, 80 percent of the plutonium remains locked up in spent reactor fuel. As long as it stays locked up, terrorists or their patron nations can't steal or divert the 15 pounds needed to build a bomb. But one-fifth of the plutonium produced in power reactors has been separated out, and some countries want to separate even more to fuel their current generation of power reactors or to use in breeder reactors that produce *additional* bomb-usable plutonium. By the year 2000, according to some estimates, if current trends continue, there will be as much as 390 tons of bomb-usable plutonium, nearly twice the combined plutonium stockpile of the two superpowers.

If these two trends—one in terrorism, the other in nuclear technology—should finally converge, the national security nightmare we fear could come all too true. For as the separated plutonium used for nuclear power increases, so does the risk it will fall into terrorists' hands. As the sophistication of terrorists increases, so does the likelihood they can use that plutonium to build a bomb.

These converging trends lead to an inescapable conclusion: *to prevent the nightmare of nuclear terrorism, we must deny terrorists the ability to build or obtain bombs.* This means halting the further worldwide spread of nuclear explosives material—both plutonium and highly enriched uranium—along with the technology to produce it.

The rising tide of international terrorism now makes the Faustian bargain we struck under Atoms for Peace look like an especially bad deal, for we may have unwittingly traded away our national security. During the Ford and Carter administrations, we tried to renegotiate the terms of that Faustian bargain by forestalling the use of nuclear explosive material as fuel for civilian nuclear power plants. I am particularly proud of the efforts by Congress and the Carter administration, through the Nuclear Nonproliferation Act, to stop the civilian use at home and the proliferation abroad of nuclear bomb material and technology. We required countries receiving our nuclear exports to apply safeguards on all their nuclear facilities. We also required them to give "timely warning" of a theft or diversion of nuclear material or technology to build a bomb. It was only a beginning, but we made progress toward our ultimate goal of preventing the further spread of bomb-usable material or technology throughout the world.

Now this President and his administration seem bent on undoing the past bipartisan effort to stop nuclear proliferation. They have dangerously and systematically tried to dismantle the Nuclear Nonproliferation Act. They have taken a foolishly cavalier attitude toward the global spread of nuclear explosives material. Indeed, they have aided and abetted it. Their "laissez-faire" attitude toward nuclear exports has led them to approve shipments of sensitive technology even to countries that have not signed the Nonproliferation Treaty and taken its pledge to forego nuclear weapons.

It's just madness. Look at the record:

- In 1981, the administration approved the shipment of heavy water process control equipment from a U.S. company to Argentina.
- In 1982, the administration arranged for France to supply uranium fuel to India, although we were blocked from doing so by our own Nonproliferation Act.
- In 1983, the administration approved the retransfer of 146 metric tons of heavy water from West Germany to Argentina.
- Last year, the administration failed to stop the export to Israel of 600 krytrons, firing pins for an atomic bomb. When a Pakistani was caught shipping out krytrons, the administration slapped his wrist and paid his way home.

This list alone constitutes a serious bill of indictment. But there's more. This administration has also adopted a promiscuous plutonium policy. Many experts, including the International Atomic Energy Agency and our Nuclear Regulatory Commission, concede that current safeguards can't give timely warning that plutonium has been stolen before it's turned into a bomb.

Yet this administration has abdicated all leadership in trying to halt the growing commercial use of separated plutonium worldwide. The Nonproliferation Act gave us control over the further use by other countries of plutonium from U.S.-supplied materials or technology. Since then, we have authorized other countries to separate 19,000 kilograms—or 3,000 bombs' worth of plutonium. Eighty percent was authorized by this administration. The administration now wants to give some countries a blank check to use plutonium. With this blank check, known as a programmatic approval, a country need no longer submit to congressional oversight each time it wants to use or retransfer plutonium.

The bill of indictment continues—and gets worse. Last year, for the first time ever, the administration approved a shipment of bomb-usable plutonium outside of Europe. It allowed the ocean shipment of 40 bombs' worth from France to Japan. The Defense Department, aware of the grave security risks, strongly opposed the shipment, and then they spent nearly one million dollars to protect it. The Defense Department is now resisting, again on security grounds, a pending request to transfer plutonium from U.S.-origin fuel from France to Switzerland.

If his Defense Department worries about the threat to our security of separated plutonium, I urge this President to worry with them. But defenders of our promiscuous plutonium policy argue that these approvals only go to "proliferation-resistant countries"—countries we can trust not to build a bomb. *Proliferation*-resistant countries, however, are not necessarily *terrorism*-resistant countries. Often those we deem the least likely to proliferate, such as Italy and West Germany, are the most likely to have terrorist gangs that may try to steal plutonium to build a bomb. This administration has driven us headlong toward a worldwide plutonium economy where nuclear explosive material, although vulnerable to theft by terrorists, will move in international commerce. Soon we may even trade it on world commodity markets along with steel and pork bellies.

This brings me to the ultimate irony: Ronald Reagan likes to talk tough on defense, yet he's soft on defense against nuclear terrorism. Let me say that again: this President is soft on defense against nuclear terrorism. His "hands off" proliferation policies have set a dangerous example for the rest of the world. In effect, he's told other nuclear countries that it's all right to stockpile, traffic in, and use separated plutonium. That could make nuclear explosive material readily available to would-be terrorists.

We still have a chance to reverse course. We still have a chance to keep nuclear explosives out of the terrorist's hands.

First, we can begin by recognizing terrorism in general—and nuclear terrorism in particular—as a direct and serious threat to our national security. To mobilize our nation's resources against this threat, we should appoint an assistant secretary of defense for terrorism.

Second, we must steer the world away from plutonium as a reactor fuel. It makes no economic sense for a country to use plutonium when it can get the same energy at one-third the cost from low-enriched uranium, a fuel that's abundant as well as unsuitable for building bombs. In fact, our country finally realized that plutonium makes no economic sense, and Congress curbed this administration's plutonium appetite by cancelling the Clinch River breeder reactor and permitting the mothballing of the Barnwell Reprocessing plant. The U.S. could *increase* the incentive for other countries *not* to use plutonium by supplying, at a substantial discount, low-enriched uranium fuel with an energy value equal to the plutonium not used.

Third, we must reverse this administration's promiscuous plutonium policy by denying foreign requests to obtain or transfer plutonium from U.S.-supplied materials or technology.

Fourth, we should place plutonium use and nuclear proliferation high on our list of foreign policy concerns. We have tremendous diplomatic and economic leverage to influence our allies and nuclear trading partners not to traffic in nuclear explosives material. We should use it. We should quit shortchanging our long-term security interest in halting the further spread of nuclear weapons for some short-term, and often short-lived, diplomatic gain.

Fifth, we should begin immediately to negotiate with all other nuclear nations to freeze the production of nuclear explosives material for both civilian and military uses. A plutonium freeze could serve as an important new step toward comprehensive arms control. It would also stop the growth in commercial inventories of bomb-usable plutonium and highly enriched uranium.

Sixth, we should work to upgrade the safeguards system administered by the IAEA. The current system *neither* is "safe" nor does it "guard." As we strive to keep plutonium out of international commerce, we should target our resources to strengthen IAEA safeguards only where they work well, for facilities that don't handle nuclear explosives material.

Finally, other countries obviously have legitimate energy needs and seek independence from foreign sources. We should assist them in developing and using alternative energy technologies to discourage them from using plutonium fuel. With this assistance, many countries may come to view nuclear power as the energy source of last, not first, resort.

These policies, if we adopt them, could return us to a path away from a fearful world awash in plutonium, toward a future secure from the peril of nuclear terrorism.

I recognize that the U.S. alone cannot halt all further spread of nuclear bomb material. We must redouble our efforts, through forums like the coming review conference for the Nonproliferation Treaty, to enlist other nations in the fight to keep plutonium out of international commerce—and out of the hands of terrorists. If the President won't lead in this effort, then we in the Congress must. For, in the last analysis, the responsibility lies on our doorstep. While several distinguished Senators—Alan Cranston, John Glenn, Charles Percy, and William Proxmire—as well as Representatives—John Dingell, Edward Markey, Richard

Ottinger, and Howard Wolpe—have kept alive the issue of nuclear proliferation, too often it slips from our agenda of urgent concerns.

As caucus chair, I intend to change that. I don't want history to record that we squandered the chance to prevent today's struggle against terrorists who threaten the lives of our airline passengers from becoming tomorrow's war against nuclear terrorists who threaten the future of civilization. We still have time to head off this nightmare, but the clock is ticking.

INTERNATIONAL TERRORISM — THE NUCLEAR DIMENSION

U.S. Senator Jeremiah Denton

The subject of nuclear terrorism is one that cannot be considered in isolation. It must be considered in the overall context of worldwide terrorism, as one part of the spectrum of violence, and especially in the context of the growing problem of state-sponsored and state-supported terrorism as a means to advance revolutionary foreign policy.

Acts of terrorism, as they have occurred within the United States, have been largely the work of remnants of the Weather Underground, the Black Liberation Army, the FALN, and the May 19th Communist organization. These groups, operating under various names, have been largely responsible for our domestic violence. As you may know, there has recently been a marked decline in terrorism as it has occurred in the United States for the years 1982 through 1985. I believe that the FBI's highly successful federal investigative efforts in cooperation with state law enforcement agencies deserve much of the credit for the improvement. The FBI is now in the pro-active mode with respect to conventional terrorist operations, and we on the Subcommittee on Security and Terrorism, which has oversight of the FBI, intend to help them keep it that way at all costs. We must remember, however, that apart from a few attacks by Armenian and Croatian terrorists, the FBI has been dealing with a home-grown kind of terrorist, usually from the middle class, often guilt-ridden and highly anti-establishment. That is a very different breed from the terrorist that the United States has to face internationally, such as the fanatical Shia Muslim groups whose members relish the idea of dying in battle and whose espoused hatred of the United States is exceeded only by the zealotry for their religion.

On the international level, Senate hearings on terrorism during the last several years have brought out sufficient evidence to conclude that there is more to terrorism than just a series of unrelated violent events perpetrated by a number of unrelated groups. We are now able to see clearly the relationship among Marxist-Leninist propaganda, drug trafficking, insurgency, and the terrorism directed against western democracies. There is a clear pattern in Soviet-supported and -equipped insurgencies seeking to destabilize, by revolution, whole regions such as in southern Africa, to politicize established religion, such as in Nicaragua, and to export violence against the democratic governments of neighboring states in order to divert attention from the insurgency itself, as Nicaragua is doing in El Salvador and Costa Rica. It has happened in North Korea; north, central, and South Africa; the Caribbean; and now Central America. Repeatedly, it has happened in Ethiopia, South Yemen, and Afghanistan. And as we are all painfully aware, it continues in the Mid-East today.

The trends are clear. Cooperation among terrorist groups is increasing. In some instances, drug money finances the violence. The lethalness of the action is becoming greater as more powerful and sophisticated weapons are employed. There is increasing disregard for the innocent, and greater willingness to use kamikazes for the cause. More diplomats and world leaders are targets. More states are supporting terrorism through asylum, training, arms, funds, explosives, and advisors. The USSR, Libya, Syria, Iran, South Yemen, Ethiopia, Bulgaria, Nicaragua, Cuba, East Germany, North Korea, Vietnam, Angola are all supporting terrorist activities.

The pattern that emerges from studying the testimony obtained in more than 60 hearings before the Subcommittee on Security and Terrorism, and more recently in joint hearings with the Foreign Relations Committee, is that terrorism is the most widely practiced form of modern warfare. It has the strategic advantages of low risk, low cost, and total deniability. The blood is only on the hands of the fanatics, the surrogates in this kind of warfare.

The trends and patterns are emerging clearly. Set against a Marxist-Leninist revolutionary backdrop, wars of national liberation are plunging the poor deeper into poverty, greater repression, and worse famine. That is happening while established Western democratic governments are being tied down in efforts to confront a growing burden of terrorism directed against them. Only token levels of harassment are directed at the Communist bloc countries. The intense violence is aimed against the free governments of the world, and those other governments, perhaps incrementally, somewhat less democratically aligned with them.

How are we dealing with this form of warfare against our commerce, soldiers, diplomats, facilities, and leaders? Not that well. We in Congress and in the Administration sometimes adopt self-defeating, even contradictory, measures that often put us at odds with our allies and friends. Most people are outraged at the violence of terrorism, as depicted by the daily news, but that rage is short-lived. Few realize how we are being distracted from dealing with the underlying problem. Some governments appear to take a hard line on dealing with terrorists—no negotiations—while others give in readily to terrorist demands, releasing convicted terrorists in order to avoid violence and confrontation at home.

Recently we saw the case of one hardliner state, Israel, exchanging 1,100 terrorists for a handful of Israelis, an act inconsistent with the announced policy of that country and one that brought back into circulation some of the worst criminals who have ever walked the face of the earth. Moreover, some commentators believe that this highly disproportionate exchange set the stage for the drama unfolding in Beirut today. Some nations advocate the use of economic sanctions against states that foster terrorism, while other nations increasingly undercut the sanctions. Seldom are economic sanctions applied consistently, or even-handedly, or for the long term.

The direct costs of terrorism to the United States have been high. Since 1980, terrorist incidents overseas have taken over 300 American lives, and more than 400 Americans have suffered injuries. More than 100 Americans are acknowledged to have been kidnapped or taken hostage. I want to emphasize that many more are victims, but the ransoms are often paid quietly by companies seeking to avoid publicity and that write off the ransoms as a business expense. We have come to a point in our history that requires that we establish both a foreign and domestic policy for dealing with the obvious threat.

Currently, U.S. policy on terrorism is fragmented and only partially developed. I believe that it is essential that we determine the degree of the threat to our interests, set our goals and objectives, and then develop policy. From there, we must explain our policy so that we can build a consensus that will enable us to persevere and to succeed over the long haul.

It is in the context of coping with increasing violence, of countering state support and sponsorship of terrorism as a means of advancing state interests, and of the necessity of developing goals and objectives to set policy that we face the threat of nuclear terrorism in a world where there is an ever-increasing proliferation of nuclear weapons and materials. The International Association of Chiefs of Police, in its *Quarterly Intelligence Reporter on Terrorist Trends*, warns:

> Nuclear power and weapons facilities will continue to be the focus of demonstrations and small scale actions (trespass, blockade, vandalism), with increasing probability of a major action being conducted against a nuclear weapons production facility or weapons transport vehicle over the next 18 to 24 months.

Many believe that we have already had warning signs that the nuclear aspect of terrorism is very real and has to be faced. Between 1966 and 1977, there were 10 terrorist incidents against European nuclear installations. In a 1979 case, environmental terrorists succeeded in inflicting $20 million in damage on a French nuclear plant. In 1982, five rockets were fired into the French Creys-Malville nuclear facility. Fortunately, in that case, the damage was minor. The United States has not escaped the violence, either. Between 1969 and 1975, in addition to 240 bombing threats against U.S. nuclear facilities, there were 14 actual and attempted bombings. Moreover, we have seen 32 acts of intentional damage or suspected sabotage in domestic nuclear facilities going back to 1974.

In 1980, a former nuclear plant employee was convicted and sentenced to 15 years' imprisonment for stealing uranium oxide after he attempted to extort $100,000 from authorities by threatening to release it into the atmosphere. Many of us know of General Dozier's kidnapping by the Red Brigades and successful rescue by Italian authorities, but few know that, while confined, he was interrogated by his kidnappers about NATO and U.S. nuclear weapon locations. Members of Germany's Red Army Faction have been apprehended with maps and drawings of nuclear storage sites and security patrol routes. In 1983, four West Germans forced their way into a Pershing missile site and tried to destroy a missile with crowbars.

Daily, we have shipments of nuclear fuel and nuclear waste moving all over the world. We have all heard about reported losses, apparently through misaccounting, waste, or theft. On April 30, 1965, the AEC noted 93.8 kilos of U-235 missing from a single U.S. plant. While intensive investigations of the situation at NUMEC in Apollo, Pennsylvania, by federal law enforcement agencies have been inconclusive regarding concrete information concerning the final disposition or location of any missing material, some knowledgeable observers believe that the material was stolen and diverted to Israel for its nuclear weapons program. Moreover, in 1980, the General Accounting Office reported 145 kilos of plutonium could not be accounted for at the Savannah River nuclear power plant. The Nuclear Control Institute estimates that there is more than 9,600 pounds of enriched uranium and plutonium unaccounted for in the United States. We place substantial emphasis on trying to prevent terrorists from building their own bomb with stolen nuclear materials. Certainly the technology to build a bomb has been public for at least 10 years. Despite the volume of missing nuclear material, some experts believe that terrorists will most probably acquire a nuclear device in one of two ways: It will be furnished as part of a state-supported terrorist act, or it will be stolen, intact.

In this context, one must also consider the underlying question of increased nuclear proliferation. The Nuclear Nonproliferation Treaty of 1968 has worked reasonably well for those nations that are signatories. Nations generally have not built the massive nuclear arsenals that were once predicted. But, like the old adage, "locks are for honest people," the Nuclear Nonproliferation Treaty has kept only well-meaning nations from building and stockpiling nuclear weapons. It has not been effective in preventing nations intent on gaining a nuclear weapons capability from so doing.

Five countries have officially acknowledged possessing nuclear weapons: the United States, Great Britain, France, China, and the USSR. Unofficially, the following countries have or soon will have weapons: India, South Africa, Israel, and Pakistan. In South America, we see Argentina, driven by old rivalries, achieving a capability of two bombs per year and its own enrichment facility in only a few years. In addition, Brazil appears to be seeking world power status with a bomb of its own, and building its own enrichment plant independently.

A further problem to consider is whether terrorist acquisition of a nuclear device could result from the overthrow of an established government. The shah of Iran sought a nuclear capability for his air force. If he had succeeded, where would we be today, given the events in Iran and the "war" that his successor has declared on the United States? I have no doubt that a nuclear weapon in Khomeini's hands would indeed be used to instill terror in the West—and probably much worse. Who can say that, by this time next year, we will not face a new revolutionary leader in one of those countries now unofficially developing a nuclear weapons capability? How will we face this?

Consider the case of Libya and Qaddafi. He has actually sought a nuclear weapon for at least 15 years. He tried direct purchase from China in 1970, to no avail. In the early 1970s, he poured millions into Pakistan's nuclear development effort, hoping to share in the fruits. President Zia, when he came to power in 1977, wisely cut him out, but not before Pakistan got from Niger, with Libya's help, the 400 tons of uranium oxide it needed to produce bomb-quality enriched uranium. Qaddafi then sought technology from India. But India stood firm on supplying information for peaceful use only, so, in retaliation, Qaddafi cut off oil deliveries to India, more than 7 million barrels per year. Since then, Qaddafi has received a 10-megawatt research reactor, furnished by the USSR, but staffed and controlled by more than 100 Soviet technicians. At the moment there appears to be no opportunity for Libya to divert fuel from the reactor—the Soviets have a lock on all of it, and the Soviets *do* what is in their best interest. The Secretary General of the Libyan Liberation Organization, an arch enemy of Qaddafi, has said, "If Qaddafi is after a bomb, he will get his ready made, by hiring terrorists to steal it." Qaddafi seeks to be the leader of the Arab world, so the question is not what he *would* do with a nuclear weapon, but what wouldn't he do?

Even though a terrorist group might not need actually to build its own nuclear weapon, that does not mean it would not try to get nuclear material and threaten or seek to carry out an environmental attack with it.

The peaceful use of the atom for energy and research has resulted in more than 300 nuclear power plants in 28 countries. We alone have 129 such plants in 32 states. The demands for nuclear fuel, uranium, and enriched uranium, and the creation of "spent fuel" rich in plutonium, which has to be processed and disposed of, have led to an international industry for enrichment, reprocessing, transport, and waste storage. Nuclear materials move from plant to plant, state to state, and nation to nation almost daily. A French transport ship carrying tons of uranium destined for the USSR sank last year in a disaster at sea. It was not terrorism—but it could have been.

Any capture and threatened release by terrorists of nuclear material, be it uranium, or plutonium, or spent fuel containing both, would horrify the world, gain unprecedented notoriety for the terrorists, and probably give them a better than even chance of achieving their demands. The potential threat applies not only to nuclear material, of which there is certainly enough available; it also applies to nuclear power plants.

Nuclear power plants are relatively soft targets of opportunity to various types of exploitation by terrorists for their own ends. The world's countries using nuclear reactors have not agreed upon a standard to secure and protect those facilities. The possibilities of attack, capture, sabotage, and subsequent environmental disaster are quite real. Even without a hint of terrorism, U.S. nuclear power plants have had at least two "near misses"—in 1966, the Fermi plant had a local fuel melting, and in 1979 Three Mile Island had a partial meltdown. We have no empirical data on the effects of a meltdown, but one study says it would in the extreme case be lethal to life within a 5-mile radius, damage life out to 10 miles, and affect life out to 100 miles. That does not include the damage to subterranean water supplies.

You and I know that U.S. nuclear weapons and weapon systems have built-in safeguards and special fail-safe devices that would prevent a nuclear detonation if terrorists tried to use them. I offer you a thought about that: Even those safeguards do not go far enough! I believe that if a U.S. nuclear weapon even comes into terrorist hands, especially in Western Europe, the political ramifications of the event could be quite severe, and the opportunity for the Soviets to capitalize on and exploit it for its propaganda value could be substantial. This could erode our position in Europe, thereby altering the balance of power in that important region. Terrorist theft of a weapon, terrorist capture of a storage site, even a conventional accident involving one of our nuclear systems, could be the precipitating cause of an avalanche of protest calls that would be clearly contrary to our interests and those of our allies.

Given the Soviet support for terrorist activities, and their goal of smashing NATO, I do not believe for a single moment that they would be deterred from acting if they thought they could get away with it. The stakes are always high in nuclear safety and security, but in this context they are astronomical. There can be no tolerance for nuclear terrorism where U.S. interests are concerned.

Nuclear terrorism approaches the ultimate catastrophe. The consequences could be so severe and widespread that they would affect not just the balance of power, but also the environment, the health, and the welfare of the population. We cannot permit it to happen. Any nation, group, or individual willing to embark on acts of terrorism involving nuclear materials knows what is at stake, and thus knows the terrible consequences of its act. U.S. policy for dealing with the nuclear aspect of terrorism should take as an assumption that the nuclear terrorist fully appreciates the consequences and is automatically willing to pay the price.

Countering nuclear terrorism calls for deadly force, and no quarter should be given. We do not want to wait around negotiating with a terrorist team while a captured nuclear reactor goes into meltdown. Likewise, the threat of a large-scale environmental release of waste, fuel, or material such as plutonium must be stopped before it occurs. Where we have nuclear weapons in host countries, there should be full agreement that we, and they, will act decisively, and forcefully, to defend them against destructive theft or seizure.

I foresee, in dealing with nuclear terrorism, that the national security interest is of the highest order, and therefore the President, acting as commander-in-chief, should be responsible for the management of any response that could become necessary. Jurisdiction must not be allowed to become an issue. I can envision scenarios when joint military, FBI, NEST, Coast Guard, intelligence, and diplomatic resources would have to be rapidly mobilized and orchestrated to deal with a situation. It occurs to me that it would be helpful to have legislation or an executive order clearly delineating jurisdiction before the fact.

What should we be doing now, today, before we are confronted? One thought that occurs to me is that, although I think that we are doing better domestically in protecting weapons, reactors, enrichment facilities, and reprocessing facilities, we may need to look more closely at the security of transporting and storing nuclear waste materials. I am heartened by the fact that the army came to Congress seeking to reprogram funds so that it can better protect Pershing missiles against terrorist attacks. I am pleased with the Department of Energy's approach in actually testing the ability of its facilities and personnel to defend against terrorist attack. It occurs to me that perhaps we should create strong incentives for other signatory nations to the Nonproliferation Treaty to take greater steps year by year to improve their protection against terrorism. I would certainly support such incentives.

In closing, I would like briefly to review for you our legislative initiatives in dealing with terrorism. I am pleased to report that the Congress passed three of the President's anti-terrorism bills in the 98th Congress. Two of these bills involved legislation for international agreements, the first dealing with aircraft sabotage, and the second with hostage-taking. The third bill provides for monetary rewards for people informing on terrorist organizations.

In the 99th Congress, I have introduced the Anti-Nuclear Terrorism Act in order to help develop a way to screen nuclear power plant employees who have unescorted access to the facilities. The bill would amend the Atomic Energy Act of 1954 to allow the Nuclear Regulatory Commission to take fingerprints of employees and applicants, and to send them to the FBI for classification and comparison with identification files in order to determine if the applicant or employee has a criminal history. The bill would make infiltration of a U.S. nuclear facility more difficult by weeding out potential problems. Screening based on the federal criminal history would make it impossible for an employee fired for industrial sabotage or equally serious acts from simply going to another state and applying for employment. It would permit plant operators to check the criminal history records of on-board, as well as, prospective hires, to help ensure that anyone who might engage in violence and sabotage is weeded out. There would be a balancing of industry's need for that kind of sensitive information with the right of privacy of the individuals about whom information would be sought.

This year, I also introduced the Anti-Terrorism Act of 1985, which would for the first time make terrorism a crime in the United States, with a possible death penalty for terrorist acts that result in the loss of life. Surprisingly, there is no federal crime of terrorism in the United States, and much of the jurisdiction for terrorist-related crimes is fragmented among the FBI, BATF, FAA, Secret Service, and so forth. Moreover, homicide, the most basic of the terrorist acts, is not a federal offense except when it relates to the murder of a president or designated elected or appointed federal officials.

I have also introduced a bill to amend the Freedom of Information Act so we can legally withhold foreign counter-intelligence and terrorism information.

Finally, I am in the process of drafting a bill to deal with international terrorism by providing for extra-territoriality with regard to terrorist acts committed against United States persons or property abroad. More than half of the acts are committed against United States businessmen, diplomats, and soldiers serving overseas.

Appendix A

World Inventories of Plutonium

David Albright

INTRODUCTION

The amount of plutonium produced in commercial nuclear reactors is steadily increasing as the large number of plants built over the last decade come on line. Even if no additional commercial nuclear power plants are built, the amount of plutonium in used, or "spent," fuel will continue to grow as existing plants operate.

An efficient 1,000 Megawatt (MWe) light water reactor, the dominant commercial type, will discharge about 230 kilograms (506 pounds) of plutonium a year. The 260 nuclear power plants in the non-communist world operating at the beginning of 1985, with a combined capacity of about 200,000 MWe,[1] discharge roughly 45 metric tons (45,000 kilograms or 100,000 pounds) of plutonium a year. By the year 2000, the Western nuclear electricity capacity will be around 350,000 to 400,000 MWe, and about 80 to 90 metric tons of plutonium will be discharged each year.[2] A nuclear explosive can be built with eight kilograms of plutonium from commercial power reactors.

In order to use the plutonium in a nuclear explosive, it must first be chemically extracted from the spent fuel, a time-consuming operation and, because the spent fuel remains highly radioactive for a long time, a very hazardous one. But once plutonium is separated, it can be fabricated into a nuclear explosive within days or weeks. Thus, the "once through" fuel cycle, where the plutonium remains locked in the spent fuel and is disposed of permanently, is considered more "proliferation-resistant" than the "closed" fuel cycle, where the plutonium is chemically extracted in a reprocessing plant and used to fuel the current generation of reactors and breeder reactors. (Breeder reactors are designed to produce more plutonium than they consume. Ultimately, they would fuel themselves and thus provide a permanent replacement of the current generation of reactors, which require a continuous source of uranium to operate.)

If plutonium comes into widespread use as a commercial fuel (i.e., in a "plutonium economy"), the amounts of separated plutonium would greatly increase, along with the risks of undetected diversions from civilian to weapons use. As reprocessing technology develops, there would inevitably be intense efforts by the less-developed countries to obtain such technologies for themselves, and aggressive efforts by the industrialized supplier countries to export these technologies. As these reprocessing technologies spread, a significant technical barrier to proliferation would be destroyed in industrialized and developing countries alike. A large number of countries would gain access to enormous quantities of weapons-usable plutonium in the absence of an international verification and accounting system ("safeguards") capable of assuring that significant amounts of plutonium are not diverted to the manufacture of nuclear weapons. Furthermore, the risks of hijackings and thefts by terrorists will increase in proportion to the growing amounts of separated plutonium that are introduced into world commerce.

In the 1960s, many nations, particularly the United States, thought that breeder reactors would be firmly established by the end of this century and would eventually replace the current reactors, as worldwide uranium resources necessary to continue fueling them were depleted. The reprocessing of spent fuel from conventional reactors would supply the separated plutonium necessary to start up the breeder reactors. Afterwards, primarily plutonium-based breeder fuels would be reprocessed in order to extract the plutonium for reuse in the breeders.

By the early to mid-1970s, many in the United States and abroad began to see that the development of the commercial use of plutonium was unnecessary and could lead to wide-scale proliferation of nuclear weapons. The Ford and Carter administrations became so concerned that they ordered a halt to domestic reprocessing and curtailed the plutonium breeder development program. The Carter administration went further and sought, with limited success, to influence other nations to follow the U.S. example.

The Reagan administration resumed active promotion of reprocessing and breeder development at home and abroad. In 1983, however, the U.S. Congress cancelled the construction of the United States' one demonstration breeder, the Clinch River Breeder Reactor. Even though the U.S. government now maintains a large breeder research and development program, it will not fund the construction of any other demonstration-size breeders. Without government support, the U.S. nuclear industry is apparently unwilling to build either a demonstration breeder reactor or commercial reprocessing facilities, and thus it has effectively abandoned further large-scale development of these technologies until at least the next century.[3]

Several countries have remained committed to the development of both reprocessing of spent fuel from conventional reactors and to the complete breeder reactor fuel cycle, despite rising costs and increased political opposition. They believe that the benefits of energy security from the recycle of the separated plutonium and of waste disposal outweigh the proliferation risks. Faced with a drastic reduction in the number of planned breeder reactors, European countries and Japan are beginning to accelerate their plans to recycle their separated plutonium in conventional light water reactors.[4] The French electricity company announced in June that it will recycle its large, impending surplus of plutonium into its light water reactors.[5] The French utility will now have the largest commercial program for the recycle of plutonium in light water reactors in the world.

PLUTONIUM PRODUCTION

Plutonium is produced in any reactor fuel containing uranium-238 (U-238).[6] The isotope plutonium-239 (Pu-239) is produced when U-238 absorbs a neutron and becomes transformed into Pu-239. Some of the Pu-239 undergoes fission, and some of it absorbs an additional neutron. This lowers the fractional amount of Pu-239 in the resulting plutonium and increases the amounts of other plutonium isotopes, mainly plutonium-240, plutonium-241 and plutonium-242. Other reactions lead to the production of small amounts of plutonium-238.

Any discussion of the specific amounts and isotopic content of the plutonium produced in a nuclear reactor is complicated by the fact that these quantities depend not only on the type of reactor, but also on the way in which the reactor is operated. In particular, they depend on the initial fractional amount of uranium-238 in the fuel (its enrichment) and the mode of operation, especially the burnup of the fuel (that is, the degree of exposure of the fuel to neutrons).

Normally, commercial power reactors operate at a high rate of fuel burnup. Table A.1 lists the annual amount of plutonium discharged in spent fuel from the major types of commercial reactors if they ran year round at these high burnups.[7] Also shown in Table A.1 is the isotopic composition of this plutonium. At the fuel burnups typical of most spent fuel, the plutonium that is "reactor-grade" plutonium contains more than 19 percent Pu-240. In contrast, military reactors operate at a low burnup, and the resulting "weapon-grade" plutonium contains less than 7 percent Pu-240.[8,9]

The normal operating conditions of nuclear power reactors are designed to minimize the cost of the electric power produced. Any of the major power reactors, however, including the light water reactors, can be operated to produce weapon-grade plutonium, although there will be economic penalties in doing so. For example, a 1,000 MWe CANDU reactor run in a military production mode produces about 1,100 kilograms of weapon-grade plutonium per GWe (net) per year if the reactor runs year-round.[10]

The plutonium discharge rates in Table A.1 are normalized to nuclear power plants having a net electrical output of 1000 megawatts (MWe-net) all year. No reactor, however, operates at full power continuously. All reactors must shut down some of the time for refueling, maintenance, inspection and testing. The capacity factor provides a measure of what fraction of time a plant is at full power. It is defined as the ratio of the total electricity actually produced by a power reactor over a given time to the theoretical maximum output of the plant at its rated power level. Capacity factors vary a great deal among various types of reactors and among utilities and countries operating the reactors.

Most of the light water reactors (LWRs) in operation today are refueled once a year, although some now refuel less often.[11] The other major types of reactors, the CANDU reactor, the gas-graphite reactor or magnox reactor, and the light water graphite moderated reactor (LWGR), are refueled almost continuously. Thus the production rate for each type of reactor represents the total amount of plutonium that has been discharged from a reactor at the end of a one-year period under normal operating conditions. For LWRs that refuel less than once a year, the production rate is an average amount discharged over several years.

The plutonium discharge rate for a specific reactor can be computed by multiplying the discharge rate at a 100 percent capacity factor in Table A.1 by its capacity factor and its rated electric power output. For example, a 1,000 MWe light water reactor operating at a 70 percent capacity factor will discharge about 230 kilograms of plutonium each year. A 500 MWe LWR operating at the same capacity factor will discharge about 115 kilograms of plutonium a year.

PLUTONIUM DISCHARGED IN SPENT FUEL

Through the end of 1984, the total amount of plutonium discharged in spent fuel from conventional power reactors in the western world is estimated to be about 300 metric tons of plutonium, of which about two thirds is from LWRs (see Tables A.2, A.3, and A.4).[12] Through 1990 and 2000, the estimated amount of plutonium in spent fuel is about 650 and 1,350 metric tons, respectively, of which about three quarters will be from LWRs.[13] Some of the plutonium discharged has already been separated at reprocessing plants.

From 1984 through 2000, the amount of plutonium from western LWRs alone will grow fivefold, while the installed nuclear power capacity will only double. This reflects the fact that the amount of spent fuel discharged, and therefore the amount of plutonium, continues to grow each time a reactor is refueled.

For other types of reactors, the amount of plutonium discharged will triple by the year 2000. Over a third of this plutonium will be from gas-graphite reactors, almost all of which will have been shut down by the end of this century.

Table A.5 estimates the amount of plutonium in spent fuel in the communist world, as well as the amount of plutonium that will be discharged in the future. Because of the large uncertainties in the future nuclear capacities of communist countries, the amounts in Table A.5 are mainly given for comparative purposes.

WORLDWIDE REPROCESSING FACILITIES

Over 15 countries have been known to be involved in civilian fuel reprocessing activities.[14] Most of these programs have been relatively small, and some of them have processed fuels with only trace amounts of plutonium.[15]

Currently, five countries operate reprocessing plants to extract plutonium in spent fuel from conventional power reactors. France and the United Kingdom have the largest programs and offer reprocessing services to several other countries that normally take back the plutonium and residual uranium (see next section). India, Japan and West Germany have pilot reprocessing plants. All of these countries are planning to expand their reprocessing capabilities. The French and British programs will expand the most, while West Germany and Japan have recently approved the construction of commercial reprocessing plants, and India is building a new plant and planning another one.

Several additional countries are building facilities to reprocess power reactor fuel. Argentina and Brazil are each building a pilot plant.[16] Pakistan is still trying to build a pilot reprocessing plant,[17] has operated an experimental-scale facility at Pinstech and completed another facility nearby called New Labs.[18] The New Labs facility can separate up to 10 to 20 kilograms of plutonium a year, although as of mid-1985 it apparently had not processed any plutonium-containing fuel.[19]

Finally, Belgium has postponed its decision to restart the old Eurochemic commercial reprocessing plant. It has doubts about the cost-effectiveness of reprocessing and has encountered problems in obtaining enough foreign customers to finance its operation.[20]

Tables A.6 and A.7 detail the present and future reprocessing capacities for spent fuel from conventional reactors for the major non-communist facilities.

The Soviet Union and the United States do not operate full-size reprocessing plants to reprocess power reactor spent fuel, although both operate several large reprocessing plants to recover plutonium from government production reactors for nuclear weapons. Presently, it is doubtful that the United States will build a commercial-size plant. Little information exists about Soviet intentions, although, because of a slowdown in their breeder reactor program, their plans for building a commercial-size reprocessing facility for power reactor fuel have apparently been deferred for quite some time.[21] However, they do have a pilot plant that reprocesses both light water reactor and breeder reactor spent fuel.[22]

China is currently reprocessing spent fuel to obtain plutonium only for nuclear weapons. China, however, has expressed interest in developing large-scale reprocessing facilities for power reactor fuel, since it is planning to build several nuclear power plants in the next couple of decades. In addition to reprocessing Chinese spent fuel, these facilities might also reprocess some foreign fuel. China has offered to take spent fuel from nations in Europe with the option to reprocess the fuel later.[23] The West German government has reversed its earlier objections to the shipment of German spent fuel to China.[24] The government will now consider the shipment of a small amount of spent fuel to China.

Israel reportedly has a reprocessing facility that is separating weapon-grade plutonium for use in nuclear weapons. The reprocessing facility probably began operation after 1969,[25] although little public information exists about the amount of plutonium separated there.

As of mid-1985, no other country is known to be attempting to obtain reprocessing technology to extract plutonium, although some countries still might harbor hopes of eventually obtaining reprocessing technology, most notably South Korea and Taiwan. Both countries tried to obtain reprocessing plants in the 1970s from France; however, the United States stopped the sale of these plants.[26]

South Korea admits in one of its recent annual atomic energy reports that the "prospects for reprocessing spent fuel are uncertain in the near future."[27] Whether it has abandoned all hopes of eventually reprocessing its spent fuel (which, incidentally, will contain a considerable amount of plutonium at the end of this century) is unclear. (See Table A.2.) Two recent incidents suggest otherwise.

Last year the U.S. State Department pressured the Canadian government to stop a joint research program with South Korea that would have looked at a "tandem fuel cycle" in which uranium recovered from spent light water reactor fuel would be recycled into a Canadian CANDU reactor.[28] The studies were part of the first phase of a technology exchange process between Canada and South Korea. Whether anything would have developed is unclear. Following phases might have involved the transfer of some technology from Canada to South Korea. What would have been the fate of the plutonium in the LWR spent fuel is not totally clear, although Canadian officials have strongly denied that the program with Korea involved plutonium extraction technologies.[29] An Atomic Energy of Canada Ltd. spokesman said that the project needed approval from the United States and "for a variety of reasons" the United States refused.[30] One probable reason for U.S. refusal is that the United States has a long-standing policy to oppose any type of reprocessing in Korea. However, some suspect that there were commercial reasons for blocking the joint study.[31] U.S. firms are bidding to sell South Korea light water reactors and might have felt that the joint research program would damage their chances of selling Korea the reactors.

The second incident was the announcement that Britain will be willing to help South Korea build a reprocessing plant around the turn of the century.[32] Sir Walter Marshall, chairman of the Central Electricity Generating Board, said in Korea last spring that once Korea has a "large" nuclear power program, around the turn of the century, it will have a legitimate reason to build a reprocessing plant.[33]

Some countries are also reprocessing small amounts of spent plutonium fuel from breeder reactors and have plans to expand their programs to reprocess greater amounts of fuel. Britain and France operate the largest facilities, while Japan and the Soviet Union operate small ones. Several countries are building facilities to reprocess small quantities of breeder fuel. These include the United States, Italy, India and, possibly, West Germany. Moreover, plutonium fuel used in light water reactors and heavy water reactors will also be reprocessed in the future.[34] A detailed treatment of these facilities, however, is outside the scope of this report.

REPROCESSING FOREIGN SPENT FUEL IN BRITAIN AND FRANCE

Commercial reprocessing cannot be discussed without mentioning the reprocessing services offered by Britain and France. These services have been a magnet to foreign customers since the 1960s. Initially, the service was limited to fuel irradiated in gas-graphite reactors, but now primarily involves spent fuel from light water reactors. Without the contracts with foreign customers to reprocess light water reactor spent fuel, it is unlikely that commercial-scale reprocessing facilities for this type of fuel would have developed.

Britain first began offering reprocessing services to foreign customers in the 1960s at the Windscale reprocessing plant. Since that time they have regularly reprocessed spent fuel from the Italian and Japanese gas-graphite reactors. Britain also began reprocessing foreign LWR spent fuel in 1969 at a facility at Windscale; however, because of an accident it was closed in 1973.[35]

Soon afterward, in 1976, France began processing foreign spent LWR fuel at the La Hague facility. Its customers include Belgium, West Germany, Japan, Netherlands, Sweden and Switzerland. Most of the light water reactor fuel reprocessed at La Hague so far has been from foreign customers (see Table A.8). France has also reprocessed spent fuel from the Spanish gas-graphite reactor, although in this case France has kept the recovered plutonium.

Britain and France are greatly expanding their capacity to reprocess foreign spent LWR fuel. France is constructing a new facility at La Hague, UP3, with a capacity of 800 metric tons of uranium a year, while Britain is constructing a new facility at Sellafield (formerly Windscale), called THORP, with a capacity of 600 metric tons of uranium.[36] Both are expected to begin operation around 1990. Japanese and West German utilities are the largest customers, while Belgian, Dutch, Italian, Swedish and Swiss utilities have also contracted to have spent fuel reprocessed (see Table A.9). Recently, the Swedish utilities decided to drop all their reprocessing contracts and are now looking for substitutes to take over their contracts.[37] The best prospects are the Japanese and Germans.

France has minimized its financial risks of building and operating the new UP3 facility (historically commercial reprocessing is a very expensive and accident-prone business) by requiring the foreign customers to pay for the investment of the entire facility (a portion of it in advance) and the first 10 years of its operation, plus an additional 25 percent fee. The British have used a similar financing method, although some of the fees are paid by British utilities whose oxide fuel will also be reprocessed at THORP. Moreover, all the customers must take back all of the radioactive waste.

France has so far committed to reprocess about 7,200 metric tons of spent LWR fuel at La Hague. About 1,200 metric tons are being reprocessed in the existing UP2 facility. A large percentage of this spent fuel has already been reprocessed (see Table A.8). France is committed to reprocess 6,000 metric tons of foreign spent fuel in UP3 during its first 10 years of operation. France now expects to process 7,000 tons during this same time period. Since foreign utilities contracted for percentages of the capacity of UP3 during its first 10 years of operation, not exact tonnages, the extra capacity is theirs.[38] Even if they do not use the extra capacity, they still must pay the same amount.

The United Kingdom has contracted to reprocess 4,000 metric tons of foreign spent LWR fuel.[39] Originally, Britain planned to reprocess only 3,100 tons, but the reprocessing needs of British customers have turned out to be less than expected.

In total, about 12,000 metric tons of foreign LWR spent fuel are expected to be reprocessed in Britain and France, mostly from West Germany and Japan. Since LWR spent fuel contains about 0.9 percent plutonium, this fuel will yield about 110 metric tons of plutonium (see Table A.9).

The amount of spent fuel contracted to be reprocessed by Britain and France could increase, as both continue to seek out new customers. Because the French UP2 facility is performing more smoothly than in the past (when it was plagued by frequent stoppages because of accidents), France has offered to reprocess an additional 1,000 metric of spent fuel in the UP2 facility, prior to the time it is converted into UP2-800 in the early 1990s.[40] (UP2-800 is reserved primarily for French spent fuel.) It is unclear whether France will find any takers for the new offer, particularly because Sweden can be expected to underbid any French offer in order to get rid of its contracts. Britain is also beginning to look for customers for the second 10 years of THORP's operation.[41]

PLUTONIUM SEPARATED IN CIVILIAN AND MILITARY NUCLEAR PROGRAMS

Some 60 metric tons of plutonium, which was produced in civilian power reactors, have been separated at major reprocessing facilities in the non-communist world through 1984 (see Table A.10). Thus, only about one fifth of the total non-communist world civilian plutonium inventory of 300 metric tons has been separated from power reactor fuel. Most of this plutonium has been separated from gas-graphite reactor spent fuel in France and the United Kingdom. So far, only a small portion of the plutonium from light water reactor spent fuel, which contains most of the plutonium in the spent fuel, has been separated. Most of this plutonium has been separated in France and Japan.

A much smaller quantity of plutonium has been separated from research and prototype reactor fuel. While an estimate of the amount of plutonium separated from spent fuel from these reactors is outside the scope of this paper, this inventory of separated plutonium should not be overlooked. Israel uses a research reactor to produce its plutonium. Moreover, India's nuclear detonation in 1974 used plutonium separated from research reactor fuel at the Trombay reprocessing plant. This facility was partially decommissioned in 1972 but has recently restarted. It will have sufficient capacity to reprocess fuel from India's two main research reactors. The spent fuel from these reactors has a low burnup and, as a result, contains weapon-grade plutonium. Each year these reactors will produce about 35 kilograms of weapon-grade plutonium.[42]

Plutonium from a Canadian research reactor might have been used in U.S. nuclear weapons. Weapon-grade plutonium produced in a Canadian heavy water research reactor was sold to the United States in the 1950s and early 1960s.[43] The spent fuel was transported to the United States and reprocessed at U.S. military reprocessing facilities. The resulting weapon-grade plutonium was clearly intended to be used for military purposes and most likely ended up in U.S. nuclear weapons.[44]

By far the largest inventories of separated plutonium are found in the nuclear weapons stockpiles of the five nuclear weapons states. The Soviet Union and the United States each has roughly 100 metric tons of weapon-grade plutonium in their stockpiles.[45] Britain, France and China have considerably smaller stockpiles of weapon-grade plutonium. Each country's stockpile is estimated to contain less than 5 metric tons of weapon-grade plutonium.[46-48]

Another significant inventory of non-civilian plutonium is the fuel-grade plutonium produced in the weapon-states' dual purpose reactors. Britain has produced about 5 metric tons of fuel-grade plutonium in its military reactors,[49] and the United States has produced about 8 metric tons of fuel-grade plutonium in the "N" reactor at Hanford, Washington.[50] Any fuel-grade plutonium in the Soviet stockpile is already included in the estimate of its total plutonium stockpile mentioned above.

In sum, about 60 metric tons of plutonium have been separated from civilian spent fuel. Military stockpiles of plutonium are estimated to contain somewhat over 200 metric tons of plutonium. Because the exact amount of plutonium in each nuclear weapon state is classified, these estimates of military plutonium contain a great deal of uncertainty. However, it is clear that the current military stockpile of plutonium is considerably larger than the civilian stockpile of plutonium.

THE FUTURE GROWTH IN CIVILIAN SEPARATED PLUTONIUM

The rate at which plutonium is currently separated from power reactor spent fuel in the non-communist world is about 7 metric tons a year.[51] A little over half of the plutonium is from fuel irradiated in gas-graphite reactors and the rest from spent light water reactor fuel. Until about the mid-1990s, the rate at which plutonium is separated from gas-graphite fuel will remain roughly constant. Afterwards, the amount separated each year will decrease, since most of the gas-graphite reactors will shut down in the 1990s. On the other hand, the rate at which plutonium is separated from light water reactor spent fuel will grow to about 7 metric tons by 1990, about 25 metric tons by 1995, and reach 30 metric tons in the year 2000.[52]

The amount of plutonium in power reactor spent fuel is already larger than the amount in weapons. If the commercial reprocessing industry continues to grow, it will eventually extract more plutonium from power reactor spent fuel than will be in the nuclear weapons stockpiles. The rate at which plutonium will be extracted from civilian fuel in the 1990s will greatly exceed the rate at which plutonium is projected to be separated from military spent fuel. Sometime in the mid to late 1990s the total amount of plutonium extracted from civilian spent fuel will exceed the total amount of plutonium that will be in the nuclear weapon stockpiles. Because of uncertainties in any estimate of future military stockpiles of plutonium, particularly in the Soviet Union, the exact date is difficult to predict.

Through 1990, the total amount of plutonium that will be separated from power reactor fuel, if current reprocessing plans are realized, is about 110 metric tons of plutonium. Through the year 2000, about 390 metric tons of plutonium will be separated.[53]

The above estimate assumes that the reprocessing capacity in Table A.7 for light water reactor spent fuel will be fully utilized. Current indications are that the capacities might not be. Already Belgium has encountered difficulty in obtaining orders from foreign customers for its facility, and France might not be able to find enough customers for its current facility at La Hague (see previous section). Moreover, any of the plants could experience operating difficulties that could severely hamper their performance. And, finally, the planned Japanese and German plants could encounter significant delays because of political opposition to their construction.

A slightly different estimate of the total amount of plutonium to be separated by the end of the century can be derived from information about the amount of spent fuel each country has already contracted for reprocessing abroad or has committed to reprocessing in a domestic plant. Table A.11 shows that about 350 metric tons of plutonium will be separated from such fuel through 2000. These stockpiles will accumulate in countries, the majority of which are non-nuclear weapon states.

CONCLUSION

By the end of this century, about 350 to 400 metric tons of plutonium will have been separated from power reactor spent fuel in the western world, if commercial reprocessing develops as outlined in this paper. Beginning at the end of the 1990s, an additional 30 metric tons of plutonium will have been separated each year in these commercial facilities. In the first decade of the next century, another 300 metric tons of plutonium will be separated from civilian spent fuel, increasing the total amount of plutonium that will be separated to about 650 to 700 metric tons of plutonium, which will be almost double the amount of plutonium that will be separated through the year 2000.

Today, about 7,500 nuclear weapons could be constructed from the 60 tons of plutonium already separated, with more than 30,000 potential weapons in the 240 metric tons remaining in unreprocessed spent fuel.[54] If 390 metric tons of plutonium are indeed separated through the year 2000, then the number of "bomb equivalents" would be some 49,000 nuclear weapons.

Although it is not suggested that this many weapons would or could be built, it does help to illustrate an important point. The plutonium necessary for a nuclear weapon is just a minute fraction of the amount already separated, let alone the amount that will be separated. As a result, separated plutonium must be carefully safeguarded against diversion by nations and secured against theft by terrorists. Yet it is doubtful that the best possible safeguards and security could provide absolute assurance against losses of small but weapon-significant amounts of plutonium.

Inevitably, in any system involving reprocessing and the commercial use of plutonium, some of it will be lost, and accounting errors and other uncertainties might mask small diversions. If only 1 percent of the plutonium is unaccounted for through the end of this century, then as much as 4 metric tons—or enough for almost 500 bombs—will have been "lost" somewhere in the system. It would be impossible to know if several bombs' worth of plutonium had been diverted or stolen.

Currently, only 20 percent of the total inventory of plutonium produced in power reactors in the western world has been separated, leaving 80 percent of the plutonium still "locked" in highly radioactive spent fuel. This plutonium is inaccessible for making nuclear weapons. Thus the danger of proliferation is reduced when commercial reprocessing is avoided. There is still time to steer away from our present path toward a plutonium economy.

NOTES

1. L.R. Howles, "Nuclear Station Achievement 1984, Annual Review," *Nuclear Engineering International*, May 1985, pp. 53-57. Only reactors that produce more than 150 MWe are counted in this survey.
2. Future estimates of nuclear capacity in the western world are highly uncertain. See Energy Information Administration, "Commercial Nuclear Power 1984, Prospects for the United States and the World," DOE/EIA-0438(84), Washington, D.C., November 1984, and Nuclear Energy Agency, "Summary of Nuclear Power and Fuel Cycle Data in OECD Member Countries," April 1985.
3. For example, a spokesman for Bechtel National, which had proposed starting the nearly completed Barnwell reprocessing plant, with the federal government as the principal customer, said, "If the government doesn't do something [to back reprocessing], there is nothing the private sector can do." *Nuclear Fuel*, May 7, 1984.

4. For a more complete discussion of this point, as well as the entire question of deferring any further reprocessing, see: D. Albright and H. Feiveson, "The Deferral of Reprocessing," *F.A.S. Public Interest Report*, Journal of the Federation of American Scientists, Vol. 38, No. 2, Washington, D.C., February 1985.
5. "EdF Takes the Mox Recycle Plunge to Utilize Reprocessed Pu, U Stocks," *Nucleonics Week*, June 13, 1985, pp. 1-2.
6. The main types of nuclear power reactors in the world are the light water reactor (LWR), the graphite moderated gas-cooled reactor (also called the magnox reactor), a heavy water moderated reactor called the CANDU reactor, and a light water graphite moderated reactor (LWGR) found in the Soviet Union. The liquid metal fast breeder reactor (LMFBR) is now under commercial development.
7. Often, the rate at which plutonium is discharged in spent fuel is called the plutonium production rate, although, strictly speaking, the amount of plutonium produced annually in a reactor operating at a high fuel burnup is considerably greater than the amount listed in the table, since much of the plutonium fissions. In fact, enough plutonium fissions in a LWR while the fuel is being irradiated to produce about one-third of the energy released by the reactor. The plutonium discharged in the spent fuel is also not the entire inventory of plutonium in a reactor—substantially more plutonium remains in the reactor.
8. There are two other grades of plutonium: fuel-grade plutonium contains between 7 and 19 percent Pu-240 and supergrade plutonium contains less than 3 percent Pu-240.
9. Pu-239 and Pu-240 are "fissile," that is, fissionable by thermal or "slow" neutrons that are produced in conventional reactors. All plutonium isotopes, however, are fissionable by the "fast" neutrons produced in a nuclear explosive. While reactor-grade plutonium and fuel-grade plutonium are less desirable for use in a nuclear explosive than weapon-grade plutonium and may have less predictability of explosive yield, nuclear weapons designers have repeatedly stated that reactor-grade plutonium could be used directly in nuclear explosives.
10. "Heavy-Element Concentrations in Power Reactors," SND-120-2, NUS Corporation, Clearwater, Florida, May 1977. The weapon-grade plutonium has 94 percent plutonium-239, which corresponds to a burnup of 1,200 MWt-d/MTU and 1 kilogram of plutonium per MTU. The thermal efficiency of the CANDU is assumed to be 0.28. The total amount of plutonium discharged after one year when low burnup fuel is used is greater than when high burnup fuel is used. The amount of plutonium in each metric ton of spent fuel decreases at low burnup, requiring significantly more uranium fuel to be run through the reactor.
11. Op. cit., Howles.
12. The amount of plutonium discharged in spent fuel in each country in the western world through 1984 is calculated from the electricity production of each reactor. The gross electricity production for each reactor in the western world through 1984 is listed in *Nucleonics Week* (January 31, 1985). Unfortunately, the net electricity production is not available. As a result, the plutonium discharge rates or conversion factors in Table A.1 have been adjusted to account for gross rather than net electricity production. In general, this adjustment lowers these rates by about 5 to 10 percent depending on the type of reactor. (The necessary information to derive the change in these values can be found in "General Information," *Nuclear Engineering International*, October Supplement, October 1984.)

The use of a fixed plutonium discharge rate leads to only a rough approximation of the actual amount of plutonium discharged in spent fuel. In actuality, the fuel burnup in an individual reactor can change considerably over its lifetime. Further, the average burnup achieved in each type of reactor has increased over time. Consequently, the method outlined above underestimates the amount of plutonium discharged each year if the burnups are actually lower than assumed and overestimates it if they are higher. The values in the tables, however, should in general be accurate to within about 10 to 20 percent, although in some cases considerably larger errors could result, particularly in countries with an inexperienced or small program.

13. The amount of plutonium discharged after 1984 is based on estimating future electricity production in each country. The projected net nuclear electricity capacity of the western world is from an estimate developed by NUKEM, Inc. ("NUKEM Market Report on the Nuclear Fuel Cycle," 5/84, May 1984, NUKEM, GmbH, Hanau, Federal Republic of Germany). NUKEM's projection has been modified in some cases to account for more recent information. NUKEM estimates the nuclear power capacity of the western world in 1990 at about 280 GWe (net) and in 2000 at almost 370 GWe (net). Estimated capacity factors for each country and type of reactor are extrapolated from actual performance to date (for example, see Howles, op. cit.). In general, the capacity factors varied between 55 and 70 percent, with the LWRs in the United States at the low end and the LWRs in European countries and CANDUs in Canada at the high end. Reactors in some countries like Finland and Switzerland are projected to have significantly higher capacity factors, while reactors in countries such as Pakistan and India are currently expected to have lower capacity factors.

The future estimates of plutonium discharged in spent fuel have several additional uncertainties (see previous footnote). The largest one is the estimation of the future nuclear power capacities that have historically been considerably overoptimistic, although the NUKEM estimates appear to be conservative. Another unknown is whether capacity factors will increase. The general trend today is toward higher capacity factors, although it is not certain that this trend will be sustained over the next 10 to 20 years as the existing plants become older.

Not included in this analysis is the effect on plutonium production of the extended fuel burnup programs, the deterioration in the capacity factor attributable to reactor aging, and plutonium recycled into LWRs. All of these effects will tend to lower the amount of plutonium discharged in spent fuel in the future.

14. P.J. Mellinger, K.M. Harmon and L.T. Lakey, "A Summary of Nuclear Fuel Reprocessing Activities Around the World," Pacific Northwest Laboratory, PNL-4981, November 1984. This report lists 17 countries known to be or have been engaged in fuel reprocessing activities. The 15 countries that have been involved in civilian reprocessing are Argentina, Belgium, Brazil, Canada, France, Federal Republic of Germany, India, Italy, Japan, Mexico, Pakistan, Spain, the Soviet Union, the United Kingdom and the United States. Six countries separate plutonium for nuclear weapons. These countries are China, France, the Soviet Union, the United Kingdom, the United States and, reportedly, Israel. Spain no longer has a reprocessing program, and Canada currently operates only a small reprocessing research and development program. The one remaining small facility in Italy will reprocess breeder reactor fuel. Mexico was thought at one time to be building a pilot-scale facility.

Taiwan is suspected of having operated a small reprocessing facility. U.S. government intelligence reports indicated that Taiwan had been secretly engaged in reprocessing in the early or mid 1970s (see S. Weissman and H. Krosney, *The Islamic Bomb*, New York: Times Books, 1981, p. 153). Several countries in Europe, such as Sweden and Yugoslavia, have operated small lab-scale reprocessing facilities.

South Korea and Taiwan operate "hot cells" to examine spent fuel. These facilities are not reprocessing facilities because they do not extract the plutonium in the spent fuel; however, possession of a hot cell enables a country to acquire experience in chemically dissolving spent fuel and in handling highly radioactive materials.
15. For example, Spain's facility reprocessed research reactor fuel that contained highly enriched uranium (enriched to over 90 percent in the isotope uranium-235). Such fuel contains only trace amounts of plutonium.
16. Brazil also operates a lab-size facility. See L.S. Spector, *The Spread of Nuclear Weapons 1984, Nuclear Proliferation Today* (New York: Vintage Books, 1984).
17. Originally France was to have supplied the facility, although it stopped its assistance in the late 1970s. Pakistan has continued to try to build the facility, although with limited success (see *Nuclear Fuel*, March 26, 1984).
18. Thomas W. Graham, "South Asian Nuclear Proliferation and National Security Chronology," Center for International Affairs, Massachusetts Institute of Technology, Cambridge, Mass., 1985.
19. Op. cit., Graham.
20. "Synatom Sets Up Belgoprocess," *Nuclear Engineering International*, May 1985, p. 7.
21. See Mellinger, op. cit., or "Soviet Turning to Spent Fuel Storage as Breeder Slowdown Delays Reprocessing," *Nuclear Fuel*, September 27, 1982, p. 15.
22. Op. cit., Mellinger.
23. "West Germany Consortium Sends Offers to Take Spent Fuel to China," *Nuclear Fuel*, July 16, 1984, pp. 2-3.
24. "Bonn Will Consider Sending to China about 150 MTU of German Spent Fuel," *Nuclear Fuel*, June 17, 1985. The shipments of spent fuel to China would be in the context of an eventual Chinese purchase of a German nuclear reactor. The Chinese would have to guarantee that the spent fuel would remain under international safeguards and would be used for peaceful purposes. The spent fuel, according to the China Nuclear Energy Industry Corp., would be stored until about 2010 next to a planned reprocessing facility.
25. Op. cit., Spector, p. 146.
26. Op. cit., *Islamic Bomb*.
27. Ministry of Science and Technology, Republic of Korea, "1983 Atomic Energy Activities in Korea," Atomic Energy Bureau, Korea, p. 13.
28. T. Shorrock and O. Gadacz, "U.S. Intervention in Nuclear Fuel Project Still a Mystery," *Business Korea*, April 1985, p. 47.
29. Op. cit, Shorrock.
30. P. Taylor, "Ottawa Denies U.S. Killed A-deal," *Toronto Globe and Mail*, October 16, 1984.
31. Op. cit., Shorrock.
32. *Nucleonics Week*, June 7, 1985, p. 11.
33. Ibid.
34. For example, see footnote x in Table A.7.
35. The facility might restart during 1985 as a small R&D facility for oxide fuel reprocessing.
36. THORP's nominal capacity is 1,200 metric tons of uranium per year, but only 6,000 metric tons of uranium will be reprocessed during the first 10 years of its operation.
37. For example, see, "Swedish and German Utilities Exploring Spent Fuel Swap," *Nucleonics Week*, February 14, 1985, and "Part of Swedish Share in UP3 Production Transferred to Chubu Electric Power Co.," *Nuclear Fuel*, June 3, 1985.

38. "Secondary Market for Reprocessing Seen after Cogema Raises Capacity Projection," *Nuclear Fuel*, June 20, 1983.
39. "U.K. AGR Slowdown and Higher Burnups Free up 900 Tonnes of THORP Capacity," *Nuclear Fuel*, September 13, 1982, p. 3.
40. "Cogema Offering More Near-Term Reprocessing," *Nuclear Fuel*, October 22, 1984.
41. "BNFL Reprocessing Prices Could Drop If Order Books Grow by 6,000 MT," *Nuclear Fuel*, May 21, 1984.
42. The CIRUS research reactor is a 40 MWt natural uranium heavy water research reactor. CIRUS produces about 9.4 kilograms of Pu-239 each year (Office of Technology Assessment [OTA], *Nuclear Proliferation and Safeguards*, Appendix 2, Part 1, 1977, Table B-2, p. 230) and has a fuel inventory of 10.5 MTU (*Directory of Nuclear Reactors*, vol. III, Research, Test and Experimental Reactors, International Atomic Energy Agency [IAEA], Vienna, p. 281).

    Western scientists have speculated that the CIRUS reactor produced at least 50 kilograms of plutonium during the decade 1964-74 and that it would later have yielded roughly 10 kilograms per year ("India Will Run FBTR with Mixed-Carbide Fuel Next Year—Probably with Cirus Plutonium," *Nuclear Fuel*, February 28, 1983.

    The yearly discharge of plutonium from the CIRUS reactor can also be estimated from public information. Generally, the fuel burnup of heavy water natural uranium research reactors is low (OTA, op. cit., pp. 97, 98). According to the IAEA *Directory of Nuclear Reactors*, the average burnup of CIRUS fuel is 900 MWt-d/MTU. Using data for the CANDU reactor, which is similar to the CIRUS reactor, the fuel at this burnup has a plutonium content of about 0.9 kilograms of plutonium per MTU ("Heavy-Element Concentrations in Power Reactors," SND-120-2, NUS Corporation, Clearwater, Florida, May 1977, fig. C-2). At this burnup, the plutonium contains about 95 percent Pu-239 ("Heavy Element," op. cit., fig. C-3). The yearly discharge of spent fuel from the CIRUS reactor can be estimated by the following method. The amount of energy produced by the fuel in a core of 10.5 MTU at a burnup of 900 MWt-d/MTU is 9,450 MWt-d. At a power of 40 MWt, the core lasts for 236 full-power days, which is consistent with the core being replaced roughly once a year. Thus, in one year, about 9.5 kilograms of plutonium are produced, or about 9.0 kilograms of Pu-239, which agrees with above value listed by OTA.

    The R-5 or Dhruva research reactor is a 100 MWt natural uranium heavy water reactor that will begin operation in 1985. Since it is similar to the CIRUS reactor, the annual discharge of spent fuel and plutonium from Dhruva can be calculated by simply scaling the data on the CIRUS reactor. Therefore, each year Dhruva produces about 25 kilograms of weapon-grade plutonium and discharges about 25 metric tons of uranium.
43. W. Eggleston, *Canada's Nuclear Story* (London: Harrap Research Publications, 1966).
44. It is estimated that roughly 100 or 200 kilograms of weapon-grade plutonium were sold to the United States during this period. The amount of plutonium is estimated from details about the operating history of the NRU reactor (Eggleston, op. cit.) and plutonium production data ("Heavy Element," op. cit.).
45. Frank von Hippel, David Albright and Barbara Levi, "U.S. and Soviet Stockpiles of Fissile Material," Report #PU/CEES 168, Princeton University, Center for Energy and Environmental Studies, 1985, forthcoming. The U.S. estimate was made in collaboration with Thomas B. Cochran and Milton Hoenig of the Natural Resources Defense Council, who have made similar estimates. Their results will be

published in Thomas Cochran, William M. Arkin and Milton M. Hoenig, *Nuclear Weapons Databook, Volume II: U.S. Nuclear Weapons Management, Resources, and Production* (Cambridge, MA.: Ballinger, forthcoming).

46. The British are estimated to have a little less than 3 metric tons of weapon-grade plutonium (J. Simpson, *The Independent Nuclear State, the United States, Britain, and the Military Atom* (London: MacMillan Press Ltd., 1983), appendix 4.

47. France has several sources of weapon-grade plutonium. Its G1 reactor produced a small amount of plutonium. A publicly unknown amount of weapon-grade plutonium was produced in its early gas-graphite power reactors. Another amount comes from its prototype breeder reactor, Phenix (see below). Plutonium for the military has also been produced in the twin Celestin reactors located at Marcoule. But most of its weapon-grade plutonium was produced in two small reactors, the G2 and G3 gas-graphite reactors.

The total amount of plutonium produced in the G2 and G3 reactors can be estimated from the electricity production of these reactors. Multiplying together the following terms gives the amount of plutonium produced in them: electricity production (*Nucleonics Week*, various issues), a thermal efficiency of 0.153 ("General Information," *Nuclear Engineering International*, October Supplement, October 1984), and a weapon-grade plutonium conversion factor of 0.83 to 0.91 grams of plutonium per MWt-d (S.E. Turner, et al., Southern Sciences Applications, Inc., "Criticality Studies of Graphite-Moderated Production Reactors, SSA-125, prepared for the U.S. Arms Control and Disarmament Agency, January 1980). Thus, in total, G2 and G3 have produced about 2.5 to 2.8 metric tons of weapon-grade plutonium (see also footnote d in Table A.10).

The amount of weapon-grade plutonium produced in the blanket of the Phenix breeder reactor can be crudely estimated. Phenix can produce up to 115 kilograms of plutonium in its blanket each year; however, a more realistic figure is about 75 kilograms of weapon-grade plutonium (Jean-Pierre Pharabod, Laboratoire de Physique Nucleaire des Hautes Energies, Ecole Polytechnique, personal communication, 1984). Phenix has operated since 1974 and thus has produced about 0.7 metric tons of plutonium.

In sum, the "G" reactors and Phenix have produced about 3 to 3.5 metric tons of plutonium. The other French sources of weapon-grade plutonium should not increase this quantity significantly.

48. Little information exists about the Chinese stockpile of plutonium. It is known that much of the fissile material in Chinese nuclear weapons has been weapon-grade uranium. Thus, this suggests that the Chinese have not produced a large plutonium stockpile. Moreover, it is doubtful that this stockpile is larger than either the British or French stockpiles. China is estimated to have fewer warheads than either the British or French and to have fewer tactical weapons, which tend to use more plutonium (see Nuclear Weapons Databook Staff, "Nuclear Weapons," in *World Armaments and Disarmament: SIPRI Yearbook 1985*, Philadelphia: Taylor and Francis, 1985).

One of the few sources of information on the rate at which weapon-grade plutonium is produced in China is H.M. Gobbel, *VR China: Atomwirtschaft und Politik* (Munich: Tridont-Verlag, 1980) (results quoted in H. Grupp and A. Schmalenstror, *Atome Fur Den Krieg*, Ein Projekt am Institut fur Energie und Umweltforschung Heidelberg e.V. [Verlag Kilner Volksblatt, 1983]). Gobbel was a German exchange scientist who spent some years in China. Her book contains a brief description of several of the fissile material production facilities in China. She lists two plutonium production reactors and a tritium production reactor. The larger plutonium production reactor (600 MWt), which is located at the Yumen reactor complex, began operation in 1967 and produces about 200 kilograms of weapon-grade plutonium a year. The other one at Bautou has a power of 100 MWt and began in 1964. She states that it produces only 10 kilograms of weapon-grade plutonium a year. The tritium production facility apparently can also be used to produce plutonium.

49. Op. cit., Simpson, appendix 4.
50. Op. cit., Cochran.
51. Based on data in Table A.7, it is estimated that about 4 metric tons of plutonium will be separated from gas-graphite fuel and about 3 metric tons from light water reactor spent fuel. The light water reactor and gas-graphite spent fuel are estimated to contain, respectively, 9 kilograms of plutonium per metric ton of uranium and 2.5 kilograms of plutonium per metric ton of uranium.
52. These estimates on the amount of plutonium separated from LWR spent fuel are based on an increase in reprocessing capacity described in Table A.7. The spent fuel is estimated to contain about 9 kilograms of plutonium per metric ton of uranium.
53. The estimates are derived from information in Tables A.4, A.7 and A.10. Through 2000 most of the plutonium will be separated from light water reactor spent fuel. Based on data in Tables A.7 and A.10, about 270 metric tons of plutonium will have been separated from LWR spent fuel through 2000. Using data in Table A.4 and assuming that almost all the gas-graphite spent fuel will be reprocessed by the year 2000, about 110 metric tons of plutonium will have been separated from gas-graphite fuel by the end of this century. The rest of the plutonium will be from CANDU spent fuel and advanced gas reactor spent fuel.
54. Each warhead is assumed to require eight kilograms of reactor-grade plutonium.

Table A.1. Plutonium Discharge Rate and Isotopic Composition, by Type of Power Reactor.

Reactor	Plutonium Discharged[a] (kg. Pu/GWe [net]-year)	Typical Isotopic Composition of Plutonium in Spent Fuel[b] (percent by weight)				
		Pu-238	Pu-239	Pu-240	Pu-241	Pu-242
LWR[c]	330	2.5	58.5	24	11	4
CANDU[d]	650	—[e]	68	24.5	6	1.6
Magnox[f]	800	—[e]	76	20	4	—
LWGR[g]	300	0.7	48	35	10.3	6
LMFBR[h]						
Core plus blanket	220	—	70	25	3	2
Blanket only	365	—	97	3	—	—
Core only	−145	—	58	34	5	3

Footnotes on following page

Note: The main types of commercial nuclear power reactors are the light water reactor (LWR), the graphite moderated gas-cooled reactor (also called the magnox reactor), a heavy water moderated reactor called the CANDU reactor, and a light water graphite moderated reactor (LWGR) found in the Soviet Union. The liquid metal fast breeder reactor (LMFBR) is under commercial development.

[a]The rate at which plutonium is discharged in spent fuel for each type of reactor is the typical amount of plutonium that is discharged in the spent fuel each year by a 1,000 MWe (net) plant operating for 365 days, i.e., one that has a 100 percent capacity factor, in a mode optimized for electricity production. (The net electricity production, as distinguished from gross or total electricity production, is the energy produced by the reactor, less the energy to produce and operate the reactor.) The actual discharge rate for a specific reactor depends on the reactor's capacity factor for that year, its thermal efficiency, the frequency of fuel reloading, the extent to which the fuel is reshuffled during refueling, and the fuel's enrichment.

[b]The isotopic composition of the plutonium is that present at the time the plutonium is discharged from the reactor. Because Pu-241 has a half-life of only 13.2 years, after the end of one year the amount of Pu-241 will have decreased by about 5 percent.

[c]U.S. Department of Energy, *Nuclear Proliferation and Civilian Nuclear Power*, Report of the Nonproliferation Alternative Systems Assessment Program, Volume IX: Reactor and Fuel Cycle Descriptions, Washington, D.C., pp. 13, 14. The plutonium discharge rate for the pressurized water reactor (PWR) is 325 kilograms of plutonium per GWe (net) per year and for the boiling water reactor is 340 kilograms of plutonium per GWe (net) per year. Since roughly two-thirds of the reactors are PWRs and one-third are BWRs, the value listed in the table is an average for this specific combination of reactors. The PWR used as a standard in the DOE study uses fuel that is 3 percent enriched uranium and achieves an average burnup of 30,400 MWt-d/MTU. The BWR uses 2.9 percent enriched uranium and achieves an average burnup of about 28,000 MWt-d/MTU. The isotopic composition of the plutonium listed above is typical of these burnups.

[d]Y. A. Chang and C. Till, "Alternative Fuel Cycle Options," ANL-77-70, Argonne National Laboratory, September 1977 (also in a set of tables entitled "Fuel Cycle Options and Fueling Modes," circa 1977). The burnup of the spent fuel is 7,500 MWt-d/MTU, and the plutonium production rate is normalized to a 100 percent capacity factor.

[e]Negligible quantities.

[f]A fairly typical discharge rate for British gas-cooled reactors is 800 kilograms of plutonium per GWe (net) per year (Official Report of the House of Commons, Hansard, July 27, 1983, column 439; this rate was supplied by the Secretary of State for Energy). Another estimate can be derived from data on a French gas-graphite reactor (Syndicat CFDT de l'Energie Atomique, *Le Dossier Electronucleaire* [Editions du Seuil, 1980], p. 51). For a French reactor whose fuel is discharged at a burnup of 4,000 MWt-d/MTU, the spent fuel contains 2.5 kilograms of plutonium per MTU, with the isotopic composition listed in the table. Dividing these numbers gives the plutonium production rate in terms of thermal power—228 grams of plutonium discharged per MWt-year. French gas-graphite reactors have an average thermal efficiency of about 0.28 based on net electricity production and about 0.30 based on gross electricity production ("General Information," *Nuclear Engineering International*, October Supplement, October 1984). Thus, the plutonium discharge rate in terms of electricity production is 815 kilograms of Pu/GWe (net)-year and 760 kilograms of Pu/GWe (gross)-year, which agrees reasonably well with the British government estimate mentioned above if the corresponding spent fuel has a burnup of 4,000 MWt-d/MTU. The isotopic composition data in the table are for 4,000 MWt-d/MTU (*Le Dossier*, op. cit.).

In general, the burnup of the fuel in both French and British gas-graphite reactors is now about 4,000 to 5,000 MWt-d/MTU. In the past it was significantly lower, and in the future it might be even higher.

[g]The discharge rate for the LWGR is for both types, the RBMK-1000 and the RBMK-1500. The fuel is enriched to 1.8% and discharged with a nominal burnup of about 18,000 MWt-d/MTU (I. Ya. Emel'yanov, A. D. Zhirnov, V. I. Pushkarev and A. P. Sirotkin, "Increasing the Efficiency of Uranium Utilization in the RBMK-1000 Reactor," translated from *Atomnaya Energiya*, Vol. 46, No. 3, March 1979, pp. 139–141, Plenum Publishing Corporation). The isotopic composition of the plutonium is interpolated from burnup data for 18,000 and 20,000 MWt-d/MTU (T. S. Zaritskaya, A K Kruglov, and A. P. Rudik, "The Formation of Transuranium Nuclides in Connection with the Combined Use of VVER and RBMK Power Reactors," translated from *Atomnaya Energiya*, Vol. 46, No. 3, March 1979, pp. 183–185, Plenum Publishing Corporation).

[h]J. Bussac and P. Reuss, *Traite de Neutronique* (Herman, 1978, pp. 583–588). The values from this book are normalized to a 1,000 MWe plant and a 100 percent capacity factor. Unlike the other reactors in this table, which use uranium fuel that initially contains no plutonium, the breeder reactor's fuel contains about 15 to 25 percent plutonium. Thus, the discharge rates for the breeder reactor core refer only to the net increase or decrease in the plutonium. The amount of plutonium discharged in breeder spent fuel is considerably greater than the amount discharged in the spent fuel of the other reactors in this table. A 1,000 MWe breeder reactor operating at a 70 percent capacity factor will discharge roughly 1,500 to 2,000 kilograms of plutonium each year, depending on its design and mode of operation (DOE, *Nuclear Proliferation*, op. cit., p. B-30).

Table A.2. Plutonium Discharged in Spent Fuel from Power Reactors in the Western World: Cumulative Total (metric tons).[a]

Country[b]	Through 1984	Through 1990	Through 2000
Argentina	2.0	4.4	13
Bangladesh	—	—	?
Belgium	5.0	12	27
Brazil	0.1	1.4	8
Canada	28	63	140
Egypt	—	—	2
Finland	3.0	6.3	13
France	36	93	210
Germany, West	17	45	99
India	1.75	4.8	16
Italy	3.6	5.4	15
Japan	27.7	64	153
Korea, South	1.5	8.4	30
Libya	—	—	?
Mexico	—	0.8	3.5
Netherlands	1.5	2.1	4.3
Pakistan	0.3	0.5	2.4
Philippines	—	0.5	1.9
South Africa	0.1	1.9	6
Spain	6.0	14	28
Sweden	10	22	40
Switzerland	5.1	9.4	18
Syria	—	—	?
Taiwan	3.0	9.3	23
Turkey	—	—	?
United Kingdom	41.7	58	87
USA	100	200	400
Yugoslavia	0.4	1.0	3
TOTALS[c]	300	630	1,350

[a]The sources for this table are described in Tables A.3 and A.4 and in the text.

[b]Other countries, such as Iran and Iraq, might also have nuclear reactors in operation by the end of this century.

[c]Totals rounded off.

Table A.3. Plutonium Discharged in Light Water Reactor Spent Fuel in the Western World: Cumulative Total (metric tons).[a]

Country	Through 1984	Through 1990	Through 2000
Bangladesh	—	—	?[b]
Belgium	5.0	12	27
Brazil	0.1	1.4	8
Egypt	—	—	2
Finland	3.0	6.3	13
France	21	71	180
Germany, West	17	45	99
India	1.0	1.4	2
Israel	—	—	1
Italy	1.4	2.7	12
Japan	26	62	150
Korea, South	1.0	6.3	25
Libya	—	—	?[c]
Mexico	—	0.8	3.5
Netherlands	1.5	2.1	4.3
Pakistan	—	—	1.4[d]
Philippines	—	0.5	1.9
South Africa	0.1	1.9	6
Spain	2.6	8.9	21[e]
Sweden	10	22	40
Switzerland	5.1	9.4	18
Syria	—	—	?[f]
Taiwan	3.0	9.3	23
United Kingdom	—	—	3[g]
USA	100	200	400
Yugoslavia	0.4	1.0	3
TOTALS[h]	200	460	1,050

[a]The cumulative totals ignore reductions in the amount attributable to the decay of Pu-241, half of which decays every 13 years.

[b]The Soviet Union has offered to finance Bangladesh's 440 MWe pressurized water reactor. Whether the government will accept is unknown. See *Nuclear Engineering International*, February 1985, p. 7.

[c]Libya might receive twin 440 MWe pressurized water reactors from the Soviet Union. A Belgian company was to have participated in the construction of the reactors, but pressure from the United States led the Belgian government to refuse to allow the company to participate in the construction.

[d]Pakistan is having great difficulty finding someone to sell it a reactor. The Soviet Union decided not to sell it one, and other suppliers will only do so after Pakistan has placed all its nuclear facilities under safeguards.

[e]In 1984 the Spanish government froze construction of five nuclear units until after 1992. The estimate in the table assumes that none of the five plants will be finished by the end of this century.

[f]The Soviet Union has agreed to help Syria build a nuclear power plant (*Nuclear Engineering International*, January 1985, p. 6).

[g]A decision to build a pressurized water reactor in Britain has not yet been made. The estimate for the cumulative amount of plutonium assumes that the first reactor begins operation in 1995 and is quickly followed by the operation of three more units this century ("NUKEM Market Report on the Nuclear Fuel Cycle," May 1984, NUKEM, GmbH, Hanau, Federal Republic of Germany).

[h]Totals rounded off.

Table A.4. Plutonium Discharged in Western Non-Light Water Reactor Spent Fuel: Cumulative Total (metric tons).[a]

Country	Reactor Type	Through 1984	Through 1990	Through 2000
Argentina	CANDU	2.0	4.4	13
Canada	CANDU	28	63	140
France	Magnox[b]	15	22	30
India	CANDU	0.75	3.4	14
Italy	Magnox[c]	2.2	2.7	3
Japan	Magnox[d]	1.7	2.2	3
Korea, South	CANDU	0.5	2.1	5
Pakistan	CANDU	0.3	0.5	1
Spain	Magnox[e]	3.4	4.9	7
United Kingdom	Magnox[f]	39	50	64
	AGR[g]		2.7	8.4	20
TOTALS[h]		96	165	300

[a]The cumulative totals ignore reductions in the amount attributable to the decay of Pu-241.
[b]The estimate of plutonium production in French gas-graphite reactors through 1984 uses a different plutonium discharge rate than the one in Table A.1. The average burnup of the fuel is assumed to be only 3,000 MWt-d/MTU (for fuel reprocessed at La Hague through 1981 see Nuclear Regulatory Commission translation of Raimond Castaing, et al., *Rapport du Groupe de Travail sur la Gestation des Combustibles Irradies*, Paris: Ministere de la Recherche et de l'Industrie, 1982, Attachment 4, "Analysis of the Dosimetric Results of the External Exposure," Table VIII). Through 1984, the conversion factor is 810 kilograms of Pu per GWe (gross) per year. At a fuel burnup of 3,000 MWt-d/MTU, the amount of plutonium discharged is about 2 kilograms per MTU (*Le Dossier*, op. cit., see footnote f, Table A.1). The average thermal efficiency of the reactors is about 0.30 for gross electricity production ("General Information," *Nuclear Engineering International*, October Supplement, October 1984).

After 1984 the fuel burnup is assumed to be 4,000 MWt-d/MTU, and the value in Table A.1 is used. The gas-graphite reactors are expected to close down in the 1990s. The date when they close is estimated by assuming that each reactor lasts 25 years. The amount of plutonium in the last core is estimated to be 2.0 metric tons of plutonium per GWe (Nuclear Energy Agency, *Nuclear Energy and Its Fuel Cycle, Prospects to 2025*, Paris: OECD, 1982. This reference lists 1.8 MT of fissile plutonium per GWe. It is assumed that the final fuel has a fairly low burnup, and the fissile fraction is crudely estimated to be about 85 to 90 percent.)

[c]The Latino gas-graphite reactor operates at a burnup of about 3,000 MWt-d/MTU ("Technical Data," *Nuclear Engineering International*, October Supplement, October 1984). At this burnup, about 2.0 kilograms of Pu are contained in each metric ton of spent fuel (*Le Dossier*, op. cit.). The thermal efficiency of Latino is about 0.3 for gross electricity production and 0.28 for net electricity production ("General Information," op. cit.). Thus, the plutonium discharge rate is about 810 kilograms of Pu per GWe (gross) per yr and 870 kilograms of Pu per GWe (net) per yr. It is assumed that Latino will shut down in 1992 after 25 years of operation (see footnote b).

[d]The Tokai gas-graphite reactor operates at a burnup of about 3,000 MWt-d/MTU ("Technical Data," op. cit.). The thermal efficiency of this reactor is 0.28 for gross electricity production and 0.27 for net production ("General Information," op. cit.). It is assumed that Tokai will shut down in 1994.

[e]The burnup of the Vandellos 1 gas-graphite reactor is estimated to be about 6,000 MWt-d/MTU ("Technical Data," op. cit.), which corresponds to 3.3 kilograms of Pu per metric ton of uranium (*Le Dossier*, op. cit.). Its thermal efficiency is 0.27 for net electricity production and 0.28 for gross production ("General Information," op. cit.).

The reactor is jointly owned by France and Spain, and all Vandello's spent fuel is shipped back to France where it is reprocessed. The reprocessed plutonium is kept by France.

[f]The plutonium discharge rate for gas-graphite reactors in Table A.1 is used as a basis to compute the plutonium accumulation for British gas-graphite reactors. Because the ratio of total net electricity production to gross electricity production is about 0.85 ("General Information," op. cit.), about 680 kilograms of Pu are produced per GWe (gross) per year.

Since no more gas-graphite plants will be built, the only unknown in estimating future nuclear capacity is when they will be shut down. Presently, they are expected to last 30 years instead of 25 years, as originally estimated (A. W. Clarke and C. J. Marchese, "CEGB Nuclear Station Performance—Current Status," *Nuclear Europe*, 1/1985, January 1985, p. 1317). Final cores are estimated to contain 2 metric tons of plutonium per GWe (see footnote b).

[g]The advanced gas reactor is only built in the United Kingdom. Its plutonium production rate is about 250 kilograms of Pu per GWe (net) per year (Official Report of the House of Commons, Hansard, July 27, 1983, column 439). Converting from net to gross electricity production gives a plutonium production rate of about 230 kilograms of Pu per GWe (gross) per year ("General Information," op. cit.). The date when the facilities under construction begin operation is taken from Atomic Industrial Forum, *AIF International Survey*, Bethesda, Maryland, April 17, 1985.

[h]Total figures rounded off.

Table A.5. Plutonium Discharged in Spent Fuel from Major Power Reactors in Communist Countries: Cumulative Totals (metric tons).

Country	Reactor Type	Through 1984	Through 1990		Through 2000	
			Lower Estimate	Upper Estimate	Lower Estimate	Upper Estimate
Bulgaria	PWR[a]	1.6	5.5	—	13	15
China, Peoples Republic of[b]	PWR	—	—	—	5.4	6.9
Cuba	PWR	—	0.3	0.5	1.1	2.1
Czechoslovakia[c]	PWR	1.0	5.2	5.2	17	20
Germany, East	PWR	2.0	3.8	12	13	17
Hungary	PWR	0.2	2.2	2.2	5.7	5.7
Poland	PWR	—	—	—	3.4	5.6
Romania	CANDU	—	0.8	0.8	5.6	6.2
U.S.S.R.[d]	PWR	10	27	38	60	160
	LWGR[e]	14	34	34	74	74[f]
TOTALS[g]		29	79	90	200	300

Note: The uncertainties of the values in the table reflect primarily the limited amount of information available about nuclear reactor programs in communist countries and the oftentimes overly optimistic Soviet forecasts of the number of reactors that will be built. For a general discussion of these problems, see Office of Technology Assessment, *Technology and Soviet Energy Availability*, Washington, D.C., November 1981.

The amount of plutonium discharged in the spent fuel is derived from an estimate of the electricity production of the reactors. The primary source for the nuclear capacity of the communist countries is the Atomic Industrial Forum, *AIF International Survey*, April 17, 1985, Bethesda, Maryland. The electricity production in each country is converted into plutonium production by assuming that the capacity factor is 65 percent for all these reactors and by using the conversion factors in Table A.1. In the case of the pressurized reactors, the plutonium discharge rate is found in footnote c to Table A.1 and is 310 kilograms of Pu per MWe (gross) per year at 100 percent capacity.

Two estimates of future plutonium inventories in spent fuel are used: a "lower estimate" that represents reactors operating, under construction or ordered, and an "upper estimate" that, in addition to the above categories, includes planned reactors. In both cases, reactors are included only if an anticipated date of commercial operation is publicly known.

[a] Pressurized water reactor, a type of light water reactor.

[b] The amount of plutonium estimated to be in Chinese spent fuel assumes that the lower estimate of the nuclear electricity capacity in 2000 will be 4.1 GWe and that the upper one will be 6.1 GWe.

[c] The startup dates of several of the reactors under construction in Czechoslovakia have been postponed by several years from the ones in the Atomic International Forum list of reactors.

[d] The nuclear capacity for the Soviet Union before 1982 is from B. A. Semenov, "Nuclear Power in the Soviet Union," *IAEA Bulletin 25*, June 1983, p. 48, and after 1982 is derived primarily from Atomic Industrial Forum, *AIF International Survey*, April 17, 1985, Bethesda, Maryland. After 1990, the upper estimate for the PWRs includes both the PWRs and the LWGRs. The upper estimate for plutonium accumulation through 2000 assumes that the total nuclear capacity in the Soviet Union will reach 55 GWe by 1990, 75 GWe by 1995 and 100 GWe by 2000 (see footnote f below).

[e] Light water cooled, graphite-moderated, reactor.

[f] The number of LWGRs that are planned to be built is not publicly known. Generally, only the total future nuclear capacity is publicly announced, not the number of each type of reactor that will be built. Since it is known that most of the future reactors will be PWRs, it is assumed for the sake of this calculation that all new reactors will be PWRs. This assumption will not affect the total plutonium accumulation for the Soviet Union, because each type of reactor produces almost the same amount of plutonium per GWe per year.

[g] Totals rounded off.

Table A.6. Reprocessing Capacities of Major Civilian Reprocessors of Power Reactor Fuel.[a]

Country	Facility	Type of Reactor Fuel[b]		Year Operational	Capacity (MTU/year)
Argentina	Ezeiza	Oxide	(CANDU)	1988?	5
Belgium	Mol	Oxide	(LWR)	1992?	120
Brazil	Resende	Oxide	(LWR)	1989	3
France	La Hague				
	UP2	Metal	(magnox)	1967–86	800[c]
		Oxide	(LWR)	1976	400[c]
	UP2-800	Oxide	(LWR)	1991 or 92	800
	UP3	Oxide	(LWR)	1989	800
	Marcoule UP1	Metal	(magnox)	1958	500[d]
West Germany	Karlsruhe	Oxide	(LWR)	1971	20
	Bavaria	Oxide	(LWR)	1992	350
India	PREFRE	Oxide	(CANDU)	1979[e]	100
	Kalpakkam[f]	Oxide	(CANDU)	1987?	100
	Western India	Oxide	(CANDU)	?	350
Japan	Tokai Mura	Oxide	(LWR)	1977	210[g]
	Rokkashomura	Oxide	(LWR)	1995	800
Pakistan	Chashma	Oxide	(CANDU)	?	100
United Kingdom	Sellafield	Metal	(magnox)	1964	2,500[h]
	Thorp	Oxide	(LWR&AGR)	1990	1,200[i]

[a]Unless otherwise noted, the data in this table are compiled from Table A.7. Some of the capacities in this table are design capacities of the plant. In these cases, more realistic yearly throughputs of fuel are listed in Table A.7.

[b]Many of the reprocessing facilities will process other types of fuel. The above table only lists the main type of spent uranium fuel that is reprocessed at this facility. In addition, only spent fuel that contains significant amounts of plutonium is included.

[c]Since 1976, both gas-graphite and LWR spent fuel have been reprocessed at the UP2 facility. The values for the fuel capacity refer to the nominal capacity for each type of fuel if only that type was reprocessed during the year. Actual capacities for the last several years are listed in Table A.7. Breeder reactor fuel has also been reprocessed in UP2.

[d]This value is for only power reactor fuel. Fuel from military reactors has also been reprocessed in UP1.

[e]From 1979 until sometime in 1982, only metal fuel (probably from the CIRUS reactor) was reprocessed. In late 1982, the facility began reprocessing spent fuel from the Rajasthan reactors.

[f]This facility will also reprocess breeder reactor fuel.

[g]This value is the nominal capacity of Tokai Mura.

[h]The actual capacity of the metal reprocessing facility is only about 1,250 MTU per year of civilian power reactor metal fuel (see Table A.7).

[i]The actual average capacity during the first 10 years of operation of THORP will be only about 600 MTU per year.

Table A.7. Projected Reprocessing Capacities of Major Civilian Reprocessors
(Metric tons of uranium per year).

Country	Facility	Type of Reactor Fuel		1982	1983	1984	1985	1986	1987	1988	1989	1990
Argentina	Ezeiza[a]	Oxide	(CANDU)	—	—	—	—	—	—	5?	5	5
Belgium	Mol[b]	Oxide	(LWR)	—	—	—	—	—	—	—	—	—
Brazil	Resende[c]	Oxide	(LWR)	—	—	—	—	—	—	—	3	3
France	La Hague											
	UP2, UP2-800[d]	Oxide	(LWR)	154[e]	221[f]	255[g]	250	250	250[h]	250[h]	350[h]	350
	UP2	Metal	(magnox)	226[j]	117[k]	185[l]	250[m]	?[m]	0	0	0	0
	UP3	Oxide	(LWR)	—	—	—	—	—	—	—	100[n]	300[n]
	Marcoule UP1[o]	Metal	(magnox)	?	500	500	450	500	500	500	500	500
West Germany	Karlsruhe[p]	Oxide	(LWR)	0[q]	20[q]	20	20	20	20	20	20	20
	Bavaria	Oxide	(LWR)	—	—	—	—	—	—	—	—	—
India	Trombay[s]	Metal	(research reactor)	—	—	?	10?	40	40	40	40	40
	PREFRE[t]	Metal	(res. reactor)	?	0	0	0	—	—	—	—	—
		Oxide	(CANDU)	?	20[t]	30?	50	50	50	50	50	50
	Kalpakkam[u]	Oxide	(CANDU)	—	—	—	—	—	—	30	50	50
Japan	Tokai Mura	Oxide	(LWR)	50[v]	3[w]	0	70[x]	140[x]	150[y]	150	150	150
	Rokkashomura[z]	Oxide	(LWR)	—	—	—	—	—	—	—	—	—
Pakistan	New Lab[aa]	?		—	—	—	?					
	Chashma[bb]	Oxide	(CANDU)	—	—	—	—	?				
United Kingdom	Sellafield[cc]	Metal	(magnox)	1,250	1,250	1,250	1,250	1,250	1,250	1,250	1,250	1,250
	THORP[dd]	Oxide	(LWR&AGR)	—	—	—	—	—	—	—	—	0

Continued on following page

[a] Cold startup is not expected until mid-1987, and no date has been set for radioactive operation ("Argentina Denies Receiving West German, Italian Reprocessing Know-How," *Nucleonics Week*, May 30, 1985, p. 4). Initial capacity projections for the plant are 10 to 15 kilograms of plutonium a year, or 5 metric tons of spent fuel a year ("Argentina Looks to Reprocessing Plant to Fill Own Needs Plus Plutonium Sales," *Nuclear Fuel*, November 8, 1982). The plant is designed for relatively easy expansion to an industrial scale.

[b] "Synatom Sets up Belgoprocess," *Nuclear Engineering International*, May 1985, p. 7 (see also p. 31, "World Survey"). The estimated annual capacity is 120 metric tons of heavy metal a year. The annual capacity during the initial years is estimated. If the plant operates, it would be devoted to reprocessing Europe's nonstandard fuel, such as the smaller fuel from earlier light water reactors, fuel from other kinds of reactors such as the French Monts d'Arree gas-cooled heavy water reactor, and LWR mox fuel. A decision to restart the plant is currently in doubt, because of Belgian utility doubts that reprocessing is economic and a lack of foreign interest in contracting for reprocessing services ("Belgians Dither over Reprocessing Plant," *Nuclear Engineering International*, December 1984, p. 13).

[c] Nuclear Assurance Corporation, *Reprocessing Status Report*, Atlanta, Georgia, October 1982.

[d] UP2 is being upgraded to reprocess up to 800 tons a year through a project known as UP2-800.

[e] J. Megy, "Reprocessing Spent Fuel in France," *Nuclear Engineering International*, March 1983, pp. 40–42.

[f] "Cogema Exceeds Reprocessing Target by 20%," *Nuclear Fuel*, November 21, 1983, p. 8.

[g] *Nuclear Fuel*, February 25, 1985.

[h] COGEMA expects to have a capacity at UP2 of 350 MTU per year rather than 250 MTU per year sometime in the late 1980s and early 1990s before it is converted into UP2-800 ("Cogema Aiming to Offer Fixed-Price Reprocessing," *Nuclear Fuel*, January 28, 1985).

Continued on following page

1991	1992	1993	1994	1995	1996	1997	1998	1999	2000	Total MTU Reprocessed from the End of 1984 Through 2000
5	5	5	5	5	5	5	5	5	5	65
—	30	60	90	120	120	120	120	120	120	900
3	3	3	3	3	3	3	3	3	3	36
150[i]	310[i]	475[i]	640	800	800	800	800	800	800	8,075
—	—	—	—	—	—	—	—	—	—	250
500[n]	700[n]	900[n]	900	900	900	900	900	900	900	8,800
500	500	500	500	500	500	500	500	500	500	7,950
20	20	20	20	20	20	20	20	20	20	320
—	50[r]	125[r]	200	275	350	350	350	350	350	2,400
40	40	40	40	40	40	40	40	40	40	610
—	—	—	—	—	—	—	—	—	—	?
50	50	50	50	50	50	50	50	50	50	830
50	50	50	50	50	50	50	50	50	50	630
150	150	150	150	150	150	150	150	150	150	2,310
—	—	—	—	100	225	350	475	600	600	2,350
?										?
?										?
1,250	1,250	1,250	1,250	1,250	1,250	1,250	1,250	1,250	1,250	20,000
100	235	370	510	650	650	650	650	650	650	5,115

[i]UP2-800 will become operational in 1991 ("Progress in URG Shareholders' Projects," *Reprocessing News*, United Reprocessors GmbH, Karlsruhe, Federal Republic of Germany, May 1984, p. 4), although its startup might be delayed one year. Its capacity during the first year is estimated to be 150 tons of spent fuel and will reach its full capacity of 800 tons per year four years later (Nuclear Regulatory Commission translation of Raimond Castaing, et al., *Rapport du Groupe de Travail sur la Gestation des Combustibles Irradies*, Paris, Ministere de la Recherche et de l'Industrie, 1982, Attachment 3) (known as the "Castaing Report"). The capacities from 1992 through 1994 are estimates based on a linear increase in capacity from 1991 until 1995.

[j]COGEMA, Washington, D.C., personal communication, February 1983.

[k]COGEMA, Washington, D.C., personal communication, 1984.

[l]*Nuclear Fuel*, February 25, 1985.

[m]The reprocessing of metal fuel will be transferred to the UP1 plant in Marcoule in 1986 ("France: Cogema's 1984 production programme for La Hague," *Reprocessing News*, United Reprocessors GmbH, May 1984, p. 6).

[n]UP3 is scheduled to start up in 1989 ("Progress in URG Shareholders' Projects," *Reprocessing News*, United Reprocessors GmbH, May 1984, p. 4). Another source states that active service is scheduled for mid-1988 ("Cogema Profitable in 1983," *Nuclear Fuel*, July 2, 1984, p. 13). UP3's capacity during its first year is estimated to be 100 tons per year and will reach its full capacity year four years later ("Castaing Report," op. cit., Attachment 3). The capacities from 1989 through 1992 are estimates based on a linear increase in capacity from 1988 through 1992. A COGEMA official said to *Nuclear Fuel* (June 20, 1983) that "the plant should be able to reprocess 920-936 MT per year beginning around 1990, with smaller quantities for the first two years of operation in 1988 and 1989." The increase in capacity to 900 metric tons a year in Table A.7 above corresponds to COGEMA's offer to reprocess 7,000 metric tons of spent fuel rather than 6,000 ("Customers See Little Choice in Cogema 'Offer' of Extra Reprocessing," *Nucleonics Week*, June 9, 1983).

Continued on following page

oEstimated, but see footnote d in Table A.11. (See also "Summary of Nuclear Power and Fuel Cycle Data in OECD Member Countries," Nuclear Energy Agency, Organization for Economic Co-Operation and Development, March 1984, p. 17.) Because all magnox fuel will be concentrated at Marcoule after 1986, the UP1 facility is being modified and extended, most notably with the construction of a new spent fuel storage and decladding complex, MAR-400 (A. Cruickshank, "Cogema Looks to Wider Markets," *Nuclear Engineering International*, September 1984, pp. 30-39).

pNuclear Assurance Corporation, op. cit. The nominal capacity is 35 metric tons of uranium per year for fuel with 20,000 MWd/MTU and 10 to 15 metric tons per year for fuel with 30,000 MWd/MTU.

qThe reprocessing plant at Karlsruhe was shut down in May 1980 and reopened in late 1982. From the date when the plant was restarted through late June 1983, about 20 metric tons of uranium fuel was reprocessed ("FRG: Successful Operation of the WAK-plant," *Reprocessing News*, United Reprocessors GmbH, November 1983, p. 3). During late 1983, a small amount of spent fuel from the nuclear ship *Otto Hahn* was reprocessed ("FRG: Successful Operation," op. cit.).

r"DWK Selects Site for Reprocessing Plant," *Nuclear Fuel*, February 11, 1985, p. 7. I estimate that the capacity will increase in a similar way as with the French reprocessing plant UP3 at La Hague. This estimate is consistent with estimates by the German reprocesser, DWK ("Cogema, SGN and DWK Sign Reprocessing Accord," *Nuclear Fuel*, July 16, 1984, p. 4).

sThe nominal capacity of the plant is about 40-60 metric tons per year. The yearly increase in the capacity is an estimate. Trombay went into operation in 1964 with a nominal capacity of 30 MT per year (*Annual Report*: 1983-84, Government of India, Department of Atomic Energy, p. 5). This facility supplied the plutonium for the bomb India exploded in 1974 ("India Reprocesses Rapp Fuel under IAEA Eyes," *Nuclear Fuel*, February 14, 1983). It was partially decommissioned in 1972. It restarted in late 1984 or early 1985. Spent metallic fuel from the Dhruva reactor (scheduled to start operation in 1985) and CIRUS research reactor will be reprocessed at this facility ("The Reprocessing Plant at Trombay Is Ready for Recommissioning," *Nuclear Fuel*, May 9, 1983, and *Annual Report*: 1983-84, Government of India, Department of Atomic Energy, p. 26). It is estimated in the main text of the article that about 35 metric tons of fuel will be discharged per year from these reactors. The capacity has been rounded up to 40 metric tons of fuel per year.

tPREFRE began reprocessing spent fuel from the Rajasthan Atomic Power Station (RAPS) in late 1982 ("India Reprocesses Rapp," op. cit., but see footnote f in Table A.11 about metal fuel reprocessed earlier). From late 1982 through late 1983, about 20 metric tons of RAPS fuel were reprocessed (A. Abraham, "Plutonium Missing in Tarapur Plant," *The Sunday Observer* [Bombay, India], October 16-22, 1983). The fuel reprocessed had a low burnup and is reported to have contained only 25 kilograms of plutonium (Abraham, op. cit.).

It is possible to derive an upper bound on the annual amount of plutonium that will be separated at PREFRE. The nominal daily reprocessing capacity of the PREFRE facility is 0.5 tons of uranium per day ("India's Significant Efforts on Reprocessing and Vitrification," *Nuclear Europe*, January 1983, pp. 45-46). Assuming the plant will operate for 300 days a year, it could then process up to 150 metric tons of fuel a year. The French discovered that their nominal capacity had to be further reduced by another factor of one third to account for unscheduled shutdowns ("Castaing Report," attachment 1, op. cit.), which results in an annual capacity of 100 MTU. The amount of plutonium in each metric ton of spent fuel depends on whether it is CANDU or BWR spent fuel and on the burnup of the spent fuel. If only CANDU fuel is reprocessed and burnups reach 5,000 to 7,000 MWt-d/MTU, about 3 to 4 kilograms of plutonium are contained in each metric ton of fuel ("Heavy Element Concentrations in Power Reactors," SND-120-2, NUS Corporation, Clearwater, Florida, May 1977). Thus, about 300 to 400 kilograms of reactor-grade plutonium could be produced each year. If low burnup fuel is reprocessed, about 1 kilogram of plutonium is contained in each metric ton of fuel, and 100 kilograms of weapon-grade plutonium can be separated each year.

Besides the difficulty most countries have had achieving nominal reprocessing capacities, there is another problem that India must face in actually reprocessing 100 MTU per year. There might not be sufficient spent fuel to reprocess. The purpose of the Tarapur reprocessing facility is to handle spent fuel from both the Tarapur reactors and the RAPS reactors. However, the yearly discharge from these reactors (under normal operating conditions) is only about 70 metric tons per year, of which about 15 to 20 tons is from the reactors at Tarapur (Nuclear Assurance Corporation, *Reprocessing Status Report*, October 1982, Atlanta, Georgia).

Moreover, it is unlikely that any Tarapur fuel will be reprocessed. Until 1980, the fuel was supplied by the United States, and its reprocessing requires U.S. consent, which India is unlikely to receive. Further, the Tarapur reactors were supplied by the United States, and under the U.S./India Agreement for Tarapur, any spent fuel supplied by another supplier would still be subject to U.S. control, although India disputes this part of the agreement. (Since 1984, France has been supplying low enriched fuel to the Tarapur reactors at the request of the United States. This arrangement with France, however, does not affect U.S. control over the spent fuel.)

Continued on following page

[u]The initial date of operation of the Kalpakkam plant is an estimate, as is the projected increase in capacity during the first few years. The nominal capacity of the Kalpakkam facility is about 100 metric tons of spent fuel per year. However, this facility is expected to have two separate reprocessing lines—one to handle spent fuel from the Madras Atomic Power Station (MAPS) and the other to handle fuel from the Fast Breeder Test Reactor (Department of Atomic Energy, *Annual Report*, 1982-83, and "India Reprocesses Rapp Fuel under IAEA Eyes," *Nuclear Fuel*, February 14, 1983). MAPS will discharge about 50 metric tons of spent fuel each year (Nuclear Assurance Corporation, op. cit.).

The 40 MWt Fast Test Breeder Reactor (FTBR) is expected to go critical this August ("India First to Use Mixed Carbide Fuel," *Nuclear Engineering International*, May 1985). It will be the first breeder reactor to use mixed uranium-plutonium carbide fuel. Breeding ratios are significantly higher for carbide fuel than the more standard oxide fuel, and thus the doubling time will be significantly less. A higher breeding ratio also means that more high quality plutonium can be produced in the blanket.

[v]The amount reprocessed in 1982 is estimated from the following information. Through June 1981, Japan's Power Reactor and Nuclear Fuel Development Corp. (PNC) reprocessed a cumulative total of 106 metric tons of spent fuel ("PNC to Reprocess 200 Tonnes in Two Years at 586,900/Tonne in Pact with Utilities," *Nuclear Fuel*, November 23, 1981). From June 1981 until August 1982, PNC reprocessed about 45 metric tons of spent fuel (*Annual Report of the Japanese Atomic Energy Commission—1982*). Until the reprocessing facility closed in February 1983, PNC had reprocessed a cumulative total of 170 metric tons of spent fuel (*Reprocessing News*, United Reprocessors GmbH, November 1983).

[w]The plant closed in February 1983. It restarted in February 1985 ("PNC Runs Tokai Reprocessing Plant," *Atoms in Japan*, February 1985, pp. 26-27). In trial runs in February 1983 and in December 1983, PNC reprocessed respectively 1 and 2 tons of BWR fuel ("PNC Fears It Won't Reprocess Substantial Quantities," *Nuclear Fuel*, February 28, 1983, p. 11, and "Tokai Tests Repaired Dissolver," *Nuclear Engineering International*, February 1984, p. 9).

[x]"Reprocessing to Resume at Tokai Mura," *Nuclear Fuel*, November 26, 1984, p. 9. In order to process the full 140 metric tons in 1986, Japan will have to obtain the approval of the United States. Beginning in 1986, Japan is likely to reprocess between 5 and 10 metric tons of spent mox fuel from its Fugen reactor ("Reprocessing to Resume at Tokai Mura," op. cit.). Finally, the capacity for spent fuel storage is to be increased from 97 to 140 metric tons ("PNC Runs," op. cit.).

[y]The capacity after 1986 is estimated.

[z]"Japan Utilizes Bare Plans to Build Fuel-Cycle Facilities at Shimokita," *Nuclear Fuel*, July 30, 1984. The nominal capacity of the plant is planned to be 1,200 metric tons of uranium a year, with a working capacity of 600 to 800 metric tons of uranium per year, with the plant's startup targeted for 1995 ("Japan Chooses Fuel Cycle Sites," *Nuclear Engineering International*, June 1984, pp. 12-13). The capacity listed in the table above is arbitrarily set at 600 MTU/year. I estimate that the capacity will increase in a similar way as with the French reprocessing plant UP3 at La Hague. Plans for this plant might be modified. It is possible that instead of a single reprocessing line, two lines would be built. The second would be built a few years after the first one, depending on need (P. Leventhal, Nuclear Control Institute, personal communication, 1984).

[aa]New Laboratory is a small facility located next to the Pinstech Laboratory; it can process about 2 to 5 metric tons of spent fuel per year (Thomas W. Graham, "South Asian Nuclear Proliferation and National Security Chronology," Center for International Studies, Massachusetts Institute of Technology, Cambridge, Mass.). There is no evidence that New Lab has processed any plutonium containing spent fuel (Graham, op. cit.).

[bb]Chashma is a 100 metric ton per year plant currently under construction. Originally, France would have supplied the plant, but the United States stopped the sale. Pakistan has continued to work on the facility, with limited success (*Nuclear Fuel*, March 26, 1984). Pakistan has agreed to a safeguards agreement on Chashma with France and the International Atomic Energy Agency (IAEA). If the facility is completed, whether safeguards will be applied will become an important and highly contentious issue.

[cc]Sellafield's (formerly Windscale) nominal capacity is 2,500 tons per year. However, its actual capacity is estimated to vary roughly between 1,000 and 1,500 tons per year (Syndicat CFDT, *Le Dossier Electronucleaire* [Seuil, 1980], pp. 194, 202, 502, and "British Nuclear Fuels Finds Profits, Pain in Reprocessing," *Energy Daily*, August 29, 1984, p. 4). Sellafield needs to reprocess about 1,300 metric tons of spent magnox fuel discharged annually from U.K. power stations and 100 to 150 metric tons of spent magnox fuel discharged annually from the Japanese and Italian magnox reactors (S. Rippon, "Reprocessing—What Went Wrong," *Nuclear Engineering International*, February 1976, p. 25).

[dd]Thorp will have a design capacity of 1,200 MTU a year. For planning purposes, an annual throughput increasing to 650 MTU a year during the first 10 years of operation is assumed ("Progress in URG Shareholders' Projects," *Reprocessing News*, United Reprocessors GmbH, Karlsruhe, Federal Republic of Germany, May 1984, p. 3). The date of initial operation is scheduled for late 1990. The plant is not expected to achieve full capacity for several years after start-up. I estimate that the capacity will increase in a similar way as the French reprocessing plant UP3 at La Hague. About one-third of the fuel that it reprocesses will be oxide fuel from advanced gas reactors.

Table A.8. Plutonium Separated from Light Water Reactor Spent Fuel at La Hague, France, Through 1983.

Country	Spent Fuel[a] (MT)	Plutonium[b] (kg)
Belgium	83.2	665
France	83.2	665
Germany	348.2	2,790
Japan	41.2	250
Netherlands	73.4	590
Switzerland	101.9	820
TOTAL	731	5,780

[a]M. Delange, "Reprocessing of LWR Spent Fuel at La Hague 1976-1982," *Nuclear Europe*, 1/1983, January 1983, table 2, p. 36, and letter to D. Albright from C. Hutchinson, COGEMA, Washington, D.C., January 4, 1984.

[b]Through 1981, the LWR spent fuel contained on average 8 kilograms of plutonium per metric ton of fuel (9 kilograms of plutonium per metric ton of uranium) (see footnote c in Table A.11). In all cases except for Japan, the former value was used. The actual value could vary. In the case of Japan, the amount that was sent back in 1984 is assumed to be all the plutonium that was extracted from the 41.2 metric tons of spent fuel reprocessed through 1983.

Table A.9. Amount of Spent Fuel (MTU) and Plutonium (MT) from Commercial Light Water Reactors Contracted for Reprocessing in France and Britain.

Country	France (MTU)			Britain (MTU)	Total (MTU)	Plutonium Total (MT)
	UP2[a]	UP3[a]	Extra UP3[b]			
Belgium	139	398	66	—	603	5.0[c]
Germany	681	2,141	357	750[d]	3,929	35[e]
Italy	—	—	—	190[f]	190	1.5[c]
Japan	151	2,200	367	2,250[g]	4,968	45[e]
Netherlands	79	120	20	60[f]	279	2.5[e]
Spain	—	—	—	150[f]	150	1.2[c]
Sweden[h]	55	672	112	140[i]	979	8.8[e]
Switzerland	132	469	78	350[j]	1,029	9.3[e]
TOTAL	1,237	6,000	1,000	3,890	12,127	108

[a]A. Cruickshank, "Cogema Looks to Wider Markets," *Nuclear Engineering International*, September 1984, pp. 33-39. All the spent fuel will be reprocessed at La Hague. The fuel contracted to be reprocessed in the UP2 facility is currently being reprocessed. The reprocessing of the spent fuel in the UP3 facility will begin in the late 1980s.

[b]COGEMA has announced that it intends to reprocess 7,000 tons of spent fuel under the UP3 contracts. The extra amounts are assigned to a country in proportion to the original amount this country contracted for reprocessing.

[c]The spent fuel is estimated to contain about 8 kilograms of plutonium per metric ton.

[d]E. Leyser, "The Back End of the Nuclear Fuel Cycle in the Federal Republic of Germany," in *The World Nuclear Fuel Market*, Proceedings of the 11th International Conference on Nuclear Energy, Florence, Italy, October 14-16, 1984, p. 152. Most of the spent fuel contracted for reprocessing in Britain was contracted in 1983, when Germany agreed to reprocess 722 metric tons at THORP (P. Hahlen, "BNFL's Additional Reprocessing Deals with Swiss, Germans, and Italians," *Nuclear Europe*, 5/1983, May 1983).

[e]The spent fuel is estimated to contain 9 kilograms of plutonium per metric ton.

[f]C. Braun, "Rationale for Low Cost Plutonium Fuel," paper presented at the American Nuclear Society Annual Meeting, New Orleans, Louisiana, June 3-7, 1984. Braun lists the total amount of spent fuel contracted by each country. He apparently does not include the extra 1,000 metric tons of uranium that will be reprocessed in UP3. Except for this difference, the amount in Braun's table agrees reasonably well with the quantities in the above table for Belgium, Germany, Japan, Sweden and Switzerland.

[g]Japan has signed LWR spent fuel reprocessing contracts with Britain and France covering about 4,600 metric tons ("Japan Eyes Interim Storage Alternatives," *Nuclear Fuel*, December 3, 1984). Subtracting the amount contracted for reprocessing in France (not including the extra fuel to be reprocessed under the UP3 contracts) leaves 2,250 metric tons.

[h]Sweden has decided to drop all its reprocessing contracts. They will probably be taken over by Japan and West Germany.

[i]"Germans and Japanese Will Take over Swedish Reprocessing Contracts," *Nuclear Fuel*, May 21, 1984.

[j]Switzerland has signed contracts to reprocess 950 metric tons of spent fuel (P. Hahlen, op. cit.). Subtracting the amount contracted for reprocessing in France (not including the extra fuel to be reprocessed under the UP3 contracts) leaves 350 metric tons.

Table A.10. Amount of Plutonium Separated from Civilian Power Reactor Fuel by Major Reprocessors (through 1984).

Country	Facility	Fuel Type[a]	Amount (kg)
Belgium	Eurochemic-Mol	Metal & oxide	683[b]
France	La Hague	Oxide	7,900[c]
		Metal	7,220 to 7,480[d]
	Marcoule	Metal	4,000[d]
			19,120–19,380
Germany, West	Karlsruhe	Oxide	840[e]
India	PREFRE	Oxide and metal	?[f]
Japan	Tokai Mura	Oxide	1,040[g]
USA	West Valley	Oxide	1,330[h]
	Savannah River Plant	Oxide	165[i]
	Hanford	Oxide	?[j]
United Kingdom	Windscale	Metal domestic	32,000[k]
		Metal foreign	3,500[l]
		Oxide	300[m]
			35,800
TOTAL			59,000[n]

[a]The types of fuel reprocessed commercially are oxide fuels from LWRs and CANDUS and metal fuels from magnox or gas-graphite reactors.

[b]Syndicat CFDT de l'Energie Atomique, *Le Dossier Electronucleaire* (Editions du Seuil, 1980), pp. 202, 203. The facility was closed down in 1974, although it might be restarted in the early 1990s. A small fraction of the plutonium was produced in non-power reactors.

[c]Through 1984, 986 metric tons (MT) of oxide fuel were reprocessed at La Hague (COGEMA, Washington, D.C., January 1985). Through 1981, 8 kilograms of plutonium were contained in each metric ton of fuel, or 9 metric tons in each ton of uranium reprocessed at La Hague (Nuclear Regulatory Commission translation of Raimond Castaing, et al., *Rapport du Groupe de Travail sur la Gestation des Combustibles Irradies*, Paris: Ministere de la Recherche et de l'Industrie, 1982, "Attachment 1, "Reprocessing Capacity of UP3 [Pressurized Water] and of HAO: Past, Present, Future," Table A.3) (also known as the "Castaing Report"). The average burnup of the spent fuel was 23,000 MWt-d/MTU ("Castaing Report," Attachment 4, "Analysis of the Dosimetric Results of the External Exposure," table VIII). The average burnup of the spent LWR fuel in 1982 and 1983 was, respectively, 21,000 and 23,000 MWt-d/MTU (COGEMA, Paris, personal communication, June 1984). According to the same COGEMA source, the burnups of foreign spent fuel, the main type reprocessed, were expected to increase. But through 1984, the average plutonium content of the spent fuel is estimated to remain about 8 kilograms of plutonium per ton of spent fuel.

[d]Through 1984, 4,641 MT of commercial metal fuel were reprocessed at La Hague (COGEMA, Washington, D.C., February 1983 and April 1984, French Embassy, Washington, D.C., February 1983, and *Nuclear Fuel*, February 25, 1985, p. 12). From the mid-1960s through 1981, 4,113 metric tons of metal fuel were reprocessed at La Hague and contained on average 1.5 kilograms of plutonium per metric ton of fuel ("Castaing Report," Attachment 1, op. cit). This quantity of plutonium corresponds to an average burnup of 2,000 MWt-d/MTU (*Le Dossier*, op. cit.), although the average burnup listed in the "Castaing Report" for the fuel is 2,600 MWt-d/MTU (Attachment 4, table VIII, op. cit.). In recent years, the burnup of the spent fuel processed at La Hague has been about 3,000 to 4,000 MWt-d/MTU, which corresponds to about 2 to 2.5 kilograms of plutonium per metric ton of spent fuel (*Le Dossier*, op. cit., p. 51). Consequently, the spent fuel reprocessed through 1981—4,113 MT of spent fuel—contains 6,170 kilograms of plutonium, and after 1981— 528 MT of spent fuel—contains about 1,050 to 1,310 kilograms of plutonium.

Continued on following page

Through 1982, 1,358 metric tons of commercial metal fuel were reprocessed at Marcoule (COGEMA, Washington, D.C., personal communication, 1983). According to *Nuclear Fuel* (December 31, 1984), slightly under 7,000 MTU of gas-graphite spent fuel will have been reprocessed at Marcoule and La Hague through the end of 1984. Subtracting from this value, the amount of fuel reprocessed at La Hague and the amount reprocessed through 1981 at Marcoule leaves 1,000 metric tons of spent fuel reprocessed at Marcoule in 1983 and 1984. It is assumed that the burnup of the fuel reprocessed at Marcoule is similar to the fuel reprocessed at La Hague. In this case, however, the fuel reprocessed through 1982 is assumed to contain 1.5 kilograms of plutonium per metric ton and after 1982 is assumed to contain 2 kilograms of plutonium per metric ton.

Fuel from the West German KKN reactor (gas-cooled heavy water reactor) and from the French EL-4 reactor was also reprocessed at Marcoule (*Le Dossier*, op. cit., p. 186), but the amount of plutonium recovered from these reactors is within the error of the total amount separated at Marcoule.

Military spent metal fuel has also been reprocessed at Marcoule. Through 1982, about 12,000 metric tons of metal fuel were reprocessed at Marcoule (J. Megy, "Reprocessing Spent Fuel in France," *Nuclear Engineering International*, March 1983, pp. 40–42). If the 1,358 metric tons of civilian metal fuel is subtracted, about 10,640 metric tons of military fuel has been reprocessed at Marcoule.

The authors of *Le Dossier Electronucleaire* (p. 186) estimated that through 1977 about 9,910 tons of metal fuel from the military reactors G1, G2 and G3 were reprocessed. They list the burnup of the spent fuel as between 100 and 1,200 MWt-d/MTU, with an average burnup of about 400 MWt-d/MTU. A maximum estimate of the amount of weapon-grade plutonium produced can be derived by assuming that it was all produced in G2 and G3. It is an overestimate, because the G1 fuel is also included in the total amount reprocessed, and it contained significantly less plutonium per metric ton of uranium than the G2 and G3 reactors. In any case, at an average burnup of 400 MWt-d/MTU, G2 and G3 each will produce about 80 kilograms of plutonium per full power year and will require about 230 MTU per full power year (S. E. Turner, *et al.* Southern Science Applications, Inc., "Criticality Studies of Graphite-Moderated Production Reactors," Report SSA-125, prepared for U.S. Arms Control and Disarmament Agency, January 1980, figures 2.3 and 2.7). Thus, the average amount of plutonium in the spent fuel is about 0.35 kilograms of plutonium per metric ton of uranium. Thus, a maximum estimate of the amount of military plutonium produced is 3.4 metric tons.

The G1 reactor ran at a very low burnup (about 100 MWt-d/MTU) and only produced about 10 kilograms of plutonium each full power year, while it required about 100 metric tons of uranium each full power year (Turner, op. cit.). G1 ran for about 12 years, so at a burnup of 100 MWt-d/MTU, it would have discharged about 800 MTU if it ran 70 percent of the time and would have produced about 80 kilograms of plutonium. The net effect of including G1 into the calculation is to lower the amount of plutonium produced in the "G" reactors to about 3.2 metric tons of plutonium.

[e]A total of 540 kilograms of plutonium were separated at Karlsruhe through 1980 (H. H. Hennies and B. Kucera, "Construction and Use of Pilot Plants in the Karlsruhe Nuclear Research Center," KfK-Nachrichten, Year 13, no. 3–4, 1981, p. 203). Most of it was from reactors that produced electric power (author unknown, KfK-Bericht 3113, Karlsruhe Research Center, April 1981, p. 98). The plant was closed from May 1980 until late 1982. In 1983, about 20 metric tons of fuel with average burnups of from 10,000 to 28,000 MWt-d/MTU were reprocessed (*Reprocessing News*, United Reprocessors, GmbH, Karlsruhe, Federal Republic of Germany, November, 1983, p. 3). I estimate that another 20 metric tons were reprocessed in 1984. If all of it was power reactor fuel with an average burnup near 20,000 MWt-d/MTU, roughly 300 kilograms of plutonium were recovered (see KfK-Bericht 3113, op. cit., for plutonium production data).

[f]India began reprocessing commercial spent fuel from the Rajasthan Atomic Power Station 1 (RAPS-1) reactor at its PREFRE facility in late 1982 under International Atomic Energy Agency safeguards ("India Reprocesses RAPP Fuel under IAEA Eyes," *Nuclear Fuel*, February 14, 1983, p. 12). Until late 1983, about 20 metric tons of RAPS spent fuel were reprocessed (A. Abraham, "Plutonium Missing in Tarapur Plant," *The Sunday Observer* [Bombay, India], October 16–22, 1983). The fuel reprocessed had a low burnup and is reported to have contained only 25 kilograms of plutonium (Abraham, op. cit.). The facility as of mid-1984 is in operation and continues to separate RAPS-1 spent fuel ("Commissioning of Vitrification Facility Affirms India's Self-Sufficiency Claims," *Nuclear Fuel*, June 3, 1985, pp. 9–11).

Prior to processing RAPS fuel, metal fuel, evidently from the CIRUS reactor, was processed in three separate campaigns starting in 1979 (reference to these campaigns and the starting date of the facility are in Government of India, Department of Atomic Energy, *Annual Report 1980-1981*, pp. 4, 31, *Annual Report 1981-82*, p. 26, and *Annual Report 1983-84*, pp. 6, 31).

[g]Through March 1983, Tokai had reprocessed a total of 172 metric tons of spent oxide fuel and recovered 1,040 kilograms of plutonium ("Japan Makes Plans for Reprocessing," *Nuclear Engineering International*, July 1984, pp. 20–21). The plant did not operate through most of 1983 and all of 1984.

[h]The total amount of plutonium separated at West Valley, which operated from 1966–1972, was 1,886 kilograms (G. I. Rochlin *et al.*, "West Valley: Remnant of the AEC," *Bulletin of the Atomic Scientists*, January 1978, p. 23, table 2). About 550 kilograms of the separated plutonium are from spent metal fuel from the Department of Energy's N-reactor at Hanford, Washington, which is a military reactor presently producing weapon-grade plutonium for nuclear weapons.

iIn 1963, spent fuel from the Dresden 1 and the Yankee-Rowe reactors was reprocessed at the military reprocessing plant at the Savannah River Plant (Atomic Energy Commission, *Annual Report to Congress of the Atomic Energy Commission for 1964*, 89th Cong., 1st sess., Senate Document No. 8, January 1965, table 4). The plutonium in the spent fuel was owned by the government, as was all special nuclear material until 1964, when Congress amended the Atomic Energy Act of 1954 to permit private ownership of these materials. The reactor owners, however, were compensated for the plutonium. Almost all of the plutonium from these power reactors was fuel-grade plutonium.

jThe blanket from the first core of the Shippingport reactor might have been reprocessed at the military reprocessing facility at Hanford, Washington in the 1960s or early 1970s. The first two cores of the Shippingport reactor had highly enriched uranium seeds and a natural uranium blanket. The blanket of the first core contained about 70 kilograms of fuel-grade plutonium. The blanket from the second core contained about 100 kilograms of plutonium (Edison Electric Institute, "Plutonium Survey-1964," EEI Pub. No. 65-41, June 1965, table B1) and was being stored at Hanford in the early 1980s. It might have already been reprocessed.

kAs of the end of March 1983, a publicly announced quantity totaling 23,000 kilograms of plutonium had been separated from Central Electricity Generating Board (CEGB) and South of Scotland Electricity Board (SSEB) metal fuel (Answer by the Secretary for Energy to Mr. Lester, MP, on plutonium production, Hansard, Record of the House of Commons in the United Kingdom, July 27, 1983, p. 440). Another classified amount of plutonium separated from CEGB and SSEB metal fuel is estimated to be 4 MT (C. Norman, "Congress, DOE Battle over British Plutonium," *Science*, Vol. 224, April 27, 1984, pp. 365-366). Another estimate using detailed information about the burnup of the fuel from the civil magnox reactors estimates that about 6 to 7 MT were exported to the United States (K. W. J. Barnham, D. Hart, and R. A. Stevens, "The Production and Destiny of UK Plutonium," submitted to *Nature*). The amount was classified, since it was part of a defense exchange agreement between the U.K. and the U.S. The agreement permitted the U.K. to obtain from the United States highly enriched uranium and tritium for its weapons program in exchange for civil plutonium from CEGB magnox reactors.

From March 1983 through 1984, it is estimated that 2,000 metric tons of metal spent fuel from British reactors were reprocessed. This estimate assumes that in all 1,250 metric tons of spent fuel were reprocessed each year (see Table A.7), of which roughly 200 tons was from the Italian and Japanese gas-graphite reactors (see below). Two hundred tons corresponds to the reprocessing of two years' worth of spent fuel from these reactors ("Technical Data," *Nuclear Engineering International*, October Supplement, October 1984). Each metric ton of spent fuel from British reactors is estimated to contain 2.5 kilograms of plutonium, which roughly corresponds to fuel with a burnup of 4,000 MWd/MTU (*Le Dossier*, op. cit.).

lSpent fuel from Italy and Japan has also been reprocessed at Windscale. Nuclear Assurance Corporation has estimated that through 1982 about 1,500 kilograms of fissile plutonium have been recovered from Italian fuel and about 1,000 kilograms of fissile plutonium have been recovered from Japanese fuel (Nuclear Assurance Corporation, "Near-Term Plutonium Market Outlook," prepared for the Department of Energy, ORNL/Sub/ 83-40111/1, March 1983). The burnup of the fuel is estimated to be about 3,000 MWt-d/MTU ("Technical Data," op. cit.), so about 85 percent of the plutonium is fissile. Thus, the total amount of plutonium recovered through 1982 is about 3,000 kilograms. In the same report, Nuclear Assurance Corporation also estimated that about 340 kilograms and 140 kilograms of fissile plutonium would be recovered from, respectively, Italian and Japanese fuel. The total amount of plutonium recovered is 550 kilograms. If only 200 metric tons was processed in 1983 and 1984, as estimated above, then only 400 kilograms of plutonium would have been recovered.

Not all the plutonium recovered from foreign spent fuel has necessarily been returned to the customers. Until 1981, 1,930 kilograms of plutonium were exported and returned to BNFL's overseas customers. The countries to which this plutonium was exported (in shipments larger than gram quantities) are Belgium, Canada, France, West Germany, Italy, Japan, and the U.S. (*Transcript of Proceedings, Sizewell B Public Inquiry*, March 17, 1983, p. 70).

mAbout 90 metric tons of oxide spent fuel were reprocessed at Windscale in the early 1970s (P. J. Mellinger, K. M. Harmon and L. T. Lakey, "A Summary of Nuclear Fuel Reprocessing Activities Around the World," PNL-4981, prepared for the Department of Energy, Pacific Northwest Laboratory, p. 50). Nuclear Assurance Corporation stated that 56 MT of this oxide fuel were from LWRs and that the LWR spent fuel was estimated to contain 237 kilograms of fissile plutonium, which corresponds to roughly 300 kilograms of plutonium (Nuclear Assurance Corporation, op. cit.). The amount of plutonium in the rest of this spent fuel is unknown.

nThe value is rounded off.

Table A.11. Source and Amount of Separated Plutonium in Various Countries Through the Year 2000[a] (metric tons of plutonium).

Country	Separated Plutonium from Foreign Reprocessing Through 2000		Separated Plutonium from Domestic Reprocessing Through 2000		Total Amount of Plutonium Separated Through 2000
	LWR Fuel	Magnox Fuel	LWR Fuel	Other Fuel	
Argentina	—	—	—	0.2[b]	0.2
Belgium	5	—	?[c]	—	5
Brazil	—	—	0.3[d]	—	0.3
France	—	—	50–75[e]	37[f]	85–110
Germany, W.	35	—	25[g]	—	60
India	—	—	?	5[h]	5
Italy	1.5	3	—	—	4.5
Japan	45	3	37[i]	—	85
Netherlands	2.5	—	—	—	2.5
Pakistan	—	—	—	?	?
Spain	1.2	—[j]	—	—	1.2
Sweden	8.8[k]	—	—	—	8.8
Switzerland	9.3	—	—	—	9.3
United Kingdom	—	—	—	73[l]	73
TOTAL	108	6	113–138	114	340–365

[a]The sources for Table A.11 are primarily Tables A.4, A.7, A.9 and A.10.

[b]The plutonium will be extracted from CANDU fuel. The spent fuel is estimated to contain 3 kilograms of plutonium per metric ton of uranium.

[c]I assume that the reprocessing facility in Belgium will not be restarted.

[d]The light water reactor spent fuel, which will be reprocessed, is estimated to contain 8 kilograms of plutonium per metric ton of uranium.

[e]The range in the amount of plutonium separated from French light water reactor spent fuel results from the uncertainty in the amount of spent fuel contracted for reprocessing by the French electricity company. The lower estimate assumes that only 5,426 metric tons of uranium have been contracted for reprocessing (A. Cruickshank, "Cogema Looks to Wider Markets," *Nuclear Engineering International*, September 1984, pp. 33–39). The upper estimate assumes that about 8,600 MTU will be reprocessed through 2000. The latter estimate is derived by totaling the amount of LWR spent fuel reprocessing capacity at La Hague (the amount from 1984 through 2000 is from Table A.7 and the amount reprocessed through 1984 is 986 MTU) and subtracting the known amount of capacity reserved or planned for foreign spent fuel (about 9,200 MTU).

[f]The amount of plutonium that will be separated from gas-graphite fuel in France includes the plutonium from the Spanish gas-graphite reactor.

[g]The spent fuel to be reprocessed in the future is estimated to contain 9 kilograms of plutonium per metric ton of uranium.

[h]The CANDU fuel reprocessed in India is estimated to contain 3 kilograms of plutonium per metric ton of uranium. Included in the amount listed in the table is roughly 600 kilograms of weapon-grade plutonium extracted from research reactor spent fuel.

[i]The fuel reprocessed at the new facility is estimated to contain 9 kilograms of plutonium per metric ton of uranium. The fuel that will be reprocessed at Tokai Mura is estimated to contain only 7 kilograms of plutonium per metric ton of uranium.

[j]The plutonium from the Spanish gas-graphite reactor is sent to France.

[k]Sweden is planning to drop its reprocessing contracts. They will probably be taken over by Germany and Japan.

[l]Most of the British inventory of plutonium is from its gas-graphite reactors. But about 9 metric tons of plutonium will be separated at THORP from about 2,000 metric tons of advanced gas reactor spent fuel.

Appendix B

U.S. Exports of Highly Enriched Uranium

David Albright

Highly enriched uranium[1] was present at the creation of the modern nuclear era. The bomb detonated over Hiroshima contained about 60 kilograms of weapon-grade uranium, that is, uranium that is enriched to over 90 percent in the isotope uranium-235.[2] All HEU can be used to make nuclear explosives, although an explosive made from uranium enriched to only 20 percent will require significantly more uranium-235 than one made with 90 percent enriched uranium. Today, weapon-grade uranium is still used in all nuclear weapons programs. The United States is estimated to have at least 500 metric tons of it in its nuclear weapons stockpiles.[3]

In addition to the weapons program, HEU is also used in civilian research reactors worldwide and in a commercial high temperature reactor. The amount of HEU that has been used in civilian programs is only a small percent of that used in the U.S. weapons program. Nonetheless, its use as a fuel in reactors presents a risk that some of the HEU will be stolen by terrorists or diverted by a national program and used to fabricate a nuclear explosive. A nuclear explosive can be constructed with only 25 kilograms of weapon-grade uranium. A 1982 General Accounting Office report commented on these facts and summarized:

> [A] single seizure of a significant quantity of HEU by an irresponsible government or terrorist group could have profound repercussions for the security of all nations and would almost certainly have a highly negative impact on all peaceful nuclear activities. . . . The dangers are not limited to material located in irresponsible nations. . . . An irresponsible nation, or a sub-national group, might seize material from the territory of the most responsible nation.[4]

An evaluation of civilian HEU's security risks must include an analysis of the amount of HEU in circulation and its distribution in the world.

The overwhelming bulk of the nuclear reactors in the world use uranium enriched to only a few percent in the isotope uranium-235. Any uranium enriched to less than 20 percent is called low enriched uranium (LEU). It cannot be used to make a nuclear explosive.

Currently, about 150 civilian research, test and power reactors in the non-communist world use highly enriched uranium. The roughly 50 civilian reactors in the United States that use highly enriched uranium are Department of Energy (DOE) civilian research and test reactors, university research reactors and a nuclear power reactor, the Fort St. Vrain high temperature reactor, in Colorado. About 35 foreign countries operate roughly 100 research and test reactors.

Each year the civilian research reactors in the non-communist world (which use HEU enriched to over 90 percent in the isotope uranium-235)[5] require about 1,100 kilograms of uranium-235. Roughly half of the HEU is used domestically, and the remainder is used overseas.[6,7]

The annual amount of HEU required by a reactor is not the total amount of HEU in circulation. A much larger quantity is in the "pipeline," which includes all the HEU being fabricated into fuel, stored at the reactor either as fresh or irradiated fuel, reprocessed, and transported between any of these facilities. For research reactors, the average amount of time for HEU fuel elements to go through their entire cycle from enrichment to reprocessing is about 4 years.[8] Thus, over 4,500 kilograms of HEU enriched over 90 percent are in continuous circulation to fuel the reactors in operation today in the non-communist world.[9]

HEU has been used to fuel many types of U.S. reactors since the 1950s. Until the 1960s, the United States—historically the major supplier of HEU—supplied primarily low enriched fuel to foreign research reactors. However, more demanding experiments required HEU fuel.[10] As a result, U.S. exports of HEU increased dramatically in the 1960s (see Figure B.1). Through 1982 almost 45 countries had received about 24 metric tons of HEU from the United States (see Table B.1). About 11.5 metric tons of this HEU were enriched to over 90 percent.[11]

Unfortunately, the data in the table represent only shipments to foreign countries and do not reflect either the returns to the United States or retransfers of HEU to other foreign countries, and therefore they do not represent the current inventory of highly enriched uranium in a country.

An important example that illustrates how the U.S. export data for HEU can be misleading is South Africa.[12] In 1975 the United States stopped any further HEU shipments to South Africa because it refused to accept international inspections of all its nuclear facilities. Until then, South Africa had received 33 kilograms of HEU directly from the United States (see Table B.1). South Africa also received U.S.-origin HEU indirectly from the United Kingdom. The United States sent HEU to the United Kingdom specifically for fabrication into fuel elements for use in a South African research reactor. The United Kingdom subsequently retransferred a total of 72 kilograms of weapon-grade uranium to South Africa.[13] Although this HEU was clearly authorized for South Africa, it is included in the amount of HEU that the United States exported to Britain. The total amount of HEU exported to South Africa was 105 kilograms, all of which was weapon-grade uranium.

When the United States stopped shipping HEU to South Africa either directly or indirectly, the total inventory of HEU in South Africa, including reductions attributable to fuel burnup, re-exports to France and the United Kingdom, and returns to the United States was 44 kilograms,[14] or over 10 kilograms higher than the total amount currently listed in the table as exported directly to South Africa from the United States.

Other countries have also exported small amounts of HEU.[15] Britain and France have supplied HEU to a few countries. France was to have supplied HEU fuel to Iraq's research reactor that was destroyed by Israel. The Soviet Union has also supplied a small amount of HEU to a few countries.

In the future some additional reactors will use HEU fuel. When the high temperature reactor in West Germany begins operation in 1985, each year it will require as much as 150 kilograms of uranium-235 in 93 percent enriched HEU.[16] The United States might restart one of its large test reactors, which would require about 150 to 200 kilograms of uranium-235 yearly, also enriched to 93 percent.

Simultaneously, many research reactors will discontinue using HEU when they convert from HEU fuel to a new type of low enriched uranium fuel. This fuel is currently being developed in several programs.[17]

Some preliminary conclusions can be drawn: First, HEU is distributed in many countries; without powerful incentives, several of them will continue to use HEU into the future. Second, in most cases the HEU in civilian programs can be replaced by the new low enriched uranium fuels. Third, unless these new fuels are utilized, HEU anywhere in the fuel cycle will continue to be a proliferation risk.

NOTES

1. Highly enriched uranium (HEU) contains over 20 percent of the isotope uranium-235.
2. J. McPhee, *The Curve of Binding Energy* (New York: Farrar, Strauss and Giroux, 1974), p. 14.
3. Frank von Hippel, David Albright and Barbara Levi, "U.S. and Soviet Stockpiles of Fissile Materials" Report #PU/CEES 168 (Princeton University, Center for Energy and Environmental Studies, in press). The weapon-grade uranium estimate was made in collaboration with Thomas B. Cochran and Milton Hoenig of the Natural Resources Defense Council, who have reached a similar conclusion. Their results will be published in Thomas B. Cochran, William M. Arkin and Milton Hoenig, *Nuclear Weapons Databook, Volume II: U.S. Nuclear Weapons Management, Resources, and Production* (Cambridge, MA.: Ballinger, in press).
4. General Accounting Office, "Obstacles to U.S. Ability to Control and Track Weapons-Grade Uranium Supplied Abroad," GAO/ID-82-21, Washington, D.C., August 2, 1982.
5. Some research reactors use HEU enriched to less than 90 percent uranium-235; however, they are not included in the quantitative analysis in this report.

6. Letter to K.L. Mattern, DOE, from J.E. Matos, Argonne National Laboratory, "Subject: RERTR Program Reactor Summary September 1982," September 22, 1982.
7. In addition to the research reactors, the commercial high temperature gas reactor at Fort St. Vrain annually requires about 125 kilograms of uranium-235 in HEU enriched to 93 percent. The core of the Fort St. Vrain reactor contains about 750 kilograms of U-235, and one-sixth of the core is unloaded each year (M.T. Simnad, *Fuel Element Experience in Nuclear Power Reactors*, an AEC Monograph, Gordon and Breach Science Publishers, 1971, p. 544). This is a maximum estimate, because the Fort St. Vrain reactor has had extensive problems that have closed the reactor for long periods of time.
8. A. Travelli, "RERTR Program Activities Related to the Development and Application of New LEU Fuels," presented at the International Symposium on the Use and Development of Low and Medium Flux Research Reactors, MIT, October 17-19, 1983.
9. Fuel in the Fort St. Vrain reactor fuel cycle is assumed to take four years to go through its fuel cycle.
10. According to Travelli (op. cit.), "As power and neutron flux were revised in research reactors to satisfy more demanding experimental requirements, greater U-235 loadings of the fuel elements began to be needed to avoid the financial penalty of a reduced fuel lifetime. The increased loadings could have been achieved either by continuing the development of fuels with higher uranium density or by increasing the uranium enrichment. Of the two choices, the latter prevailed in the 1960s."
11. Department of Energy, Nuclear Materials Management and Safeguards System (NMMSS). A large fraction of the HEU originally enriched over 90 percent has been reprocessed either in the United States or in Europe.
12. For a more general analysis of the methods used to track the amounts of HEU sent abroad, see the GAO report in footnote 4.
13. U.S. Congress, Senate Committee on Government Operations, *The Export Reorganization Act of 1975*, 94th Cong., 1st sess., 24, April 30, and May 1, 1975, pp. 100, 101.
14. Op. cit., *Export Reorganization Act*.
15. Today, while several countries in Europe have uranium enrichment plants that could produce HEU, the United States supplies over 95 percent of the HEU used in the foreign research reactors in the non-communist world (letter to K.L. Mattern, op. cit.).
16. "HEU Shipment to West Germany Raises Concern of US DOD," *Nuclear Fuel*, September 10, 1984, pp. 2-3.
17. In the United States, the reduced enrichment for research and test reactors (RERTR) program was established in 1978 by the Department of Energy in order to develop and demonstrate new types of fuel with higher uranium densities that permit the conversion of reactors presently using uranium enriched to more than 70 percent uranium-235 to uranium enriched to 20 percent uranium-235 fuel, or where necessary to 45 percent U-235 fuel. This was to be accomplished without significantly affecting reactor performance or fuel cycle costs.

The RERTR program coordinates its activities with the State Department, the Arms Control and Disarmament Agency (ACDA) and the Nuclear Regulatory Agency (NRC), as well as with many foreign reactor owners and fuel fabricators. According to the General Accounting Office, "The reduced enrichment program is one of the few concrete U.S. non-proliferation initiatives to gain widespread international support." (Op. cit., GAO, footnote 4, p. iv.)

Table B.1. Exports[a] of HEU from 1954 Through 1982.

Country	HEU (kg)[b]	Contained U-235 (kg)[b]	% U-235 (average)
Argentina	94	59	63
Austria	9.8	7.3	75
Australia	10	9.2	90
Belgium	187	159	85
Bolivia	c	c	—
Brazil	7.7	7.2	93
Canada	1,861	1,724	93
Columbia	3.1	2.8	90
Czechoslovakia	c	c	—
Denmark	26	24	92
Finland	3.9	.77	20
France	6,268	4,655	74
W. Germany	9,990	6,611	66
Greece	6.6	6.1	93
IAEA	.31	.25	81
Ireland	c	c	—
Indonesia	.018	.13	72
India	.098	.081	83
Israel	19	17	90
Iran	5.5	5.2	93
Italy	382	307	80
Japan	1,995	946	47
Korea, South	30	18	62
Malaysia	c	c	—
Mexico	30	12	42
Netherlands	63	57	89
Norway	.01	.008	80
Pakistan	5.8	5.2	90
Philippines	3.3	3.1	93
Portugal	7.7	7.2	93
Romania	39	37	93
South Africa	33	30	92
Spain	9.4	8.3	88
Sweden	148	133	90
Switzerland	8.8	8.0	91
Taiwan	9.9	9.2	93
Thailand	5.3	4.8	90
Turkey	5.3	4.8	90
U. Kingdom	2,301	2,141	93
Uruguay	c	c	—
Venezuela	.011	.009	82
Vietnam	.39	.08	21
Yugoslavia	17	5.9	35
Zaire	1.4	.28	20
TOTAL	23,590	16,980	72

[a]Figures represent shipments by U.S. to foreign countries. Returns to U.S. and retransfers to other foreign countries are not reflected in the data.
[b]Amounts rounded off.
[c]A few grams at most.
Source: Department of Energy, Nuclear Materials Management and Safeguards System.

Figure B.1. Annual U.S. Exports of HEU.

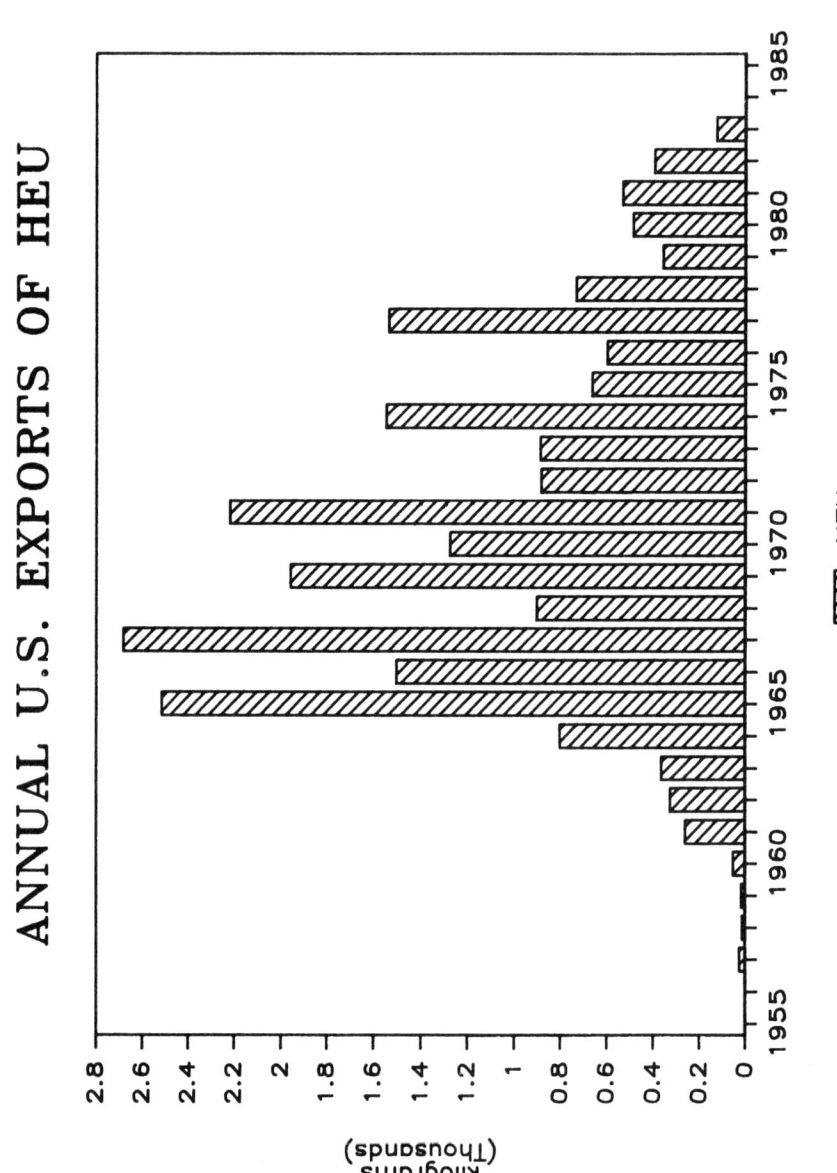

Appendix C

World Spent Fuel Reprocessing Plants

Country	Facility	Mission	Design Capacity	Operational
Argentina	Pilot plant (Ezeiza, B.A.)	Process demonstration	20 kg/d	Target: 1987
	Industrial plant	Reprocess domestic HWR fuels	—(a)	Target: late 1980s
Belgium	Eurochemic (Mol)	Demonstrate reprocessing of varied fuels; operating experience for European owners	HEU—5 kg/d LEU—350 kg/d Future—600 kg/d	1966–1974; may be recommissioned in 1986/87
Brazil	Pilot plant (Rio de Janeiro)	Process demonstration	10 kg/d	Target: 1986
	Industrial plant	Reprocess domestic LWR fuels	300 t/yr	—
China (Peoples' Republic)	Industrial plant	Reprocess military fuels	—	—
France	UP1 (Marcoule)	Reprocess military and civilian U metal (GCR) fuels	4.5–6 tHM/d	1958–present
	UP2 (La Hague)	Treat GCR fuels only Add LWR capability Expand LWR capability	5 tHM/d (GCR) 1.3 tHM/d (LWR) 4 tHM/d (LWR)	1967–present 1976–present Target: early 1990s
	UP3 (La Hague)	Reprocess foreign LWR fuels through 1995; then treat domestic fuels	4 tHM/d	Target: 1988/89

Country	Facility	Mission	Design Capacity	Operational
France *Cont'd.*	AT-1 (La Hague)	Pilot plant: FBR fuels	25 kgHM/d	1969–present
	SAP (Marcoule)	Pilot plant: process development for GCR, LWR and FBR fuels	25 kgHM/d	1962–present
	TOR (Marcoule)	New FBR fuel headend for SAP	25 kgHM/d	Target: 1985
Germany (FRG)	WAK (Karlsruhe)	Pilot plant for process and component testing—LWR fuels	175 kgHM/d	1971–present
	Jupiter	Pilot plant for process testing—HTGR fuels	2 kgHM/d	—
	WA-350 (Bavaria or Lower Saxony)	Commercial plant for LWR fuels	350 tHM/yr	Target: 1990
India	Trombay	Reprocess test reactor fuels	0.1–0.15 tHM/d	1964–1974, 1983–present
	Tarapur	Reprocess HWR, BWR fuels	0.5 tHM/d	1976–present
	Kalpakkam	Reprocess HWR, FBR fuels	0.5 tHM/d	—
Israel	Dimona	Pu production	—	—

Country	Facility	Mission	Design Capacity	Operational
Italy	Eurex (Saluggia Center)	Process demonstration; reprocess varied fuels	HEU–30 kgHM/d LEU–100 kgHM/d	1970–present
	Itrec (Trisaia Center)	Reprocess Th-U fuel from US; treat Italian FBR	10–15 kgHM/d	1975–present
Japan	Tokai-mura	Develop and test LWR reprocessing technology	700 kgHM/d	1977–present
	JNFS plant	Commercial LWR fuel reprocessing	2 tHM/d	Target: 1995
	FBR fuel reprocessing test facility	Develop FBR fuel reprocessing technology	120 kgHM/d	Target: 1991
Pakistan	Chashma	Pu production	300 kgHM/d	—
USSR	Industrial plant	Reprocess military fuels	—	1973–?
	Khlopin pilot plant (Leningrad)	Process development—LWR & FBR fuels	—	—
UK	Butex (Sellafield)	Pu production for defense fuels; new headend for oxide fuels installed in 1968	Oxide headend—1.5 tHM/d	1952–1964, 1969–1973
	Magnox (Sellafield)	Reprocess civilian and military U metal (GCR) fuels; take feed from Butex oxide plant	5–7 tHM/d	1964–present

Country	Facility	Mission	Design Capacity	Operational
UK *Cont'd.*	Thorp (Sellafield)	Reprocess civilian and foreign oxide fuels	3 tHM/d	Target: 1987
	DFR reprocessing plant (Dounreay)	Demonstrate FBR fuel—reprocessing technology	—	1959–1975 (Converted to PFR)
	PFR reprocessing plant (Dounreay)	Demonstrate FBR fuel reprocessing technology	20 kgHM/d	1980–present
USA	West Valley (NFS)	Civilian fuel reprocessing	1–1.5 tHM/d	1966–1972 (Decommissioned)
	Barnwell (BNFP)	Civilian fuel reprocessing	5 tHM/d	Target: 1974 (decommissioned)
	Midwest (MFRP)	Civilian fuel reprocessing	1–1.5 tHM/d	Target: 1972 (decommissioned)
	Idaho (ICPP)	Reprocessing of test reactor and US naval fuel	—	1953–present
	Savannah River/F	Defense fuel reprocessing	—	1955–present
	Savannah River/H	Defense fuel reprocessing; production of special isotopes (e.g., ^{238}Pu)	—	1955–present

Country	Facility	Mission	Design Capacity	Operational
USA *Cont'd.*	Hanford/B	Defense fuel reprocessing and waste processing	—	1945–1952
	Hanford/T	Defense fuel reprocessing	—	1944–1956
	Hanford/U	Recover U from B&T Plant wastes	—	1952–1958
	Hanford/Redox	Defense fuel reprocessing	—	1951–1967
	Hanford/Purex	Defense fuel reprocessing	—	1955–1972 1983–present
	EBR-II (Idaho)	Demonstrate pyrochemical reprocessing	—	1966– (shut down)

[a]Indicates information not available.

Source: Reproduced from P.J. Mellinger, K.M. Harmon, and L.T. Lakey, *A Summary of Nuclear Fuel Reprocessing Activities Around the World*, report prepared by Pacific Northwest Laboratory, Richland, Washington, for the U.S. Department of Energy under Contract DE-AC06-76RLO 1830, November 1984.

Appendix D

The World Enrichment Picture

Country	Enrichment status* Installed capacity (t SWU/yr)[a] as of January 1981		Research programmes[b]	Enrichment needs for power reactors (t SWU/yr) in 1980[c]	Uranium resources Reasonably assured (10^3 t)[d]	Production 1978 (t/yr)[e]	Status with respect to arms control treaties[f]		
							NPT[g]	PTBT[h]	Treaty of Tlatelolco[i]
USA	25300[j]	(GD)	GD,GC,AE,L,CE,PL	6000	708	14 200	R	R	PI:S PII:R
USSR	7 000–10 000	(GD)	GD,GC(?),L,CE(?)	600–1 100	?	7 000[k]	R	R	PII:R
Eurodif countries	6 000[l]	(GD)							
France	300–600[m]	(GD)	GD,GC,L,CE,PL	1 700	55.3	2183			PI:S PII:R
	(3 010)[n]								
Italy	(1 050)[n]		GD,GC,L	140	1.2		R	R	
Belgium	(670)[n]		L	175			R	R	
Spain	(670)[n]			70	9.8	191		R	
Iran	(600)[n]						R	R	
Urenco countries	458[o]	(GC)							
UK	400[p]	(GD)	GD,GC,L	240	4.5	41	R	R	PI:R PII:R
FRG	(213)[q]		GC,AE,L,PL	1000			R	R	PI:R
Netherlands	(245)[r]		GC,PL	55			R	R	PII:R
China	180	(GD)	GD,GC,L		>50[s]	?			
Japan	30	(GC)	GD,GC,L,CE	1 600	7.7	2	R	R	
South Africa	6	(AE)	AE		391	3 961		R	
Brazil	0[t]		AE		74.2			R	R
Pakistan	?		GC						
India	?		GC(?),L(?)	50	29.8	126	S	R	
Argentina					28.1	516		S	S
Australia	0[u]		GC,L,CE,PL		299		R	R	
Israel			L					R	
Canada			Stopped	30	235	6 803	R	R	
Sweden			Stopped	425	301		R	R	
South Korea				60	4.4		R	R	
Taiwan				140			R	R	
Switzerland				210			R	R	
Namibia					133	2697		R	

Enrichment status*

Country	Installed capacity (t SWU/yr)[a] as of January 1981	Research programmes[b]	Enrichment needs for power reactors (t SWU/yr) in 1980[c]	Uranium resources Reasonably assured (10^3 t)[d]	Uranium resources Production 1978 (t/yr)[e]	Status with respect to arms control treaties[f] NPT[g]	PTBT[h]	Treaty of Tlatelolco[i]
Niger				160	2060		R	
Gabon				37	1022		R	
Zaire				1.8	0[v]	R	R	
Algeria				28			S	
Central African Republic				18		R	R	
Somalia				6.6		R	S	

Note: (Present involvement of countries in uranium enrichment in relation to their nuclear power programmes, uranium resources and adherence to arms control treaties.)

* Abbreviations of processes: GD = Gaseous Diffusion; GC = Gas Centrifuge; AE = Aerodynamic; L = Laser separation; CE = Chemical Exchange; PL = Plasma separation (electromagnetic processes).

a. Included are all known enrichment plants; see country descriptions and appendix 8B.
b. Many of these programmes are mentioned in the country studies; further descriptions can be found in. (a) INFCE, see reference [35b]; (b) Interdevelopment, see reference [48]; (c) Blumkin, see reference [54]; (d) Wilcox, see reference [124]. A question mark by a process indicates that there have been occasional reports about R&D activities. The present status of these programmes, however, is unknown.
c. See appendix 8B; the figures here are rounded off.
d. Resources which are expected to be exploited at costs lower than US$ 130/kg U; see reference [41], p. 18.
e. See reference [41], p. 22.
f. S = Signed; R = Signed and Ratified; see reference [97].
g. Treaty on the non-proliferation of nuclear weapons (Non-Proliferation Treaty-NPT).
h. Treaty banning nuclear weapon tests in the atmosphere, in outer space and under water (Partial Test Ban Treaty-PTBT).
i. Treaty for the prohibition of nuclear weapons in Latin America (Treaty of Tlatelolco).

Two additional Protocols are annexed to the Treaty, referred to in the table as PI and PII.

PI:L Under *Additional Protocol I* the extra-continental or continental states which, *de jure* or *de facto*, are internationally responsible for territories lying within the limits of the geographical zone established by the Treaty (France, the Netherlands, the UK and the USA), undertake to apply the statute of military denuclearization, as defined in the Treaty, to such territories.

PII: Under *Additional Protocol II* the nuclear weapon states undertake to respect the statute of military denuclearization of Latin America, as defined in the Treaty, and not to contribute to acts involving a violation of the Treaty, nor to use or threaten to use nuclear weapons against the parties to the Treaty.

j. Partly completed capacity; full capacity of 27300 t SWU/yr is scheduled to be reached in 1983.
k. See reference [45a].
l. Partly completed capacity; full capacity of 10800 t SWU/yr is scheduled to be reached in 1982.
m. Gaseous diffusion plant at Pierrelatte.
n. The total capacity of Eurodif is divided among the participating countries in proportion to their share in the Eurodif organization.
o. Partly completed capacity; full capacity of 2000 t SWU/yr is scheduled to be reached in the late 1980s.
p. Scheduled to be closed down around 1985.
q. Size of the Urenco capacity (pilot and demonstration plants) at Capenhurst, UK [39].
r. Size of the Urenco capacity (pilot and demonstrations plants) at Almelo, the Netherlands; this includes a 200 t SWU/yr joint West German-Dutch demonstration plant [39b].
s. See country study of China.
t. A capacity of 200-300 t SWU/yr is scheduled to start operating in the mid-1980s.
u. Seriously considering construction of a commercial enrichment plant for export purposes.
v. Production before 1975 was 25600 t of uranium (reference [41], p. 22). At the beginning of the nuclear age, Zaire (Belgian Congo) had the main known uranium deposits.

Reproduced from Allan S. Krass, Peter Boskma, Boelie Elzen, and Wim A. Smit, URANIUM ENRICHMENT AND NUCLEAR WEAPON PROLIFERATION, Copyright by Stockholm International Peace Research Institute, Bergshamra, S-171 73 Solna, Sweden, 1983.

Selected Bibliography

Alexander, Yonah and Myers, Kenneth A., eds. *Terrorism in Europe*. New York: St. Martin's Press, 1982.

Alexander, Yonah and Ebinger, Charles K., eds. *Political Terrorism and Energy: The Threat and Response*. New York: Praeger Publishers, 1982.

Alexander, Yonah and Kilmarx, Robert A., eds. *Political Terrorism and Business: The Threat and Response*. New York: Praeger Publishers, 1982.

Beckman, Robert L. *Nuclear Non-Proliferation: Congress and the Control of Peaceful Nuclear Activities*. Boulder, Col.: Westview Press, 1985.

Beres, Louis René. *Terrorism and Global Security: The Nuclear Threat*. Boulder, Col.: Westview Press, 1979.

Carlton, David and Schaerf, Carlo, eds. *Contemporary Terror: Studies in Sub-State Violence*. London: MacMillan, 1981.

Cline, Ray S. and Alexander, Yonah. *Terrorism: The Soviet Connection*. New York: Crane Russak, 1984.

Cochran, Thomas B. *The Liquid Metal Fast Breeder Reactor*. Washington, D.C.: Resources for the Future, 1974.

Duffy, Gloria, and Adams, Gordon. *Power Politics: The Nuclear Industry and Nuclear Exports*. New York: Council on Economic Priorities, 1978.

Dunn, Lewis A. "Nuclear Grey Marketeering." *International Security* 1, no. 3 (Winter 1977): 107–118.

Epstein, William. *The Last Chance: Nuclear Proliferation and Arms Control*. New York: Free Press, 1976.

Ford/MITRE Report. *Nuclear Power Issues and Choices*. Cambridge, Mass.: Ballinger, 1977.

Gilinsky, Victor. "Plutonium, Proliferation, and Policy." *MIT Technology Review* (February 1977): 58–65.

Glasstone, Samuel, ed. *The Effects of Nuclear Weapons.* Revised edition. Washington, D.C.: U.S. Government Printing Office, 1964.

Jenkins, Brian. *Terrorism and Beyond.* An International Conference on Terrorism and Low-Level Conflict. RAND Publication, R-2714-DOE/DOJ/DOS/RC. Santa Monica, December 1982.

———. *The Consequences of Nuclear Terrorism.* P-6373. Santa Monica: The Rand Corporation, August 1979.

———. *The Potential for Nuclear Terrorism.* P-5876. Santa Monica: The Rand Corporation, May 1977.

———. *Will Terrorists Go Nuclear?* California Seminar on Arms Control and Foreign Policy, paper No. 64. Los Angeles: Crescent Publications, 1975.

Jungk, Robert. *The New Tyranny.* New York: Grosset and Dunlap, 1979.

Kupperman, Robert H. and Trend, D. *Terrorism: Threat, Reality, Response.* Stanford, Calif.: Hoover Institution Press, 1979.

Laqueur, Walter. *Terrorism.* Boston: Little, Brown, 1977.

LDC Nuclear Power Prospects, 1975–1990: Commercial, Economic and Security Implications. A report prepared for the Energy Research and Development Administration under Contract AT (49-1)-3665, by Richard J. Barber Associates, Inc. Washington, D.C.

McPhee, John. *The Curve of Binding Energy.* Westminster, Md.: Ballantine Books, 1975.

O'Keefe, Bernard. *Nuclear Hostages.* Boston: Houghton Mifflin Company, 1983.

Patterson, Walter. *The Plutonium Business and the Spread of the Bomb.* San Francisco: Sierra Club Books, 1984.

Potter, William C. *Nuclear Power and Nonproliferation.* Cambridge, Mass.: Oelgeschlager, Gunn and Hain, 1982.

Quester, George H. *The Politics of Nuclear Proliferation*. Baltimore: Johns Hopkins University Press, 1973.

Ramberg, Bennett. *Nuclear Power Plants as Weapons for the Enemy*. Berkeley: University of California Press, 1984.

"A Report on the International Control of Atomic Energy" (Acheson-Lilienthal Report). Prepared for the Secretary of State's Committee on Atomic Energy by a Board of Consultants. Washington, D.C. March 16, 1946.

Rosenbaum, David M. "Nuclear Terror." *International Security* 1, no. 3 (Winter 1977): 140-161.

_____. "The Threat of Nuclear Theft and Sabotage: Safeguards Report." Contained in *Congressional Record*, April 30, 1984.

Spector, Leonard. *Nuclear Proliferation Today*. New York: Vintage Books, 1984.

Sterling, Claire. *The Terror Decade: A Biopsy of International Terrorism, 1970-1980*. New York: Holt, Rinehart, and Winston, 1981.

_____. *The Terror Network*. New York: Holt, Rinehart, and Winston, 1981.

U.S. Congress. Senate. Committee on the Judiciary. *State Sponsored Terrorism*. Report prepared by Ray S. Cline and Yonah Alexander. June 1985.

_____. *Legislation to Combat International Terrorism: 98th Congress*. Hearings and Markup before the Committee on Foreign Affairs. November 9, 1983; June 7, 13, 19; and September 26, 1984. Washington: U.S. Government Printing Office, 1984.

_____. *Nuclear Security Coverup*. Hearing before the Subcommittee on Oversight and Investigations of the Committee on Energy and Commerce, House of Representatives, 98th Cong., 2d sess. February 3, 1984.

_____. *Nuclear Proliferation Factbook*. Prepared for the Subcommittee on Energy, Nuclear Proliferation, and Federal Services of the Senate Committee on Governmental Affairs and the Subcommittee on International Economic Policy and Trade of the House Committee on Foreign Affairs. Joint Committee Print, September 1980.

??????. *Export Reorganization Act of 1976.* Hearings before the Senate Committee on Government Operations, 94th Cong., 2d sess., January 19, 20, 29, 30 and March 9, 1976. Washington, D.C.: Government Printing Office, 1976.

??????. *Peaceful Nuclear Exports and Weapons Proliferation.* A compendium prepared by the Senate Committee on Government Operations. Washington, D.C.: U.S. Government Printing Office, April 1975.

??????. Office of Technology Assessment. *Nuclear Proliferation and Safeguards.* New York: Praeger, 1977.

U.S. Department of State. "Combatting Terrorism." *Department of State Bulletin.* Washington, D.C. August 1982.

Walker, William and Lonnroth, Mans. *Nuclear Power Struggles.* London: George Allen and Unwin, 1983.

Willrich, Mason and Taylor, Theodore. *Nuclear Theft: Risks and Safeguards.* Cambridge, Mass.: Ballinger Publishing Co., 1974.

Wohlstetter, Albert, et al. *Moving Toward Life in a Nuclear Armed Crowd.* Los Angeles: Pan Heuristics, 1976.

About the Editors and Contributors

HAROLD AGNEW is the former president of GA Technologies, Inc. Prior to that he was the director of the Los Alamos Scientific Laboratory. He worked in the group that achieved the first self-sustaining nuclear reaction, and he helped to develop the atomic bomb. He was scientific advisor at NATO headquarters and served as head of the Weapons Physics Division at Los Alamos before becoming director of the Laboratory.

DAVID ALBRIGHT is a physicist on the staff of Princeton University's Center for Energy and Environmental Studies. A specialist in nuclear fuel cycle issues, he is a consultant for the Federation of American Scientists and writes frequently for such publications as *Scientific American* and *Bulletin of the Atomic Scientists*.

YONAH ALEXANDER is professor of international studies and director of the Institute for Studies in International Terrorism at the State University of New York. He is also a senior research staff member of the Georgetown University Center for Strategic and International Studies. He is editor-in-chief of *Terrorism: An International Journal* and *Political Communication and Persuasion: An International Journal*.

JAMES K. ASSELSTINE is a member of the Nuclear Regulatory Commission. Prior to his appointment to the NRC, he served as associate counsel of the Senate Committee on Environment and Public Works and as minority counsel for the committee's Subcommittee on Nuclear Regulation. He was co-director of the Senate Special Investigation of the Three Mile Island nuclear accident. He also was assistant counsel for the former Congressional Joint Committee on Atomic Energy.

ROBERT L. BECKMAN is a visiting assistant professor of political science at the U.S. Naval Academy and the author of the just-published *Nuclear Non-Proliferation: Congress and the Control of Peaceful Nuclear Activities*. He consults on nuclear energy and policy, and recently completed a study for the Congressional Research Service on the NPT and the approaching review conference. He holds a PhD in International Relations and is a Vietnam veteran and former aircraft commander in the Strategic Air Command.

LOUIS RENÉ BERES is professor of political science and international law at Purdue University and the author of numerous works on nuclear issues. His most recent book is *Security or Armageddon: Israel's Nuclear Strategy*. He is also the author of *Nuclear Catastrophe in World Politics*, an exploration of possible routes to nuclear confrontation and the means to prevent them.

BERTRAM BROWN is the president and chief executive officer of Hahnemann University. He was the Director of the National Institute of Mental Health for eight years and served as a consultant to the White House on mental health issues on numerous occasions. He has received the Meritorious Service Medal and the Commendation Medal from the U.S. Public Health Service.

REAR ADMIRAL THOMAS D. DAVIES retired from the U.S. Navy to become assistant director of the Arms Control and Disarmament Agency, where he served under three Presidents. He twice chaired the U.S. delegation in arms-control treaty negotiations with the Soviet Union. While in the Navy, he was a naval aviator and aeronautical engineer and served as Chief of Naval Development and as Commander of North Atlantic Surveillance Operations during the Cuban missile crisis.

SENATOR JEREMIAH DENTON (R-Ala.) is chairman of the Subcommittee on Security and Terrorism of the Senate Judiciary Committee. In the last session of Congress, he introduced, on behalf of President Reagan, four anti-terrorism bills and obtained approval of compromise versions on three of them. He requested and received a GAO study on the role of the federal government in combatting domestic terrorism. He also serves on the Labor and Human Resources and Veterans Affairs Committees. He was a commander in the U.S. Navy, where he was shot down while leading a group of 24 aircraft, and held prisoner for over seven years. He is now a rear admiral (ret.).

DONALD DEVITO is director of the New York State Emergency Management Office and president-elect of the National Emergency Management Association. Previously he was county administrator of New York's Montgomery County. He also served in the Air Force, where he received the Distinguished Flying Cross (three times) and the Air Medal (seven times).

WILLIAM J. DIRCKS is the executive director of operations of the U.S. Nuclear Regulatory Commission. He formerly was director of the NRC's Office of Nuclear Material Safety and Safeguards and, before that, was the agency's deputy executive director. Prior to joining the NRC, he served as executive assistant to the administrator of the Environmental Protection Agency.

WILLIAM O. DOUB is a partner in the law firm of Doub & Muntzing. He formerly served as a commissioner of the U.S. Atomic Energy Commission. He is chairman of the Nuclear Non-Proliferation Committee of the Atomic Industrial Forum. He was appointed by President Reagan as the U.S. representative to the Southern States Energy Board.

ABOUT THE EDITORS AND CONTRIBUTORS

BERNARD T. FELD is a professor of physics at the Massachusetts Institute of Technology. He was actively involved in creating the first nuclear chain reaction and in forming the Atomic Energy Commission. He has published extensively in technical journals and is a consultant to the Brookhaven National Laboratory. He is a former editor of the *Bulletin of the Atomic Scientists*.

D. A. V. FISCHER is the former assistant director general for external relations of the International Atomic Energy Agency. He led the IAEA negotiation of the main safeguards agreement under which the agency operates. He is the author of several works on safeguards and non-proliferation, including the recently published *Safeguarding the Atom: A Critical Appraisal* (with Paul Szasz).

REPRESENTATIVE RICHARD A. GEPHARDT (D-Mo.), a five-term member of Congress, is chairman of the House Democratic Caucus. He is a member of the Ways and Means Committee, where he has worked extensively on health policy and social security issues. He is co-author of a comprehensive health-care reform proposal designed to make the health-care marketplace more competitive. With Senator Bill Bradley (D-NJ), he is sponsoring a major tax simplification plan. As a former member of the Budget Committee, he helped to formulate alternatives to President Reagan's economic program.

VICTOR GILINSKY currently is an independent consultant on nuclear energy issues. He is a former two-term member of the Nuclear Regulatory Commission. Before his appointment to the NRC, he was head of the Physical Science Department at Rand Corporation and assistant director of policy and program review for the U.S. Atomic Energy Commission.

LOUIS O. GIUFFRIDA is director of the Federal Emergency Management Agency. He has served as chief U.S. delegate to NATO's Senior Civil Emergency Planning Committee and to its Civil Defense Committee. He also was chairman of the International Emergency Management Committee and adviser on Terrorism and Emergency Management to the governor of California.

STEVEN GOLDBERG is professor of law and science at Georgetown University Law Center. He has served in the Office of the General Counsel of the U.S. Nuclear Regulatory Commission, where he worked on energy and environmental issues, including the Generic Environmental Statement on the Mixed Oxide (uranium/plutonium) Fuel Program (GESMO). He is the co-author of *Law, Science, and Medicine*.

JOHN PETER GOSS is executive director of Control Risks Ltd., a security consulting firm. He served as a regular officer in the British Army for 30 years, where his assignments included numerous counter-guerrilla and counter-terrorist campaigns. He also was a senior civil servant in the Cabinet office, Whitehall (Prime Minister's Secretariat).

GUENTER HILDENBRAND is senior vice-president and group executive of Kraftwerk Union, A.G., the leading supplier of nuclear facilities and equipment in the Federal Republic of Germany. Having trained as a physicist, he is responsible for KWU's activities in the nuclear fuel cycle in both the national and international contexts. Dr. Hildenbrand has participated in a number of international conferences, workshops and project groups dealing with nuclear energy and non-proliferation issues.

BRIAN M. JENKINS is director of the Rand Corporation's program on security and subnational conflict. He is the editor of *TVI Journal*, a quarterly report on political violence and has written and edited numerous books and articles on political violence. He has also served as a member of the Green Berets and General Creighton Abraham's Long Range Planning Task Group in Vietnam.

ANDRÉ KLEINMAN is deputy director of civil defense for the Canton of Geneva, in which capacity he is responsible for the underground shelter system and for instruction and supervision of civil defense, coordination with other administrative services, staff planning and public relations. He is also a captain (ret.) in the Army's medical service.

PAUL LEVENTHAL is the founder and president of Nuclear Control Institute. He has served as staff director of the Senate Nuclear Regulation Subcommittee and special counsel to the Senate Government Operations Committee. He was responsible for hearings and legislation leading to enactment of the Energy Reorganization Act of 1974 and the Nuclear Non-Proliferation Act of 1978. He was co-director of the Senate Special Investigation of the Three Mile Island nuclear accident and has been an aide to Senators Gary Hart (D-Colo.), Abraham Ribicoff (D-Conn.) and Jacob Javits (R-NY).

DAVID MABRY is the director of the Emergency Action Plans the Exercise Division of the Counterterrorism Programs of the Bureau of Diplomatic Security of the U.S. Department of State. He is also a colonel in the U.S. Marine Corps. Formerly he was battalion commander of the Marine Security Guard Battalion, which is responsible for providing security to U.S. embassies around the world. Colonel Mabry is a graduate of the U.S. Naval Academy.

JACQUES MEURANT is the director of the Henry Dunant Institute, an auxiliary of the International Red Cross in Geneva, Switzerland. Before joining the Institute, he worked with the League of the Red Cross and Red Crescent Societies as special assistant to the secretary general and then special adviser in charge of statutory and legal matters.

YUVAL NE'EMAN is currently co-director of the Center for Particle Theory at the University of Texas and Professor of Physics at Tel Aviv University. He is the former Israeli Minister of Science and Development and chairman of the Cabinet

Committee for Science and Technology. He has also served as a member of the Knesset, vice-chairman of the Israeli Atomic Energy Commission, and senior advisor to the Minister of Defense.

AMIRAM NIR is the advisor to the Prime Minister of Israel on combatting terrorism. Previously he was the military correspondent and commentator for Israel National Television. He also was a senior research fellow at the Center for Strategic Studies at Tel Aviv University, where he wrote a series of papers on such subjects as Israel's Lebanon policy, Soviet-Syrian strategic relations, and advanced weapons systems in the Middle East.

BERNARD J. O'KEEFE is chairman of the executive committee of EG&G, Inc. and previously served as the company's chairman of the board and chief executive officer. He was a principal developer of the firing circuits for the first nuclear weapons and participated in the assembly and delivery of those weapons. He worked in the Engineering Department of the Massachusetts Institute of Technology and, with an MIT colleague, formed Radiation Instruments Company before joining the three principals of EG&G in founding that company.

PETER STOCKTON is a research analyst for the Subcommittee on Oversight and Investigations of the House Committee on Energy and Commerce. He and Representative John Dingell (D-Mich.) spent over two years investigating security at DOE nuclear weapons production facilities. He also has investigated major weapons acquisitions, the death of Karen Silkwood, and the disappearance of 200 lbs. of bomb-grade uranium from the NUMEC facility in Pennsylvania.

THEODORE B. TAYLOR is chairman of the board of Nova, Inc. He is a nuclear physicist who has designed nuclear weapons and nuclear research reactors. He also has served as deputy director (scientific) of the Defense Atomic Support Agency in the Department of Defense and as an independent consultant to the U.S. Atomic Energy Commission. He is the co-author (with Mason Willrich) of *Nuclear Theft: Risks and Safeguards* and is the subject of John McPhee's *The Curve of Binding Energy*.

MERRILL WALTERS is the director of nuclear planning for NATO. Previously he was deputy director and acting director of theater nuclear forces in the Department of Defense. He has also served as chief of the Strategy and Doctrine Department of the Air War College at Maxwell AFB and as chief of the Nuclear and Chemical Section of SHAPE.

PAUL WARNKE is a partner in the law firm of Clifford & Warnke. He is the former director of the U.S. Arms Control and Disarmament Agency and chief U.S. negotiator for the second Strategic Arms Limitation Talks. He has also served as assistant secretary of defense (International Security Affairs) and general counsel to the Department of Defense. He is the chairman of the Committee for National Security.

MASON WILLRICH is senior vice president of Pacific Gas and Electric Company. Previously he was John C. Stennis Professor of Law at the University of Virginia and director of the University's Center for the Study of Science, Technology, and Public Policy. He has also served as general counsel of the U.S. Arms Control and Disarmament Agency and co-authored *Nuclear Theft: Risks and Safeguards* (with Theodore Taylor).

DATE DUE

GAYLORD PRINTED IN U.S.A.